1. Heart in Pilgrimage

HEART IN PILGRIMAGE

Heart in Pilgrimage

*Meditating Christian Spirituality
in the Light
of the Eucharistic Prayer*

MICHAEL L. GAUDOIN-PARKER

ALBA·HOUSE NEW·YORK

SOCIETY OF ST. PAUL, 2187 VICTORY BLVD., STATEN ISLAND, NEW YORK 10314

Library of Congress Cataloging-in-Publication Data

Gaudoin-Parker, Michael L.
    Heart in pilgrimage: meditating Christian spirituality in the
light of the eucharistic prayer / Michael L. Gaudoin-Parker.
      p.   cm.
    Includes bibliographical references.
    ISBN 0-8189-0696-0
    1. Eucharistic prayers — Catholic Church. 2. Spiritual life —
Catholic Church. 3. Catholic Church — Doctrines. I. Title.
BX2015.6.G38   1994
264'.02036 — dc20   94-14439
                                        CIP

Produced and designed in the United States of America by the
Fathers and Brothers of the Society of St. Paul,
2187 Victory Boulevard, Staten Island, New York 10314,
as part of their communications apostolate.

ISBN: 0-8189-0696-0

Printing Information:

Current Printing - first digit	1	2	3	4	5	6	7	8	9	10

Year of Current Printing - first year shown

1994	1995	1996	1997	1998	1999

In gratitude to
my Parents and Sister,
teachers,
Kathleen and Leslie
Marie and Maurice
Léonie and Stratford
and
in cherished memory of
Trevor and Denny,
whose music is prayer
of the heart in pilgrimage.

Great indeed, we proclaim, is the mystery of our religion:
    He was manifested in the flesh,
    vindicated in the Spirit
        seen by angels,
    preached among the nations,
    believed on in the world,
        taken up in glory.[...]
Everything created by God is good,
    and nothing is to be rejected
    if it is received with thanksgiving;
    for then it is consecrated by the word of God and prayer.
If you put these instructions before the brethren,
    you will be a good minister of Christ Jesus,
    nourished on the words of faith and of sound doctrine
    which you have followed.
Have nothing to do with godless and silly myths.
Train yourself spiritually.
Physical exercises are useful enough,
    but the value of spirituality is unlimited,
    for it holds promise for the present life
    and also for the life to come.

                              1 Tm 3:16; 4:4-8

Prayer the Church's banquet, Angel's age,
    God's breath in man returning to his birth,
    The soul in paraphrase, heart in pilgrimage,
The Christian plummet sounding heav'n and earth.

                              George Herbert

Contents

Contents

Communicating the Spirituality of the Eucharist

The well-known and often cited metaphor of Good Pope John about opening the windows of the Church to let in fresh air undoubtedly makes a useful point. But, as a figure of speech it "works" only insofar as one is prepared to ignore the fact that our houses are, for the most part, not in the lovely tranquillity of the pollution-free countryside of his birthplace, *Sotto il Monte* in Bergamo! Neither romantic nostalgia nor the sweeping metaphors of rhetoric gets us anywhere. Pope John's intention in *aggiornamento*, however, requires a tough-mindedness that awakens us to take a deeper look at the very *inner life* of the Church as the extension of the mystery of *Christ the Sacrament* — that mystery which is the vital impulse of the Church's mission of evangelization. Indeed, we need to open the windows and doors of our lives that we may go out and proclaim Christ to the world.[1] But before going out, we have to let the light of Christ in, to penetrate our hearts in order that we may *walk in the light*!

It is a most curious fact of experience that, generally speaking, we know so little about the central act of the Christian community's life, the Eucharistic Prayer. We tend to allow the words of this great Prayer — even though it has been in the vernacular for more than twenty years — to pass over us without giving them much thought or reflecting prayerfully on their implications. Whatever the reasons for this may be — lack of adequate instruction or catechesis, concern over more urgent matters of Christian commitment, or the theologi-

---

[1] The image of opening doors has often been employed by Pope John Paul II, as for example in introducing the Jubilee Year of Redemption —cf. Apostolic Letter: *Aperite portas redemptori* ["Open your doors to the Redeemer"] (6 January 1983).

cal nature of the Eucharistic Prayers itself — our intelligent participation in the sacred liturgy suffers and, moreover, the quality of our Christian life or spirituality as a result becomes impoverished. It would be a serious mistake to imagine that it is enough merely to "hear" Mass.

On the other hand, it is always a sign of living faith to be ready to question the language in which our deepest truths are handed on. We must not shy away from searching into the significance of the *Mystery of Faith* and its proclamation in the Eucharistic Prayer. The condition of childlikeness, which our Lord upholds as befitting the kingdom of God, is characterized after all not by complacency or ignorance, but by a sense of wonderment. This is simplicity! This is frequently manifest in the asking of questions. The value of this process of learning through the wonder of discovery is evident at the Jewish liturgy of the Passover during which the youngest child asks about the origin and meaning of what is celebrated; both the child and the whole community thus grow in discovering and making their own the Tradition of faith and worship — the Tradition that is the mainstay of their life as a community. A readiness to ask questions, however, in no way implies a lessening or abandoning of faith, but on the contrary implies a healthy sign of growth and deepening of faith — or simply, to borrow St. Anselm's lapidary expression, *faith seeking understanding.*[2]

---

[2] In the first chapter of the *Proslogion* Anselm expands and explains the title of this little work: *"Fides quaerens intellectum"*:

I do desire to understand a little of your truth
which my heart already believes and loves.
I do not seek to understand so that I may believe,
but I believe so that I may understand;
and what is more,
I believe that unless I do believe I shall not understand.
(translation in *The Prayers and Meditations of Saint Anselm*, Penguin Classics, 1979, p. 244)

This approach was familiar to St. Augustine who repeatedly writes in this vein commenting on a verse from Is 7:9 (in the Septuagint version): *"If you have not believed, you will not understand"* — cf. *De lib. arb.*, II; *Serm. 43*, 7.9 which is cited in the new *Catechism of the Catholic Church* (n. 158).

Xavier Léon-Dufour sums this up well: "It is obvious that those who approach the texts on the Eucharist must be ready, not to cast doubt on the faith they have received from their fathers, but to question the language in which that faith has been passed on to them." — *Sharing the Eucharistic Bread*, p. 281.

Another way of putting this is to envisage the use or utterance of religious language as the humble threshold of the mansions of wisdom —the threshold at which the Holy Wisdom of the Logos or Word of God comes out to meet and invite us to join in a chorus of praise and thanksgiving for his revelation of the mystery of communication. Our experience of reality — *"Heaven in ordinarie"* in George Herbert's telling phrase about prayer — embraces both ordinary actions and also the search for and exploration into the significance of our language about what we do or endure. We stand beggar-like on the threshold of communication.[3] This threshold of awareness is the *narrow door* of perception of the Good News of Christ, which his Spirit enables and empowers us to give gracious utterance in prayer. But we must cross this threshold and pass through Christ's door in order to discover that beyond the prosaic events of our often drab lives lies the glory of the kingdom of God. We approach this threshold because we are bidden by Christ, who stands there seeking to be acknowledged as the Light of the world.[4] The light of his presence enables us to discern the inner, rich meaning of all things and their worth. He alone as the unique Mediator, who bears in his own flesh the wounds and scars caused by our sin-fragmenting frailty, enlightens the darkness of our pride, purifies our hearts, heals all divisions between and within persons, and binds them into an integral whole — namely, his Mystical Body, that is, the great *"sacrament of love, sign of unity, bond of charity."*[5]

The gulf stretching between knowing and doing, ideals and failure to realize them, aspiration and accomplishment, dreams and reality . . . this dark abyss, which sadly at times is all that constitutes or passes for awareness in the experience of many people, is, as it were, the hell into which Christ descends in the re-presentation of his unique sacrifice at every Mass. Only he has the answer to the insoluble mystery of existence, for he is the Word and Light of Life. Only he holds and offers the key to unlock the prison of unfreedom,

---

[3] St. Augustine's description of the human condition as that of a mendicant or beggar before God is quoted in the new *Catechism of the Catholic Church* (n. 2559) regarding our need to receive the gift of prayer — cf. Augustine, *Sermones* 56, 6, 9; PL 38, 381).

[4] Cf. Rv 3:20; Jn 1:9.

[5] St. Augustine, *Tractatus in Joh. Evan.*, 26.6.13.

for he comes as Redeemer-Savior revealing that genuine spiritual liberation of the children of God.[6] Only he manifests the end of human misery, for he is our peace,[7] he is *the true Bread for the Life of the world*[8] he is *the Way, the Truth, and the Life* to the Father.[9] Christ Jesus offers and is the vision of God — *"our God made visible"* as the Preface of the Christmas liturgy proclaims — for he enables us to become *"pure of heart,"* that condition of singlemindedness without which no one can see God.[10] Jesus, the Lamb of God, purifies us of our sins, that is, he enlightens us (as the root of the word "purity" in Greek signifies) both about the folly of sin and also about our true worth as loved by God despite our sinfulness. He attracts us, as no one or nothing else can, drawing us to singlemindedness in tenderest personal devotion and service of him in the least of our brethren.

Heart in Pilgrimage suggested itself as an appropriate title for this book on the spirituality of the Eucharistic Prayer since it is rich in biblical overtones. It comes from a poem by the Anglican priest-poet George Herbert, born four hundred years ago (1593-1633).[11] This poem, which like much of Herbert's poetry is full of eucharistic imagery, beautifully summarizes the essence of prayer.[12] The well-

---

[6] Cf. Rm 8:19ff.

[7] Cf. Ep 2:14.

[8] Jn 6:51.

[9] Jn 14:6.

[10] Cf. Mt 5:8.

[11] Herbert's background was one of prestige and learning: he descended from the family of Philip Sydney on his devout mother Margaret's side, and of William Herbert, Lord Pembroke, who was Shakespeare's patron, on his father's; he must have known John Donne well, for the poet, who was his mother's friend for thirty years, gave her the manuscript of many *Holy Sonnets and Divine Poems* in 1607. After pursuing a most promising academic course at Trinity College, Cambridge, leading to his appointment as public Orator of the University in 1620, he turned aside from the bright prospects of a worldly career in 1626 and entered the Church. He was a friend of Nicholas Ferrar the devout community at Little Gidding near Cambridge and his prebend in Huntingdonshire (celebrated in T.S. Eliot's *Four Quartets*). It is to Ferrar we owe the survival of Herbert's English poems, which he sent to be published if Ferrar considered them likely to "turn to the advantage of any dejected soul."

[12] Cf. *Prayer [I]* — "banquet," "Christ-side-piercing spear," "world transposing in an hour," "Exalted Manna," "The milkie way," "The land of spices." Quotations from Herbert's poems, unless otherwise stated, are taken from *The Metaphysical Poets* (edited by Helen Gardner) Penguin, 1975.

spring of Herbert's devotion was the tenderness of divine love — a tenderness which revives him:

> Who would have thought my shrivel'd heart
> Could have recover'd greennesse?[13]

This tenderness also somehow becomes marvelously audible in his lines. He turns with amazement and praise again and again to this source of vitality which gradually converts his heart from sin and from even his talent with words to the art of living.[14] He becomes captivated by *"two vast, spacious things"* woven together in the theme of Love conquering sin[15] — as for instance in the exquisite poem *Love bade me welcome*, which is plainly eucharistic in tone.[16]

The *heart* in the biblical sense of this word is the symbol of yearning for wholeness which is entwined into the very warp and

---

[13] *The Flower.*

[14] Cf. *Jordan (II)*:
> *When first my lines of heav'nly joyes made mention,*
> *Such was their lustre, they did so excell,*
> *That I sought out quaint words, and trim invention;*
> *My thoughts began to burnish, sprout, and swell,*
> *Curling with metaphors a plain intention,*
> *Decking the sense, as if it were to sell. [. . .]*
> *As flames do work and winde, when they ascend,*
> *So did I weave my self into the sense.*
> *But while I bustled, I might heare a friend*
> *Whisper, How wide is all this long pretence!*
> *There is in love a sweetnesse readie penn'd:*
> *Copie out onely that, and save expense.*
>
> Cf. also that most uplifting hymn *"King of glory, King of peace,"* in which Herbert exclaims:
> *Wherefore with my utmost art,*
> *I will sing thee.*
> *And the cream of all my heart*
> *I will bring thee.*
>   (*Hymns Old and New*, Kevin Mayhew, n. 292)

[15] Cf. *The Agonie.*

[16] On reading this poem Simone Weil, the Christian-hearted French Jewess, an intellectual mystic, claims to have experienced most vividly a sense of God's presence, the like of which was comparable only to that on reading the Lord's Prayer in Greek. Cf. also the last couplet of *The Agonie*:
> *Love is that liquour sweet and most divine,*
> *Which my God feels as bloud; but I, as wine.*

woof of our being. *Heart in pilgrimage* crystallizes the truth realized by St. Augustine, Pascal, Antoine de Saint-Exupery and many others: that it is with the heart that one sees truly.[17] It suggests an approach to truth which is hidden from the extremes of both heady rationalism and mere sentimentality alike. This approach is itself the deepest truth about the mystery of being human: it encompasses God's revelation of our need for faith, which lives in hope and is fulfilled only by and in love. It is the focal point of the prophets' proclamation of the *new covenant* — namely, that God creates a *new heart* in us.[18] Jesus gave these prophecies flesh and blood reality! His *new and eternal covenant* is what we proclaim in the Mystery of Faith — that Mystery of his immense love which Christians strive to live in the whole of their lives. The striving becomes easier in virtue of the proclamation of the Mystery of Faith, which expresses our *Christ-ian* identity and makes us pilgrims of love. It is the truth of Christ's love that is ultimately important — that loving truth of God's heart opened to us in his sacrifice.

This book is offered as an attempt to bring about a deepening of our understanding of the truth that Christian life and spirituality are centered on the Eucharistic Prayer.[19] The approach taken here consists in showing that what we pray and live is drawn from the depth of experiencing the mystery of Christ — that experience formed from the time of the disciples and shaped through the centuries of faith in what we call "Christian Tradition," that is, a faithful "handing on" of the precious gift of the Mystery of Faith. For, if we are to *"Proclaim the*

---

[17] Cf. St. Augustine, *Confessions*, I. 1 — "Thou has made us for thyself, O Lord, and our hearts find no rest until they rest in thee"; cf. Saint-Exupery, *The Little Prince*, Penguin Books, p. 84: "And now here is my secret, a very simple secret: It is only with the heart that one can see rightly; what is essential is invisible to the eye"; cf. also Pascal, *Pensées*, IV. 277: "The heart has its reasons which reason knows nothing about."

[18] Cf. e.g. Jr 31:31ff. cited in Heb 8:8ff. and in L.G. n. 9 — the first paragraph of the chapter on the people of God's new and perfect covenant in Christ. Cf. also K. Rahner, *Theological Investigations*, Vol. 8, Herder & Herder, New York, 1971; also W. Kern, *Updated Devotion to the Sacred Heart*, Alba House Communications, Ohio, 1975; and F.J. Sheed, *The Instructed Heart*, Sheed & Ward, London, 1979. *"Cor ad cor loquitur"* ("Heart speaks to heart") was the motto on Cardinal Newman's escutcheon.

[19] The idea of writing this book originated in fact some years ago when Archbishop Couve de Murville of Birmingham (U.K.) encouraged me to publish as a separate pamphlet or booklet an article which I presented in *Adoremus* (1988, No. 2) on the Eucharistic Prayer.

Mystery of Faith" (as we are invited to do at every Mass) should we not endeavor to know and understand a bit better just what we proclaim and appreciate something about what lies under the words of the Eucharistic Prayer or what these words, which are drawn from the experience of others, point to? Will our learning ever cease — particularly that learning to live what we say and do at the Mass in fidelity to our Lord's command: "Do this as my memorial," not "say this. . ."!

After considering the need for a eucharistic catechesis based on a clear understanding of the rhythm and structure of the Eucharistic Prayer (chapters I and II), there follows an examination of the main *anaphoras* approved for general use in the English-speaking world (chapters III-VIII). This examination is carried out primarily from the point of view of Christian spirituality rather than from an historical, theological or liturgical standpoint, though insights from these angles must play some part. The book concludes with a final chapter on the primary significance of the Word (Logos) which is articulated in the Church's *proclamation of worship*. For ultimately it is Christ, *the Word of Life*, who imparts significance to everything we are and do — his Spirit-filled Logos inspiring and empowering the prayer and lives of his followers, whom it impels towards the evangelization of all peoples.

The Eucharistic Prayers of the Church proclaim the manifold dimensions of the mystery of God's love which reveals the mystery of humanity. They school the *Heart in pilgrimage* in the diverse aspects of learning to love, without which there can be no communication or hope for mankind's yearning for community — to say nothing of its more fundamental and eternal desire for communion with God.

Without love — the supreme revelation of the Word-made-flesh —there can be no learning; and, without the proclamation of faith in the Spirit-filled Word in the Eucharistic Prayer and Sacrament of Love, our words would be ineffective and powerless to communicate the Good News of salvation. The Sacraments and especially the Eucharist is the heart of evangelization, which is the primary mission of the Church. We learn to live fully in a human way only through and because of God's love. Learning to love — to live in love — entails more than a journey of the mind. It calls for a response of our whole selves: the surrender of our senses, imagination, emotions, intelligence, power of self determination, dynamism to value or will — as well as our endeavors to communicate daily in words and deeds. Anything less than this surrender of our whole selves would be selfishness — not love. But paradoxically in surrendering ourselves entirely to Christ we are made whole: we discover the wholesomeness or peace of being in harmony or communion with the whole of creation in God. In essence, the love of Christ calls and empowers us to journey to the heart of reality. This is the journey or pilgrimage of the heart, in which our inmost being becomes gradually oriented toward the depths of God. The Spirit of truth, whom Jesus promised at the Last Supper, transforms not merely the gifts of bread and wine, but our whole lives because he creates our hearts anew to be worshippers whom the Father seeks. In the worship of the Eucharistic community especially we discover our worth in taking responsibility for one another and the whole of creation. Here we learn to receive and communicate understanding and forgiveness and the vital art of trust, without which there can be no solidarity in society. Here we are strengthened through the support of others' faith in Christ to journey beyond the barriers of our fears to risk the cost of loving and of venturing forward not merely to the horizons of the unknown, but to the mystery of God's presence.

The *truth of love*, which is what the Church proclaims in the Eucharist, is what St. Peter Julian Eymard pointed out in his last sermon in Paris before leaving his brethren to continue the congregation he founded as adorers and evangelists of the Lord's Gift of the Holy Eucharist:

> We have known the charity of God (1 Jn 4:16). To believe in love is everything! It is not enough to believe in truth: we must believe in love. The love, that is, that our Lord Jesus Christ shows in the Blessed Sacrament . . . Men may teach you the subtleties of its dogma, but Jesus alone can give you belief in it. Come and receive not only its consolation; be strengthened in faith. Yes, you have the Eucharist! What more do you want?[20]

---

[20] Sermon on 16 July 1868 to his confrères in the Congregation of the Blessed Sacrament, which he founded barely twelve years earlier.

In the course of twenty five years of experiencing the power of the Eucharist as a minister of Christ's word and sacrament I have become increasingly aware of the need for deeper catechesis of the Eucharistic Prayer in order that we may make our own the Second Vatican Council's rich insights and respond to the call to inner renewal of the Church in holiness. I am equally convinced that if catechesis were related merely to theological writings, it would risk becoming too narrow and "inward looking." Treating a matter such as the Eucharistic Prayer requires us to pay careful attention to points of theological, liturgical and pastoral significance, as well as sensitivity to language. In the course of this book, therefore, I have drawn extensively on the insights of many scholars, reference to whose works are provided throughout for further reading. But, since my primary intention is to point to the Eucharistic Prayer as our richest expression and, indeed, source of Christian spirituality, I have at times felt impelled to indicate or quote also from other writers — poets and literary figures whose insights either echo or help to deepen the significance of the words we use when we pray the Eucharist. For, especially at this crucial stage of historical transition, which is full of uncertainty and fraught with a tendency to relativize everything, we have a responsibility to rediscover, relate and reinterpret how our cultural tradition — the *ensemble* of our beliefs, values, ethos, needs, symbols, etc. — is rooted in the language and action of prayer. While it is no doubt to a wide, often "irreligious," cultural context that the Church's faith reaches out in evangelization, it is *within* this very culture — and none other — that Christians pray and proclaim Christ's *Mysterium Fidei*, the heart of spirituality for which the contemporary secular world implicitly yearns.

Whatever else it may or may not express, however, I hope this book will be a small token of my sense of profound gratitude to others who have shown me so much about the joy of journeying ever towards the heart of the *Mystery of Faith*, which we proclaim at Mass. I have to acknowledge that I have learnt from them more than I have been able to impart pastorally in the ministry of breaking the *Word of Life* with them.

If I may be permitted a personal note, I trust that the following reminiscence will illustrate how being thankful to those whom one serves expresses something of the significance of the proclamation at the heart of the Eucharistic Prayer. I can clearly recall the first time I experienced a sense of gratitude for being entrusted with the service of the Eucharist. While I was a student-deacon at the Church of the Canadian Martyrs in Rome I was asked by a priest to preach the homily at the Mass he was celebrating at a nearby convent. The Gospel was on the use of the Talents. I remember my fresh enthusiasm and also the glow of satisfaction I felt — not only because I sensed I had made a decent job of communicating (in Italian, to boot!), but also because I had "preached the Eucharist." The theme of my homily was about how the Eucharist is our best Talent, our Lord's greatest Gift to us. The natural pride I felt was, however, soon deflated. For as I was assisting in distributing Holy Communion I became struck by an indescribable sense of awe and wonder at the humility of God himself who communicates his Treasure in the silence of the Blessed Sacrament. What we cannot express for all our way with words or even the best of our art, God says so simply in this manner of revealing the grace and truth of his Real Presence! Furthermore, his "simultaneous translation," as it were, of the Word of Life into the people's loving response of adoring faith awakened in me immense gratitude. It seemed that *I* was the recipient —rather than being the communicator — of the deepest lesson of Love's truth: the humility of God both in the great silence of the Blessed Eucharist and also in the silent endeavor of his people to respond to his Gospel in their lives. In that instant I knew what gratitude is. I experienced *Eucharist*, that is, the inner worth of being full of thanksgiving.

Thus, in beginning this book on the spirituality of the Eucharistic Prayer, I do so both in the spirit of indebtedness to God for calling me to hand on to others what I myself have received and also as a tribute to all through and with whom I have been privileged to discover the joy of living what we proclaim in our Lord's Gift of the Eucharist. The rich truth that we celebrate at the Eucharist dawns gradually on us as we begin to realize that the fulness of life means thanksgiving. This "eucharistic" realization is borne home to us in discovering, remembering and reflecting on how we become bonded to others — a bonding that is possible only because the Father makes us one by his Holy Spirit in the Mystical Body of Christ. This sense of gratitude then overflows into the deeds of Christlike love. Every deed of this love flows from *Eucharist* and leads into the freedom of Christ, who is the *Light of the nations.*[21] This sense of loving gratitude reveals the profound sense of *praxis*[22] and also the well-spring of Christian hope in the great mercy of God, for which

> e'en eternity's too short,
> to extol thee.[23]

At the end of our hearts' pilgrimage — as the Church sings each evening at Vespers — we shall realize our Eucharistic Prayer transformed into the eternal *Magnificat* which we proclaim with the Blessed Virgin Mary and all the saints:

> The Almighty works marvels for me.
> Holy is his name!
> His mercy is from age to age,
> on those who fear him . . .
> the mercy promised to our fathers,
> to Abraham and his sons for ever.

Feast of the Assumption of Mary into Heaven

---

[21] Cf. Jn 3:21; 8:12, 32. *"Lumen Gentium,"* the opening words of the Second Vatican Council's great Constitution on the Church, were the leitmotif of the recent International Eucharistic Congress in Seville, 7-13 June 1993.

[22] *Praxis*, without excluding the sense of the "practical," must not be restricted merely to pragmatism — or it would soon be abandoned through becoming frustrated at every turn by humanly insurmountable obstacles and circumstances. *Praxis* is not the opponent, but the ally of contemplation (*"theoria"*), just as contemplation is its closest friend. For both are focused as responses to the deep truth of gratitude (*"eucharist"*), without which living cannot be called human. It is the profundity of graced love and its wisdom that the liberation theologians, who rightly insist on *praxis*, must learn from someone like the recently beatified Franciscan John Duns Scotus: "It is proved that love is truly *praxis*" — Prologue to *Ord.*, n. 303 (Ed. Vat., I, 200), cited by Pope Paul VI in his Apostolic Letter (*Alma Parens*, 14 July 1966) to the Bishops of England, Wales and Scotland on the occasion of the Second Congress of Scholasticism at Oxford and Edinburgh to mark the seventh centenary of Scotus' birth.

[23] The last two lines of George Herbert's *"King of glory, King of peace"* (loc. cit.). Cf. Ps. 88 (89):2, *"Misericordias Domini in aeternum cantabo"* ("I shall sing of the Lord's mercy for ever"). It is said that this verse was the sustaining hope of the great St. Teresa of Avila.

My special gratitude
is due to an Australian friend,
Father Donald Cave, s.s.s.
who kindly permitted me to use his triptych of
the Emmaus event and the two other biblical scenes,
Philip baptizing the eunuch and the Visitation.
This ensemble, in cruciform shape,
aptly depicts the central theme:
HEART IN PILGRIMAGE.
For Christ meets us along the journey we begin at baptism,
reveals himself in the "breaking of bread"
and strengthens us in the power of his love
to become his missionaries of charity,
like the Blessed Virgin Mary,
in proclaiming
the marvels which the Lord has done
and in serving the people of our times.

Biblical Abbreviations

OLD TESTAMENT

Genesis	Gn	Nehemiah	Ne	Baruch	Ba
Exodus	Ex	Tobit	Tb	Ezekiel	Ezk
Leviticus	Lv	Judith	Jdt	Daniel	Dn
Numbers	Nb	Esther	Est	Hosea	Ho
Deuteronomy	Dt	1 Maccabees	1 M	Joel	Jl
Joshua	Jos	2 Maccabees	2 M	Amos	Am
Judges	Jg	Job	Jb	Obadiah	Ob
Ruth	Rt	Psalms	Ps	Jonah	Jon
1 Samuel	1 S	Proverbs	Pr	Micah	Mi
2 Samuel	2 S	Ecclesiastes	Ec	Nahum	Na
1 Kings	1 K	Song of Songs	Sg	Habakkuk	Hab
2 Kings	2 K	Wisdom	Ws	Zephaniah	Zp
1 Chronicles	1 Ch	Sirach	Si	Haggai	Hg
2 Chronicles	2 Ch	Isaiah	Is	Malachi	Ml
Ezra	Ezr	Jeremiah	Jr	Zechariah	Zc
		Lamentations	Lm		

NEW TESTAMENT

Matthew	Mt	Ephesians	Ep	Hebrews	Heb
Mark	Mk	Philippians	Ph	James	Jm
Luke	Lk	Colossians	Col	1 Peter	1 P
John	Jn	1 Thessalonians	1 Th	2 Peter	2 P
Acts	Ac	2 Thessalonians	2 Th	1 John	1 Jn
Romans	Rm	1 Timothy	1 Tm	2 John	2 Jn
1 Corinthians	1 Cor	2 Timothy	2 Tm	3 John	3 Jn
2 Corinthians	2 Cor	Titus	Tt	Jude	Jude
Galatians	Gal	Philemon	Phm	Revelation	Rv

Abbreviations

AAS Acta Apostolicae Sedis
A.G. Ad Gentes, Vatican II Decree on the Church's Missionary Activity
CCC Catechism of the Catholic Church (1994)
C.L. Christifideles Laici, Apostolic Constitution on the Calling and Mission of the Lay Faithful (Pope John Paul II)
C.T. Catechesi Tradendae, Apostolic Constitution on Catechesis (Pope John Paul II)
D.M. Dives in Misericordia, Encyclical Letter (Pope John Paul II)
D.O. The Divine Office
DS Denzinger-Schönmetzer
D.V. Dei Verbum, Vatican II Constitution on Divine Revelation
E.M. Eucharisticum Mysterium, Instruction on the Eucharistic Mystery
E.V. Evangelii Nuntiandi, Apostolic Constitution on Evangelization (Pope Paul VI)
GIRM General Instruction on the Roman Missal
G.S. Gaudium et Spes, Vatican II Constitution on the Church in the Modern World
ICEL International Committee for English in the Liturgy
I.E.C. International Eucharistic Congress(es)
L.G. Lumen Gentium, Vatican II Constitution on the Church
P.D.V. Pastores Dabo Vobis, Apostolic Exhortation on the formation of priests in the circumstances of the present day (Pope John Paul II)
PG Patrologia Graeca (Migne)
PL Patrologia Latina (Migne)
P.O. Presbyterorum Ordinis, Vatican II Decree on the Life and Ministry of Priests
R.H. Redemptor Hominis, Encyclical Letter (Pope John Paul II)
R.M. Redemptoris Missio, Encyclical Letter (Pope John Paul II)
R.P. Reconciliatio et Paenitentia, Apostolic Exhortation on reconciliation and penance in the mission of the Church today (Pope John Paul II)
SC Sources Chretiennes
S.C. Sacrosanctum Concilium, Vatican II Constitution on the Sacred Liturgy
S.R.C. Sollicitudo Rei Socialis, Encyclical Letter (Pope John Paul II)
U.R. Unitatis Redintegratio, Vatican II Decree on Ecumenism

HEART IN PILGRIMAGE

1

Catechesis of the Eucharistic Prayer

[T]hrough catechesis the Gospel kerygma (the initial ardent proclamation by which a person is one day overwhelmed and brought to the decision to entrust himself to Jesus Christ by faith) is gradually deepened, developed in its implicit consequences, explained in language that includes an appeal to reason, and channelled towards Christian practice in the Church and the world. All this is no less evangelical than the kerygma, in spite of what is said by certain people who consider that catechesis necessarily rationalizes, dries up and eventually kills all that is living, spontaneous and vibrant in the kerygma. The truths studied in catechesis are the same truths that touched the person's heart when he heard them for the first time. Far from blunting or exhausting them, the fact of knowing them better should make them even more challenging and decisive for one's life. [. . .] Catechesis is necessary both for the maturation of the faith of Christians and for their witness in the world.[1]

Frequently throughout the documents of the Second Vatican Council the phrase *"pastoral charity"* recurs.[2] This expression indicates a rich understanding of the Church's divinely entrusted mission and re-

---

[1] Pope John Paul II, Apostolic Exhortation, *Catechesi Tradendae* [C.T.], n. 25; translated by St. Paul Publications & Catholic Information Services, p. 26. Cf. also his Apostolic Constitution (*Fidei Depositum*, 11 October 1992) at the publication of the *Catechism of the Catholic Church*, n. 3.

[2] Cf. e.g., P.O., n. 14 to which Pope John Paul II refers in P.D.V., n. 23: *"The internal principle, the force which animates and guides the spiritual life of the priest inasmuch as he is configured to Christ the Head and Shepherd, is pastoral charity, as a participation in Jesus Christ's own pastoral charity, a gift freely bestowed by the Holy Spirit and likewise a task and a call which demand a free and committed response on the part of the priest."* (English translation: Libreria Editrice Vaticana, 1992, p. 46.)

1

sponsibility in handling the *"mysteries of God"* (cf. 1 Cor 4:1). The essential content of pastoral charity, as Pope John Paul II states, is *"the gift of self,* the total gift of *self to the Church,* following the example of Christ."[3] Pastoral charity was the motivating energy of the Fathers of this Council in authorizing a thorough reform of the Church's liturgy in order that all the faithful might

> be brought to take that full, intelligent, active part in liturgical celebration which the nature of the Liturgy itself requires, and which, in virtue of their baptism, is the right and duty of the Christian people, "a chosen race, a royal priesthood, a holy nation, God's own people" (1 P 2:9; cf. 2:45).[4]

The first of the Conciliar documents, which was significantly devoted to the Sacred Liturgy, emphasizes the unsurpassable worth of worship —particularly "in the divine sacrifice of the Eucharist, the 'work of our redemption,'" since worship enables "the faithful to express in their lives and show forth to others the mystery of Christ and the real nature of the true Church."[5] Since all genuine renewal of Christian life springs from the liturgy, at the heart of which is Christ's sacrifice and table of love, the focus of the Church's activity,[6] the Second Vatican Council authorized liturgical reforms and adaptations which were meant to be far-reaching and profound — deeper than merely a revision of external or structural changes. For the Council's aim was to foster a rediscovery or renewal of the Christian community's very life of relationship or communion (*"koinonia"*) with God.

To achieve this aim the Council fostered a rediscovery of liturgical piety, that is, spirituality centered in the sacramental exten-

---

[3] Ibid. He goes on to quote from his homily at adoration during the I.E.C. of Seoul (7 October 1989): *"Pastoral charity is the virtue by which we imitate Christ in his self-giving and service. It is not just what we do, but our gift of self, which manifests Christ's love for his flock. Pastoral charity determines our way of thinking and acting, our way of relating to people. It makes special demands on us...."*

[4] Constitution on the Sacred Liturgy (S.C.), n. 14; CTS Do 386, p. 12.

[5] Ibid., n. 2 (citing the *Roman Missal,* Prayer Over the Offerings, 9th Sunday after Pentecost).

[6] Cf. Ibid., n. 10.

sion of Christ's Paschal Mystery.[7] The depth and very nature of the community's relationship with the God of the covenant cannot be exhausted merely in the human experience of *"togetherness"* or in attempts to make the liturgy more *"meaningful"* and *"relevant"* — however well-intentioned or, even, needful it may be to find an incarnational rooting and expression for the mystery of God's communication of *his love.* The focus of the community celebrating divine worship should be not itself — as is sometimes all too evidently the tendency — but the Lord. Only then will the persons making up the praying Christian community discover themselves free and capable for genuine communication in the bonds of fraternal charity. Without due recognition given to the complementarity of ministries involved, without appreciation of the delicate interplay of spoken word, song and silence, without an atmosphere permitting deepest reverence for God or respect for one's neighbors' need for encountering the Savior or care for one's own similar need, we would show a grossly impoverished understanding of what the Council meant in encouraging a "full, intelligent, active participation in liturgical celebration."

"Participation" means much more — indeed something profoundly charitable! — than everyone being constrained (and feeling rather awkward) to take part in a rowdy "clap-happy" sort of jollity. The significance of Christ's mystery would be demeaned and obscured if its celebration were to depend on the theme announced for the day or on the accompanying mood music. The mystery of *participation* (*communion* or *divine fellowship*) itself would be reduced to the level of partial camaraderie instead of being a sacramental expression of the "wonderful/awesome exchange" (*"admirabile/ sacrum commercium"*) between God and humanity.[8] It is not always

---

[7] In the perspective of Vatican II it is significant that the new *Catechism of the Catholic Church* (cf. Part II) presents the sacraments within the context of the sacred liturgy and not, as formerly, in isolation from it. This perspective of the Fathers had been obscured in both the Western and also Eastern theology since the Middle Ages and Scholasticism (when treatises on *De Sacramentis* flourished) as Alexander Schmemann, an Orthodox theologian, pointed out over thirty years ago: cf. *For the Life of the World,* p. 135ff.

[8] Cf. Hans Urs von Balthasar, "The Worthiness of the Liturgy" in *New Elucidations,* Ignatius Press, San Francisco, 1986, p. 127ff. Cf. also the apposite remarks on "our over-rational, word-dominated modern liturgies" by Dr Heather Ward in *The Gift of Self,* DLT, London, 1990, pp. 84ff.

a question of aestheticism[9] or a die-hard *conservative mentality* that makes people dissatisfied with the way the liturgy is sometimes "performed" (!) — but a genuine *cri de coeur* regarding the proper respect due to the inner dignity of the Mass as our Lord's precious gift to us.[10]

Communion or participation bespeaks genuine intimacy with God to which Christ gave us access in the Eucharist, the Sacrament of Friendship *par excellence*; casual familiarity is quite another matter. Participation bespeaks the quality of sharing the life of God's love — the heart of spirituality. Rather than doing away with mystery, it gradually introduces us ever deeper into the significance of our being in the mystery of God through symbol and sacrament. Casual familiarity, on the other hand, alienates us from both God and ourselves since it rashly and irreverently presumes to grasp at meaning by external contact alone whether by rationalism or, more superficially still, by projection of ephemeral subjective feelings. What is most urgently needed is the discovery of the contemplative and prayerful spirit of the liturgy, the source of authentic Christian spirituality.[11]

---

[9] Gerard Manley Hopkins was certainly not drawn to the Catholic Church for aesthetic reasons as he states in his letter to his father (16 October 1866): "I am surprised you shd. say fancy and aesthetic tastes have led me to my present state of mind: these wd. be better satisfied in the Church of England, for bad taste is always meeting one in the accessories of Catholicism."

[10] In stimulating assessment of the challenge facing Christians today and of the way the Churches are approaching this challenge, Professor R.P.C. Hanson seems to misunderstand the revolution introduced by Vatican II in seeing it as the breakthrough for which "the Catholic modernists had wistfully longed." A revolution it was indeed if this means the process of reforms leading to renewal of spirituality, but not as a break with the Church's tradition. Thus, he fails to appreciate the significance of the renewal of the liturgy and also of the intrinsic value of what the liturgy celebrated before the reforms of the Council: "The monolithic uniformity of the Roman Church has disappeared. Some rock-ribbed Anglo-Catholics in the Church of England have found themselves in the embarrassing position of being on the right of the Pope. The ghost of the late Evelyn Waugh has been heard lamenting the loss of a liturgy which had the supreme virtue of incomprehensibility." *Mystery and Imagination: Reflections on Christianity*, SPCK, London, 1976, p. 13.

[11] In his talk at the 45th International Eucharistic Congress in Seville (1993), Cardinal Martini pointed to the importance of this by quoting Hans Urs von Balthasar's challenge to the clergy (*Who Is a Christian?*, Burns & Oates, A Compass Book, London, 1968, p. 34): "The emphasis on 'doing' or 'carrying out' the ritual celebration has (and does) run the risk of depriving our eucharistic liturgies — and hence the life and faith of our people — of their contemplative and prayerful spirit. In a provocative, though wholly honest way the theologian von Balthasar put it like this: 'Where are the

Catechesis of the sacred mysteries guarantees that formation required to prepare us for encountering the transforming grace of Christ's Holy Spirit, without whom there can be no relationship of communion with God, no spirituality or quality of eternal life.[12]

As much as there is need constantly to improve the quality in the way we celebrate the sacred liturgy, it is important to realize that this can best be done by faithfully following the reforms introduced by the Council rather than by innovations which lack the extent and depth of the Church's experience in celebrating worship. This is what someone like J.R.R. Tolkien, as full-hearted in faith as in imagination, clearly understood and endeavored to communicate in a letter to his son Michael, whose "sagging-faith" was occasioned by the slipshod way about which he complained Mass was celebrated — even before Vatican II was falsely interpreted as permitting every kind of exaggerated and casual familiarity:

> The only cure for sagging of fainting faith is Communion. [...] I can recommend this as an exercise (alas! only too easy to find opportunity for): make your communion in circumstances that affront your taste. Choose a snuffling or gabbling priest or a proud and vulgar friar; and a church full of the usual bourgeois crowd, ill-behaved children from those who yell to those products of Catholic schools who the moment the tabernacle is opened sit back and yawn — open necked and

---

worship and adoration in our up-to-date services? Thinking either that these functions are superfluous or that churchgoers aren't mature enough, the clergy have taken it into their heads to fill out the time in a practical way and with a pretty varied run of activities: there's not a moment left free. Noisy all the time; if it's not prayers out loud or Bible readings and expositions, then it's singing and responses that have to be listened to. . . .'"

[12] On the meaning of the word *catechesis* it is worth recalling that its original meaning was "to instruct" or "teach" and was applied to the act of children's repeating (or singing out in chorus) the instruction received from a teacher or answers to his questions. Cf. Philo, *Leg. ad Gaium*, 198. In this sense the word is used in the N.T. — e.g. Lk 1:4; Ac 18:25; Gal 6:6. The first known use in the sense of giving (oral) instructions about the faith occurs in the oldest homily, the Pseudo-Clementine so-called *Second Epistle to the Corinthians*, 17, 1 (prior to 150 A.D.). Tertullian was the first Latin writer to use the verb *"catechizare"* as meaning "to instruct orally"— cf. *De Cor. Mil.*, 9. Cf. also St. Augustine, *De fide et operibus*, 13 (first use of the word); also *De catechizandis rudibus*, 1.1. Cf. Joseph P. Christopher (ed.), *St. Augustine: The First Catechetical Instruction*, Westminster, MD, The Newman Press; Longmans, Green & Co., London, 1946, pp. 93f.

dirty youths, women in trousers and often with hair both unkempt and uncovered. Go to Communion with them (and pray for them). It will be just the same (or better than that) as a Mass said beautifully by a visibly holy man, and shared by a few devout and decorous people. (It could not be worse than the mess of the feeding of the Five Thousand after which [Our] Lord propounded the feeding that was to come).[13]

Among the re-*forms* of the sacraments and various liturgical rites, those concerning the Mass — particularly the Eucharistic Prayer itself — must hold pride of place and can be truly regarded as the outstanding fruit and lasting monumental achievement witnessing to the pastoral charity of the Second Vatican Council — that charity of Christ, who constantly challenges, urges, and enables his faithful to renew the inner form of their lives by the outpouring of his Spirit of holiness.[14] The aims of the Second Vatican Council have a breadth of vision which Pope John Paul II cites twenty five years after the promulgation of the Constitution of the Sacred Liturgy:

> To impart an ever increasing vigor to the Christian life of the faithful; to adapt more suitably to the needs of our own times those institutions that are subject to change; to foster whatever can promote union among all who believe in Christ; to strengthen whatever can help to call the whole of humanity into the household of the Church.[15]

Need for Catechesis of the Eucharistic Prayer

The need for catechesis or instruction concerning the "signs of the Eucharist" has been recognized and repeatedly emphasized in recent Synods of Bishops since the publication of the Instruction on

---

[13] Letter 1 November 1963 in *The Letters of J.R.R. Tolkien* (edited by Humphrey Carpenter with the assistance of Christopher Tolkien), George Allen & Unwin, London, 1990, p. 338f.

[14] Cf. 2 Cor 5:14; Rm 5:5.

[15] Apostolic Letter (4 December 1988), n. 1 (tr. in *Briefing* 89, Vol. 19, No 12, p. 251); cf. S.C., n. 1.

the Eucharistic Mystery, which applied the teaching of the Second Vatican Council and sets out the principles governing Eucharistic doctrine and worship.[16] One of the first tasks Pope John Paul II set himself on becoming pope was to write the Apostolic Exhortation, *Catechesis in Our Time (Catechesi Tradendae)*, in which he sums up the work of the Fourth General Synod, which was held in October 1977. In this document he expresses the Synod's desire to center catechesis in the liturgy and sacraments, in which it has its source and focus:

> Catechesis is intrinsically linked with the whole of liturgical and sacramental activity, for it is in the sacraments, especially in the Eucharist, that Christ Jesus works in fullness for the transformation of human beings... sacramental life is impoverished and very soon turns into hollow ritualism if it is not based on serious knowledge of the meaning of the sacraments, and catechesis becomes intellectualized if it fails to come alive in sacramental practice ... one can say that catechetical teaching... finds its source and its fulfillment in the Eucharist, within the whole circle of the liturgical year.[17]

Attention to this pastoral need has been given in different ways. However, despite the vast amount of catechetical material available in recent years, it is sadly evident that the basic reasons and thrust underlying the liturgical reforms have not always been deeply enough assimilated by people in general (not to mention their pastors too!).

On the positive side, however, with good reason we may hope that much can be achieved in endeavoring to lead people to appreciate the significance of what we celebrate and proclaim in worship especially when we take into account the fact that by now everyone is quite familiar with the format and practice of the Church's new rites of the sacraments and Eucharistic liturgy. For, now that the initial period of confusion and reaction, which was occasioned by the introduction of liturgical changes, is behind us, this moment of comparative calm is

---

[16] Cf. *Eucharisticum mysterium*, nn. 3-6.
[17] C.T. nn. 23 & 48; translation in *Catechesis in our Time*, St. Paul Publications/CIS pp. 25 & 45.

most opportune for re-approaching the task of catechesis about the inner meaning of participation in the liturgy especially regarding the Eucharistic mystery. Such a climate of calm would seem to be indeed conducive to appreciate that participation means a lot more and something much deeper than merely fulfilling formal, ritual requirements to the last jot and tittle. It means growth and consolidation in the life of the Spirit, who brings about genuine renewal which springs from the heart of Christian worship.

The same pastoral charity motivating the Council in renewing the liturgy also enjoined and encouraged a constant responsibility regarding catechesis and deepening spiritual instruction about the Mass, which celebrates the *Mystery of Faith*. The example of the Great Fathers of the Church bears ample testimony to the validity and effectiveness of that kind of catechesis called *"mystagogical"* which was developed and practiced from the second half of the fourth century until it disappeared in the Western Church due to the prominence given to allegorical interpretation in the Middle Ages.[18] *Mystagogical catechesis*, as its very name suggests, is instruction and formation in the Mystery of Christ — the heart and focal point of which is his passover. The new *Catechism of the Catholic Church*, which draws on the teaching of the Second Vatican Council, expresses the recognized need to rediscover this kind of Christian formation in our age:

> "The Liturgy is the summit towards which the Church's endeavor leads and, at the same time, the source from which springs its entire energy." It is therefore the privileged environment for catechesis of the People of God. "Catechesis is intrinsically related to the whole span of liturgical and sacramental activity, for it is in the sacraments, and above all in the Eucharist, that Jesus Christ is fully engaged in bringing about the transformation of humanity."[19]

The following paragraph of the same *Catechism* beautifully describes

---

[18] Cf. Enrico Mazza, *Mystagogy: A Theology of Liturgy in the Patristic Age,* p. 10ff.

[19] N. 1074 — citing S.C., n. 10 and John Paul II, Apostolic Exhortation *Catechesi tradendae,* n. 23.

the graced process of human transformation through the rites of the sacraments of Christ's passover:

> The aim of liturgical catechesis (which is, indeed, "mystagogy") consists in providing an introduction to the Mystery of Christ, insofar as it moves from the visible to the invisible, from signs to the reality signified, from "sacraments" to the "mysteries." Such a catechesis provides a model for all local and regional catechisms.[20]

Liturgical catechesis is itself an example of what is expressed in the ancient adage from the age of the Fathers of the Church: *"Lex orandi, lex credendi,"* that is, the faith and doctrine of the Church express the way the Church prays.[21] The revival of this mystagogical method of catechesis contributes to the Church's essential mission of evangelization, from which it is distinct, as the Basic Text of the 45th International Eucharistic Congress in Seville makes clear:

> While the Eucharist is the center of evangelization, it is not directly concerned with basic missionary endeavor. Its expression of evangelization, which is the same as that of the liturgy, is "mystagogical," that is, by means of word and sign which are unfolded for the assembly of the faithful in the liturgical action. This unfolding of the mystery, which is understood as taking place in an integral and full way, implies three moments: the time "before," "during" and "after" the celebration.[22]

---

[20] Ibid., n. 1075 (Cf. also, n. 1234). One is reminded in this succinct description of the sublime teaching and approach of such masters of mystagogical catechesis as Dionysius (the "Areopagite") or St. Maximus the Confessor.

[21] The phrase is attributed to St Vincent of Lerins, *First Notebook*, c. 23; cf. Prosper of Aquitaine: *"legem credendi lex statuat supplicandi"* — *De vocatione omnium gentium*, I. 12 (PL 51, 664c). It passed into the *Indiculus de gratia Dei et libero voluntatis arbitrio*, c. 8 (PL 51, 209C; DS (139) 246), attributed to Pope Celestine I against semi-pelagianism. The Magisterium employed this principle, which it cited in different ways in the course of the centuries, especially in recent documents apropos the liturgy — cf. *Enchiridion Documentorum Instaurationis Liturgicae*, Marietti, Torino, 1976, p. 1110. Re developing Eucharistic theology from this principle in the Eucharistic Prayer — cf. *Notitiae*, n. 259 (Feb. 1988), pp. 110-152. The French hierarchy drew up a "Credo" of the Catholic Faith around the structural lines of Eucharistic Prayer IV — cf. *Notitiae* (1979), pp. 147-152.

[22] "Eucharist and Evangelization" in *Eucharist: The Heart of Evangelization*, Éditions Paulines, Sherbrooke, Quebec, 1992, p. 31.

Only when Christ's faithful are renewed *within themselves* can they become authentic witnesses to the Good News of Christ, whom they have received, welcomed and assimilated. In summing up the work of the Fourth Synod of Bishops on catechesis, Pope John Paul II pointed to the parish community as the *"home"* where *"the bread of good doctrine and the Eucharistic Bread are broken . . . in abundance, in the setting of the one act of worship; from that home they are sent out day by day to their apostolic mission in all the centers of activity for the life of the world."*[23]

In accord with the sound principles of teaching, particular care should be taken regarding the manner in which the Church's norms and instructions are carried out concerning the liturgy. Attention should be paid to the level of understanding and background of the group to whom it is directed, and the catechesis and method of its presentation should be appropriately adapted. This does not mean a "watering down" of the Christian doctrine of the *Mystery of Faith* so that, for instance, children are introduced only to the "meal-aspect" of the Eucharist as if it were a matter of "partying with Jesus"! This shallow approach, as is all too evident in some of our modern "catechetical programs," not only distorts *the faith of the Church* and presents merely a humanistic and subjective sense of Christianity, but it also implies a very poor appreciation of the graced quality of children's imagination, which manifests a hunger and openness for what the Spirit of God offers.[24] The exercise of pastoral charity is demanded in ensuring that the Eucharistic Mystery is "considered *in all its fullness*" — as the post-Conciliar Instruction on the Worship of the Eucharistic Mystery states — "not only in the celebration of Mass, but also in devotion to the sacred species which remain after Mass and are reserved to extend the grace of the sacrifice." It would be a grave injustice if children — Christ's *little ones* — were to be deprived

---

[23] C.T., n. 67; trans. in St Paul Publications/CTS, p. 61.

[24] This is not to gainsay the pastoral task of taking account of and applying the human sciences, such as sound pedagogy. The problem of gradual initiation into the Mystery of Christ was recognized from St. Paul's day (cf. 1 Cor. 3:2). Following his imagery of weaning from "milk" to enable the taking of "solid food/meat," the early Fathers such as Clement of Alexandria energetically addressed this task with inspired pastoral charity — cf. *Christ the Teacher* (*Paidagogos*), I. 6.35-52.

of approaching him as their Lord and God while being encouraged to frequent his table merely as another "pal" or even as their best friend! Furthermore, the Instruction insists that people should be taught about the principles of Eucharistic faith and also be helped to understand "the *signs* by which the Eucharist is celebrated as the memorial of the Lord and worshipped as a permanent sacrament in the Church."[25]

Needless to say, pastoral care must be taken in explaining the nature of the Eucharistic Prayer itself — not only because of its technical and theological character, but also because of its privileged quality as expressing and communicating the central and deepest reality of the Christian mystery of life and worship. In the Fourth Part of the new *Catechism* devoted to an extensive and inspiring treatment of prayer in the life of Christ's faithful we find the following words which center the heart of all prayer in the Eucharist:

> The Eucharist contains and expresses all aspects of prayer: it is "the pure oblation" of the whole Body of Christ to the glory of his name. Both Eastern and Western Traditions regard it as "the sacrifice of praise."[26]

The document introducing the *New Order of Mass* encourages development of its guidelines according to local circumstances in order to promote active and full participation in the sacred liturgy, through which the spiritual welfare of the faithful is enhanced.[27] In another section later on, the same document stresses that care should be taken when instructing the faithful about the central significance of the Eucharistic Prayer so that its essential nature, intended by Christ, will become apparent as "the climax and the very heart of the entire celebration, a prayer of thanksgiving and sanctification."[28] There then follows a detailed description of the main elements which constitute the structure or form of the Eucharistic Prayer:

---

[25] Instruction *Eucharisticum mysterium* [E.M.] (25 May 1967), nn. 3g, 4 (italics mine); also nn. 2, 5, 6.

[26] *Catechism*, n. 2643.

[27] *General Instruction on the Roman Missal* [GIRM], n. 5.

[28] Ibid., n. 54; trans. in *Vatican Council II* (ed. A. Flannery), Dominican Publ., Dublin, 1975, p. 175.

- Thanksgiving
- Acclamation
- Epiclesis
- Narrative of the Institution
- Anamnesis
- Offering
- Intercessions
- Doxology[29]

It is strongly recommended that catechesis on the Eucharistic Prayer should include an adequate explanation of the significance of these various elements in order to bring out how the Eucharistic Prayer contains the basis of authentic Christian spirituality.

Any program of catechesis of the Eucharist should likewise present a thorough explanation of the doctrine encompassed in the various forms of the Eucharistic Prayer. These exemplify the way this Prayer may be adapted to the needs of particular groups and pastoral situations. As no single Prayer can exhaust the Eucharistic mystery in all the depth of its richness, it is fitting that there have always been various Eucharistic Prayers and rites to express the Church's worship. These reflect different theological and cultural perspectives of Christians down the centuries.

The Eucharistic Prayer is not only at the center of the Mass; it is the heart of the Mass, so that today the Mass is often simply called "the Eucharist." In the first Christian centuries many forms of the Eucharistic Prayer were in use. Indeed, before a man could be ordained a bishop it was required that he showed himself capable of spontaneously (that is, without a prepared text) improvising his own prayer during the Eucharistic celebration. In time, the Eucharistic Prayer eventually became standardized and written down from among the better examples of Prayers. This came about as the Church gradually began to recognize the need both to express a unified form of worship in different pastoral and cultural areas and also, no doubt,

---

[29] Ibid., n. 55. Though Wainwright lists ten features, they essentially amount to the same scheme — cf. *Baptism and Eucharist: Ecumenical Convergence in Celebration*, p. 102f.

to prevent the spread of heretical or partial "theologies" which appeared here and there.

In the Western Church only one Eucharistic Prayer became the standard use at Mass. This Prayer is called the "Roman Canon" since its was the standardized rule or *"canon"* for Latin Rite Catholics.[30] Though its roots go back to before St. Ambrose in the fourth century and though it was used from the eleventh or twelfth century, the Roman Canon became officially promulgated by Pope St. Pius V in response to the reforms called for by the Council of Trent. It was a momentous decision, therefore, that Pope Paul VI took in calling for the two or three new Eucharistic Prayers to be drawn up for use with the Roman Canon.[31] This responded to the endeavor of the Second Vatican Council to renew and revitalize the sacred liturgy in the Western Church. Within a few years the three "new" Eucharistic Prayers, now familiar to us for more than two decades, were carefully prepared by a committee of liturgical and theological scholars and approved by the Holy See.

After the appearance of these three "new" Eucharistic Prayers in 1969/70, the Holy See saw fit also to approve the use of other Prayers for pastoral reasons which some episcopal conferences presented. Among those approved were three Prayers for Masses with children and two for Masses of reconciliation; these were first approved in 1974 experimentally for three years and later came to be permitted definitively.[32] It would not go amiss to recognize that there are also other approved Eucharistic Prayers being used in various countries for particular pastoral occasions — for example, a Prayer for Masses with deaf and dumb children in Australia and Germany.

---

[30] St. Gregory the Great (end of the 6th cent.) confused the two senses in which some Fathers (e.g. Tertullian and St. Cyprian) used the phrase *"oratio dominica"* — either for the "Our Father" or the prayer our Lord used at the Last Supper. Only the former has come down to us verbatim; the latter has, however, been transmitted in spirit in the Church's various forms of Eucharistic Prayer. St. Gregory was wrong about the *"Lord's Prayer being used at the Last Supper,"* but correct in regarding the Eucharistic Prayer being in keeping with Christ's teaching and example of prayer.

[31] This was on 20 June 1966. Cf. Senn (ed.), *New Eucharistic Prayers: An Ecumenical Study of their Development and Structure*, p. 2f.

[32] See below — chapters VII & VIII. The account of the stages of preparation and approval is described by Alan Detscher and John Barry Ryan in *New Eucharistic Prayers*, ibid., pp. 15-62.

All these Prayers contain and express in different ways the essential structural features of Eucharistic worship.[33]

Eucharistic catechesis in general and especially regarding the Church's Great Prayer is not only necessary as a valid expression of the pastoral charity at the heart of the Church, but it also provides an indispensable service in bringing about that *life of communion of God's children.* This life drawn from the Eucharistic celebration expresses the heart of Christian spirituality to which we are called by the Father's Word, in which we are consecrated by the Holy Spirit, and of which the whole of our lives becomes a joyous proclamation of the worth of worship *in spirit and truth.* For worship is that living proclamation which manifests the fruits of the Gospel of the Eucharist, that is, it witnesses to how the Eucharist, which is the Risen Lord's gift of himself as our communication with the Father, transforms our individual human lives into his community of persons.

For the Lord's disciples, early Christians, and the Fathers of the Church, worship signified more than cult or ritual since it took in the whole sweep of human living brought before God. Worship stems from and leads to the life of genuine piety (*"latria"* and *"Eusebeia"* as St. Augustine liked to point out in tracing it to the roots of religious experience).[34] Worship characterizes the essential relation of humanity to God, its Creator, Redeemer and Savior — that relation which finds expression in *"Eucharist"* or thanksgiving and praise. Since in English the words "worship" and "worth" are etymologically related, it is clear that worship is the basis of human culture. Worship, thus, celebrates paradise-regained![35]

Liturgical worship held its place as signifying the whole of

---

[33] Collections of various Eucharistic Prayers are given in the following useful books: Della Torre (ed.), *Pregare l'Eucaristia*; Senn (ed.), *New Eucharistic Prayers,* op. cit.; Thurian & Wainwright (eds.), *Baptism and Eucharist: Ecumenical Convergence in Celebration,* op. cit. Cf. also *Eucharisties de Tous Pays,* Centre National de Pastorale Liturgie, Paris, 1975: in this book fourteen "new" prayers are presented with an excellent introduction regarding pastoral catechesis. ICEL is preparing a series of new Eucharistic Prayers, the first of which, "Eucharistic Prayer A," is in the final stages of preparation for approval.

[34] Cf. *City of God*, X. i.

[35] As the Fathers of the Church loved to speak or sing of it — cf. St. Basil, *De Spirito Sancto*, xv. 36 (PG 32, 130-131); or the many hymns of St. Ephrem, *Hymns on Paradise* (Trans. by Sebastian Brock), St Vladimir's Seminary Press, Crestwood, New York, 1990. Cf. also Alexander Schmemann, *The Eucharist: Sacrament of the Kingdom,* p. 174ff.

human living brought before God, whose saving love empowered it with a new dynamism of meaning as being a sacramental "parable" of the Mystery of Christ. In this *new creation*, which the Holy Spirit of Christ brings about through the sacred liturgy, we are introduced to and impelled towards realizing God's kingdom in our midst. Just as Jesus' parables proclaim the nearness of the *"mysteries of the kingdom of God/heaven,"* so too the sacred mysteries of Christian worship manifest God's Name being praised (*"blessed/hallowed"*) as his will is done in memory of Jesus *"on earth as it is in heaven."*

Rediscovering Roots

Before we can be sufficiently confident about developing and employing new forms of language for worship, there is an urgent need for us to appropriate the biblical roots of our faith-story, which the various Eucharistic Prayers attempt to proclaim in celebration.

The name Mass is a rather "latecomer," deriving from the Latin sentence of dismissal: *Ite missa est* — which might be translated: "Go, you are sent." *Mass* is a mission word since the reality it signifies, the Eucharistic Celebration, is the heart of evangelization.[36] The earliest names by which the Christian community described its central act of gathering for worship were: *"the breaking of bread," "assembly" (synaxis), "prayer of offering" (anaphora),* and *"Eucharist"*; other expressions were also in common use, such as *"the mysteries."*[37] When we come across such expressions in the New Testament — especially in the Acts of the Apostles and Epistles — we have traces of the central act of Christian worship.[38] Furthermore, the whole of daily living was seen as linked to the worship of God. For example, when St. Paul exhorts Christians to pray always and to do everything in the spirit of thanksgiving (*"eucharist"*),[39] could he not have had the Christian

---

[36] Cf. Christine Mohrmann, *Études sur le Latin des Chrétiens*, t. III, Edizioni di Storia e Letteratura, Roma, 1965, pp. 351-376.

[37] Cf. Jungmann, *The Mass of the Roman Rite*; cf. also C.F.D. Moule, *Worship in the New Testament* (Part II), Grove Books (n. 13), Bramcote, Notts., p. 63ff.

[38] Cf. Ildefons Herwegen, *Liturgy's Inner Beauty*, Collegeville, MN, 1955, p. 7ff.

[39] Cf. Col 3:15-17; cf. also Rm 12:1.

celebration in mind? The same Apostle's magnificent praise-poems near the opening of his great Captivity Epistles also breathe the spirit of the early Church's style of praying the Eucharist.[40] If we hope to discover the roots of the spirituality of the Eucharist it is essential to understand and contemplate the biblical roots of prayer, in which *Eucharist* came to hold a privileged place as the culminating moment of communal worship.

It may be fairly well known that the shape of our Eucharistic worship is linked with and, indeed, rooted in the Jewish table prayers and, broadly speaking, the passover celebrations. But, the fact that our Eucharistic Prayer itself owes much to Jewish origins needs to be better recognized and appreciated. This fact is becoming more and more evident thanks to the patient work and insights of some contemporary scholars.

Since the pioneering work regarding the Jewish origins of this Prayer, new questions emerged about the precise nature and kind of pattern of Jewish prayer on which the Christian celebration is based. New ground was broken when attention was focused on the literary form or *genre* rather than being directed exclusively on the religious and theological aspects of this Prayer — the former being seen as inseparable from and intrinsic to the latter. What might seem to be so obvious had somehow escaped notice until recently when it was pointed out that the Eucharistic Prayer combines the oldest Hebrew style of praying called *todah* with its later development called *berakoth*. The structure — which involves both praise and petition — hinges on the use of the indicative and imperative mood of the verbs. In other words, statements are made (confession of God's wonderful deeds or expressions of our praise) and also petitions are made (as for instance, requests for the Holy Spirit to transform our gifts and ourselves). The very word *"eucharist,"* though derived from the Greek, has a Hebrew substratum of meaning in *blessings-blessed,* which would be related to the religious attitude of *praise-thanksgiving.* This attitude found expression not only in the literary genre called *berakah,* but also derives from the more ancient *genre* called *todah,* which held in fine balance both an account of God's wonderful deeds as well as

---

[40] Cf. Ep 1:3-10; Col 1:12-20.

the petitions addressed to him.[41] The focus is clearly more God-centered in *todah* than that expressed simply by the words "thanksgiving-praise" (*berakah*) — as beautiful as the sentiments which they imply may be in recognizing benefits to oneself/one's community received from another. The very benefits or gifts somehow bind one to the benefactor.

Jewish life was — and is — permeated with the acclamations which recognize or acknowledge God's being and our total dependence on him for being. These are expressed in the *blessing prayers* for every situation in daily living, as the psalms amply witness. It is generally agreed that the Eucharistic Prayer and celebration as such developed from the grace before meals involving the blessing of the bread and from the grace after meals in which a number of blessing prayers were pronounced over the wine. Comparison with the Jewish structure and style of *"Blessings"* helps us to situate the various elements constituting our Eucharistic Prayer within an overall scheme or frame of reference: *praise-thanksgiving, commemoration, petition.* This pattern relates us to the design of God's revelation of salvation and eternal life through our experience of time, namely: present (praise), past (memorial), and future (petitionary intercession). Broadly speaking we can discern this thematic scheme in the structure of our Eucharistic Prayer.[42] But it would be a mistake to try to apply the pattern too rigidly. For is it not true that human experience of any relationship (with its needs and complexity of motives, intentions and "moments" of insight) flows in and out of time — especially

---

[41] The literary approach is developed by C. Giraudo — cf. *La struttura letteraria della preghiera eucaristica* . . . , op. cit.; Cf. also Mazza, op. cit., p. 12ff.; R. Maloney, *The Eucharistic Prayers in Worship, Preaching and Study*, p. 13ff.; also N. Lash's splendidly lucid chapter in *His Presence in the World*, pp. 64-107. Lash stated the need for English readers already in 1968: "... on the one hand, the meaning of the Mass can only be grasped through the study of the eucharistic prayer and, on the other hand, that the whole prayer must be studied: its literary form, patterns, and rhythm, not simply isolated words and phrases taken out of context" (p. 68).

[42] Cf. Maloney, op. cit., p. 16ff. I say "broadly speaking" since what is presented here is an attempt to simplify (I trust not oversimplify!) the various theories and insights of biblical and liturgical scholars regarding the origins and structure of the Eucharistic Prayer. For a useful summary of the complexity of the questions involved — Cf. David N. Power, "The Eucharistic Prayer: Another Look" in Senn (ed.), *New Eucharistic Prayers*, op. cit., p. 239ff.

in regard to the communal expression of that quite unique relationship with God in the Eucharistic Prayer. For here we — that is, individuals becoming persons by entering into the mystery of community — discover another dimension of awareness and dialogue, which is the *"mind of Christ"* or *"newness of being"* as St. Paul was at pains to describe. This dimension is celebrated in the Eucharistic Prayer, in which the Christian community proclaims the heart of its spirituality, its *life of the Spirit.*

2

The Rhythm and Structure of the Eucharistic Prayer

The starting point for seeking to understand the Eucharistic Prayer is to appreciate its ascendant quality: it is a prayer of "blessing," of thanksgiving. It supposes that there is something prior to the prayer: an event, a memorial, to which response is made. The Eucharistic Prayer is, basically, a response: the Church's response to the mystery of faith. Thanks to the biblical and ecumenical study of this century, Eucharistic theology has rediscovered the strong sense of "memorial." This category has brought together the diverse Christian traditions and become a point of contact for them in profound dialogue concerning the significance of the Eucharist. These diverse traditions meet in a wide common witness about this. But, "Memorial" as such is not the ultimate reference point, for it must be seen as referring to an Event: the mystery of Christ, our Passover, his rite of passage from this world to the Father in which he re-unites to himself God's people in the Holy Spirit.[1]

The principal elements which constitute the Eucharistic Prayer must now be examined in some detail. In providing a catechesis of these elements, however, it is important that we do not give the impression that they stand independently of each other, that they are "parts" or that they disrupt the dynamic unity of the Prayer as a whole.[2]

---

[1] Monsignor Pere Tena, "Reflections on Eucharistic Catechesis in preparation for International Eucharistic Congresses" (Conference given in 1988 at the meeting of National Delegates to the 44th I.E.C. of Seoul) in *The International Eucharistic Congresses for a New Evangelization*, p. 88f.

[2] Alexander Schmemann is quite right in emphatically objecting to an analysis of the "parts" that breaks up the unity of the Eucharistic Prayer — cf. *The Eucharist: Sacrament of the Kingdom*, op. cit., p. 171ff.

Furthermore, as noted at the end of the last chapter, it is crucial to realize that these elements taken together contribute to the overall unified sense of the Prayer's structure or form as celebrating the Christian rhythm of worship in *praise-commemoration-intercession*. Thus, though this chapter may seem disproportionately long in comparison to others in this book, it is necessarily so because we are dealing with the unified experience of the Church at prayer. In deepening our understanding of its component elements we must not lose sight of what the Eucharistic Prayer re-presents:

> When the faithful participate in the Eucharist, they must understand that truly "each time we offer this memorial sacrifice the work of our redemption is accomplished" and to this end bishops must carefully train the faithful to celebrate every Sunday the marvellous work that Christ has wrought in the mystery of his Passover, in order that they likewise may proclaim it to the world . . . Since Christ's death on the cross and his resurrection constitute the content of the daily life of the Church and pledge of his eternal Passover, the liturgy has as its first task to lead us untiringly back to the Easter pilgrimage initiated by Christ, in which we accept death in order to enter into life.[3]

Proclamation

The entire Eucharistic Prayer is proclamation — the proclamation of God's saving design of love.[4] The Liturgy of the Word (scripture readings and homily) does not exhaust the proclamation of salvation. For the action of the Liturgy of the Eucharist carries on the

---

[3] Pope John Paul II, Apostolic Letter (4 December 1988) n. 6; loc. cit., p. 253.

[4] Cf. J.D.Crichton (*Christian Celebration: The Mass,* p. 84f.) who treats "proclamation" separately as a feature of the Eucharistic Prayer, whereas the list of principal elements given in the General Instruction on the Roman Missal (n. 55 — cited above) does not include it as such. Léon-Dufour (cf. *Sharing the Eucharistic Bread: The Witness of the New Testament,* op. cit., p. 224ff.) points out regarding 1 Cor 11:26 that the Greek verb should be translated "proclaim" rather than "announce" and that it is not an imperative or new command that Paul issues, but a statement of fact: that is, the very fact that the community gathers to celebrate the Eucharist is itself a proclamation of the Lord's death until he returns.

proclamation, and is truly the fulfillment of the divine plan of salvation in sacramental deed. It is true to say that the Eucharistic Prayer is the fulness of the Gospel — the *Good News* realized (made real) in-deed. It is the *new creation* over which we too rejoice and exult with God in discovering and proclaiming created realities as "very good." The Eucharist manifests the light of God's look on creation — that look which restores it to the excellence and dignity intended from the beginning.[5]

But just what is the saving design of God's love that the Eucharistic Prayer proclaims? What is it that the Institution Narrative affirms? What is it that the power of the Holy Spirit effects and reveals to the Church, the assembly of Christ's faithful? It is the Paschal Mystery of Christ certainly. But it also proclaims the infinite implications of this reality for human life. This reality is Christ *already present in mystery* — that is, *sacramentally.*[6]

The Paschal Mystery of Christ, the Second Vatican Council teaches, is the supreme revelation of God's love which the Eucharist celebrates and proclaims. The spiritual reality of the Paschal Mystery can only be discerned by the power of the Holy Spirit, whom he promised to send during the Last Supper and whom he breathed on the disciples in the moment of his glory — that "hour," as St. John likes to highlight, when the Father's will was accomplished.[7]

---

[5] Cf. Gn 1:31. — Cf. comments of St. John of the Cross in *The Spiritual Canticle*, Stanza 5 *The Collected Works . . .* (Kieran Kavanaugh & Otilio Rodriguez) ICS Publ. Washington D.C., 1979, p. 435: "To look and behold that they were very good was to make them very good in the Word, His Son. . . . Accordingly, the Son of God proclaimed: 'If I be lifted up from the earth, I will elevate all things to Me' [Jn 12:32]. And in this elevation of all things through the Incarnation of His Son and through the glory of His resurrection according to the flesh, the Father did not merely beautify creatures partially, but rather we can say, clothed them wholly in beauty and dignity." Vatican II applies the verse from Jn 12:32 to the Eucharist — cf. L.G. n.3.

[6] Cf. L.G. n. 3 — in employing this expression (*iam praesens in mysterio*), the Council simply adopted the key insight of Dom Odo Casel, which derives from the way the Fathers of the Church interpreted St. Paul's language. It thereby takes no sides in the "mystery religion" controversy. Many studies are available on the biblical notion of "mystery" — cf. R.E. Brown's bibliography under "Mystery" in *New Catholic Encyclopedia*, 10, McGraw-Hill, New York, 1967, pp. 148-151.

[7] Cf. L.G. n. 3 (also 48); S.C. n. 5 (end) — cf. *Commentary on the Documents of Vatican II* (ed. H. Vorgrimler) Burns & Oates/Herder and Herder, 1967, p. 141f. The Council, following the Fathers of the Church, integrates both theological perspectives presented in the New Testament: the exaltation on the cross, when Christ breathed forth the spiritual life of the Church (John), and also the Pentecost event (Acts).

First of all we must be clear about what is meant by the Paschal Mystery. This English word *passover* expresses exactly what the *"Pasch"* signifies. This word derives from the Hebrew verb which literally means "to leap/pass over"; it is related to the idea of passage. In early catechetical Easter homilies we find great care exercised in explaining the original meaning of the Hebrew word, as for instance in the following text by the second century bishop Melito of Sardis:

> The very name of the feast points to the way in which it [the Jewish passover] is surpassed, if it is carefully explained. The word "Pasch" means "passage," because when the angel of death was striking down the first-born, he passed over the houses of the Hebrews. But with us the passage of the angel of death is a reality, for it passes over us once for all when Christ raises us up to eternal life . . . the sacrifice of the true Pasch is the beginning of eternal life for us . . . Now Christ is sacrificed for him [the Christian] when he recognizes the grace and understands the life this sacrifice has won for him.[8]

We notice the double sense here of *"passover"*: the figure (or type) and reality, which the Fathers delighted to explore, of the angel's/ Christ's deliverance. In virtue of this *passover* other levels of life are made possible: the *exodus* or passage from the condition of bondage to freedom — from slavery and sin to new life in the promised land or in Christ.

Throughout the long homily of Melito of Sardis on the Passover, the idea of the permanence of Christ's eternal sacrifice is poetically contrasted with the transitory quality of its Old Testament antecedents and all imperfect or incomplete attempts to worship God fittingly. Three centuries later St. Augustine energetically explains to his congregation that, despite the corruption of the sense of *"pascha,"* it really meant "to pass over" (*transitus*) since it is derived from the Hebrew, and not — as was commonly thought in his day — from the Greek verb *"paschein"* ("to suffer").[9] We, perhaps much more than

---

[8] Cf. A. Hamman (ed.), *The Paschal Mystery: Ancient Liturgies and Patristic Texts*, (tr. Thomas Halton), Alba House, Staten Island, N.Y., 1969, p. 25ff. Cf. Tillard's excellent study: *The Eucharist: Pasch of God's People*, op. cit.

[9] Apart from various sermons, clearly the most famous of Augustine's texts on this is his letter to Januarius — *Ep.* 55.2; PL 33, 205. Cf. Christine Mohrmann, *Études sur le Latin des Chretiens*, op. cit., t. I, pp. 205-222.

the Greek- or Latin-speaking Christians of Melito's or Augustine's day, have greater need to realize our religious roots!

The point of recalling the original sense of *passover* is not merely a matter of academic interest or to satisfy curiosity about etymology, which might give a useful clue in filling in cross-word puzzles! It focuses our attention on what is centrally important in our Christian life — what ought to shape our whole experience as deriving from proclaiming Christ's mystery of *passover* in the Eucharist. Though employed many times in the course of the Vatican II documents and especially in its first on the Sacred Liturgy,[10] the meaning of "Paschal Mystery" seems to be taken for granted. It is hardly explained — apart from the following brief statement:

> Christ the Lord fulfilled this work of human Redemption and God's perfect glorification — to which the marvels God did for the people of the Old Testament were a prelude. He accomplished this principally through the paschal mystery of his blessed Passion, Resurrection from the dead and glorious Ascension. In this paschal mystery he [Christ] "destroyed our death by dying and by rising restored our life."[11]

The sense of the Second Vatican Council's brief "definition" of this mystery can be found in a verse of St. Paul's Epistle to the Romans where it is thought that the Apostle is quoting from an early hymn in praise of Christ:

> The death he died to sin, once for all, but the life he lives he lives to God.[12]

This verse occurs in the section of St. Paul's teaching on becoming conformed to the sacramental *pattern/form* of Christ's Paschal Mystery. St. Paul's instruction draws out the practical consequences of faith in God's free gift received through sacramental initiation into Christ's life — the consequences of which cannot be ignored as superfluous because Christ has done everything. Rather, the very proclamation of Christ's generous achievement on our behalf impels us to imitate what we receive and handle in the sacraments as the

---

[10] Cf. S.C. nn. 5, 6, 47, 61, 81, 102-111.

[11] S.C. n. 5b — citing an Easter Preface.

[12] Rm 6:10.

Fathers of the Church constantly emphasized.[13] St. Paul insists on the absolute break between death and life — not only in the natural sense, but in the moral and spiritual senses. This is evident in the tenses of the Greek verbs employed: the aorist past in the repetition of "he died," emphasized by the adverbial phrase "once for all," is contrasted starkly by the way Paul describes Christ's actual condition in repeating *"he lives."* Christ's death is the great *passage* or *passover* through and from our human condition into the eternal presence of God's life.[14] His *passover* is an eternal event.

In it he "brothers" the whole of humanity which he represents before his Father's life of love. He would not and could not be detained in the thickets of time by death, which results from the common condition of lovelessness, namely the pride of sin, since he was about his Father's business — to reveal and recreate the world into the kingdom of love. He fulfilled this loving business in the intense atmosphere of his passion, death, resurrection, ascension and sending of his Spirit. The atmosphere of this *passover* is that of our rite of passage to life proclaimed in the Eucharistic Prayer. In joining Christ's passover we are plunged into the living presence of God's reality: we become "contemporaries" of Christ.[15] The Eucharist is the

---

[13] Especially when commenting on this text — cf. e.g. St. Cyril of Jerusalem, *Mystagogical Catecheses*, II, v. Participation means sacramental *imitation* of Christ. This imitation is not a matter of external observance, but of inner assimilation of Christ's attitude and spirit. Thanksgiving/praise was characteristic of Christ — see below where "thanksgiving/praise" is treated.

[14] Cf. Dom Odo Casel, O.S.B., *La Fête de Pâques dans l'Église des Pères*, (tr. by J.C. Didier from German in the Lex Orandi series 37), fd. du Cerf, Paris 1963, p. 98.

[15] Long before Sören Kierkegaard, "the father of existential thinking," Augustine had realized so perceptibly that to appreciate fully the significance of what it is to be human it is essential to experience the relation of being and time. Through the *Confessions*, of which the *Hymn of Beauty* (Bk. X.27) is a fine poetic resumé, he endeavors to show that his discovery of this relation is owed to the grace of Christian conversion to Christ the Word-made-flesh. The account of his own conversion illustrates well what the Danish preacher describes as the drawing together of the various strands of one's temporal being into the presence of God so that one becomes a "contemporary" of Christ — *Concluding Unscientific Postscript* (translated by David Swenson and Walter Lowrie), Princeton Univ. Press, 1941, p. 311: *"To have been young, and then to grow older, and finally to die, is a very mediocre form of human existence; this merit belongs to every animal. But the unification of the different stages of life in simultaneity is the task set for human beings."* Cf. also *Training in Christianity* (Princeton Univ. Press, 1971, p. 66ff.): "Christianity as the Absolute Contemporaneousness with Christ," ibid., p. 152f. (from the first of his seven discourses on "From on high He will draw all to Himself"): *"Christianity requires Christians [. . .] to remember one thing, the Lord Jesus Christ."*

sacrament of unity not only because it signifies and brings about unity between humanity and God and between individuals themselves, but also because it integrates into the harmonious perspective of God's real presence all our fragmented experiences, all our disjointed memories, all our divisive and frustrating moments of unachieved hopes, yearnings and dreams. It celebrates our conversion or our being turned together towards living Christ's *passover*, that eternal instant of the power of love's dynamism.[16] The Christian celebration of the *passover* is possible and realized because of the power of the Holy Spirit who draws us to Christ, the Light of the Nations, in the Mystery of Faith.[17]

In the Eucharistic Prayer the Christian community proclaims God's work in it, or rather, God *working* in its midst through the sanctifying presence and power of Christ's word and Spirit of love, who renews the face of the world.[18] The community is thus renewed in this vital act of celebrating the new reality of its life of love both in God and in itself. For in proclaiming the "wonderful deeds of God" (the *mirabilia Dei*), the Eucharistic liturgy creates a new atmosphere of grace — that environment in which, like the Blessed Virgin Mary, our hearts are drawn to magnify the presence and working of God our Savior in wonderment. Awe, adoration, reverence and loving recognition of God's transforming involvement and influence in this world — this wonderment is indeed the only appropriate response to the love of God. This atmosphere of grace (the *divine milieu*) is the ground for Christians to grow in hope and to rejoice in responsible love — that is, the responsibility of fulfilling their commitment to become co-operators with God (truly *co-workers and missionaries of charity*).[19] For from the beginning (of the world and the Church) God

---

[16] The significance of "conversion" is closely linked with "conversation," both words sharing the same Latin double-rooted word *"con-versio,"* which literally means a turning over together. Indeed, there can hardly be any conversion without conversation: "Faith comes from hearing" (Rm 10:17). This is the greatest of all revolutions! For a general treatment of the notion of conversion — cf. A.D. Nock, *Conversion*, Oxford Univ. Press, 1961; cf. also John S. Dunne, *A Search for God in Time and Memory*, Sheldon Press, London, 1975, and Walter E. Conn, *Conversion*, Alba House, Staten Island, N.Y., 1978.

[17] It fulfills what was intuitively seen and perhaps prophetically taught by Plato in his famous passage on the nature of true education consisting in turning from fascination with shadows to the full brightness of reality — cf. *Republic* VII.518ff.

[18] Cf. Gn 1:2; Ps 104:30.

[19] To borrow the names of Mother Teresa's associates!

communicates with sheer generosity his creative imagination and skill to humanity[20] to this end: that, in employing his gifts and talents, human beings may discover and proclaim the worth of living. This proclamation is living worship!

The Eucharistic Prayer as proclamation, begins with the *Preface* —which implies more than "introduction," as in modern English. The word "preface" is derived from the Latin *"prae-fatio,"* which means *"speaking-out"* or *"proclaiming."*[21] Its original meaning, though not immediately clear, was associated with prophetic utterance and activity.[22] Here it is a question of proclaiming before God and his people the Christian prayer of sacrifice. The *Preface* is thus a rich proclamation of our God-given charter of human rights in their most profound sense! In recalling God's dialogue with humanity in his saving words and deeds, this *Magna Carta* raises the tone of language to that of praise, thanksgiving, and blessing, for the *Preface* states that we are called to share in and become the Mystical Body of Christ. To be prepared for this our hearts must be open to the transformation of conversion, which the Risen Lord's Spirit brings about. We are invited and empowered to be uplifted to participate in the dynamic movement of the *passover* of Christ's Mystery: "Lift up your hearts!" In other words, we are summoned to God: Hearts awake and be alert! — *Sursum corda!*[23]

The importance of the *Preface* as an integral part of the Eucharistic Prayer has been restored in the *New Order of the Mass.* There are now over eighty in the Missal. They offer a rich variety of ways of proclaiming and celebrating God's love in salvation-history; they "enrich the Church's treasury of prayer and understanding of the mystery of Christ."[24] This variety with its rich contents also affords a

---

[20] Cf. Gn 1:27f.; Mt 25:14ff.; Ac 1:8; 1 Cor 2:7ff.; 4:12.

[21] Cf. Christine Mohrmann, "Sur l'histoire de praefari — praefatio" in *Études sur le Latin des Chretiens*, t. III, Edizioni di Storia e Letteratura, Rome 1965, pp. 291-305.

[22] Cf. Mazza, *The Eucharistic Prayers*, op. cit., p. 36ff.

[23] The earliest known Western references to *Sursum cor[da]* as a liturgical formula seem to be in the *anaphora* of Hippolytus of Rome and in Cyprian's treatise on the Lord's Prayer, *De Orat. Dom.*, 31. St. Augustine frequently cites the phrase — forty-five times at least! — and comments on it especially in his sermons to the people. It was also employed in the ancient Eastern liturgies — cf. St. Cyril of Jerusalem, *Mystagogical Catecheses*, V.4. The expression possibly has its roots in Scripture — cf. Lm 3:41; also Col 3:12 and Jn 11:41.

[24] John Paul II's Apostolic Letter (4 December 1988), n. 10; loc. cit., p. 255.

valuable source of catechetical material which may be adapted in different pastoral situations and circumstances, liturgical seasons and themes, special occasions, the needs of particular groups, etc. Care should be taken in choosing the appropriate *Preface* for season, Sunday, or occasion being celebrated.[25]

Indeed every celebration of the Eucharist is a proclamation of that important dimension of the Church's mystery which expresses the *anticipation in hope* of humanity's calling to participate in the definitive communion of the kingdom of God. This dimension of hope expresses the ultimate openness for which our Lord himself prayed when establishing the original pattern of eucharistic celebration; it is what he guaranteed at this same event by promising to send the Holy Spirit to lead his faithful to the whole reality of the truth of communion.[26] The working of Christ's Spirit has evidently enabled the Christian Churches to come closer to unity in their understanding of the nature of the Church in virtue of realizing the profound truth of what the Church does in proclaiming the mystery of the Eucharist. For, the eucharistic celebration must ever point towards and already anticipate, with the certain hope contained in this sacrament of faith *par excellence*, the deep yearning of love for Christ's return in glory, as the Apostle Paul clearly states:

> For as often as you eat this bread and drink the cup, you proclaim (*kataggellete*) the Lord's death until he comes.[27]

This proclamation of the *death* of the Lord really refers, in St. Paul's sense not merely to a factual event of the past, but to the *dying* of Jesus, that is, his constant attitude of handing himself over to bring life *out of* death.[28]

---

[25] Cf. Crichton, op. cit., chapter 10 on celebration, p. 146ff.

[26] Cf. Jn 14:16-17, 26; 15:26; 16:12-15.

[27] 1 Cor 11:26. The liturgy expresses this reality of proclamation often — particularly in the *postcommunion* prayers, such as that for the Twenty-sixth Sunday of the Year: "Lord, may this eucharist in which we proclaim the death of Christ bring us salvation and make us one with him in glory, for he is Lord for ever and ever."

[28] Thus, for instance, Jerome Murphy-O'Connor translates the expression in 2 Cor 4:10 not as "the death of Jesus," but rather as "the dying of Jesus" — *Becoming Human Together: the Pastoral Anthropology of Saint Paul,* Michael Glazier, Wilmington, Delaware, 1982, p. 45ff.

Though this is not the place to discuss how ecumenical dialogue has moved on apace through the spiritual insight afforded by teaching such as that contained in this pauline verse, it is useful to recall some sentences from the splendid agreed statement of the Joint Commission for theological dialogue between the Roman Catholic Church and the Orthodox Church:

> By the eucharist the paschal event opens itself out into church. The church becomes that which it is called to be by baptism and chrismation. By the communion in the body and blood of Christ, the faithful grow in that mystical divinization which makes them dwell in the Son and the Father, through the Spirit.
>
> Thus, on the one hand, the church celebrates the eucharist as expression here and now of the heavenly liturgy; but on the other hand, the eucharist builds up the church in the sense that through it the Spirit of the risen Christ fashions the church into the body of Christ. That is why the eucharist is truly the sacrament of the total gift the Lord makes of himself to his own and as manifestation and growth of the body of Christ, the church. The pilgrim church celebrates the eucharist on earth until her Lord comes to restore royalty to God the Father so that God may be 'all in all.' It thus anticipates the judgment of the world and its final transfiguration.[29]

This vision of the Christian *heart in pilgrimage* bespeaks a mysticism that is no longer seen as a rather esoteric phenomenon pertaining to a few or the "other-worldly," but — especially in virtue of the Eucharist, the sacrament of Christ's New Covenant *"for the many"* — its boundaries are limitless; that is, it is for *all*. This mystical,

---

[29] *The Mystery of the Church and of the Eucharist in the light of the Holy Trinity,* First Statement of the Joint Commission for theological dialogue between the Roman Catholic Church and the Orthodox Church (Munich, June 30 to July 6, 1982), n. 4b-c; (ET) *Church Eucharist Trinity,* CTS Do 553, p. 7. Cf. also ARCIC: Statement on the Eucharist, nn. 4, 11; World Council of Churches, "Lima Statement" on the Eucharist, nn. 8, 18, 22. Unfortunately the Catholic-Orthodox statement is not widely enough known. But this has been recently remedied by the appearance of a work edited by Paul McPartlan, *One in 2000: Towards Catholic-Orthodox Unity, Agreed Statements and Parish Papers,* St Paul Publications, Slough (U.K.), 1993.

that is, sacramental perspective, particularly evident in the approach of the Orthodox Church, maintains a balanced tension in proclaiming both the decisiveness of the historical incarnation-redemptive event of Christ and also the eschatological hope expressed and anticipated in the sacraments of the kingdom of God. The Eucharist, being the most existential sacrament of reality, holds together the "already" and "not yet" — as *memorial* and *pledge of future glory* — in that dynamic dimension of human awareness which both resembles and penetrates ever deeper into the mystery of divine Love which is the fullness of reality in no narrow or "objectified" sense of *Presence.*

This dimension of anticipation in hope finds expression in the Eucharistic Prayers — for example, as Eucharistic Prayer IV puts it:

> you have created all things to fill your creatures with every blessing and *lead all to the joyful vision of your light.* . .
> *looking forward to his coming in glory,* we offer you his body and blood, the acceptable sacrifice which brings salvation to the whole world . . .
> Father, in your mercy *grant also to us, your children, to enter into our heavenly inheritance* . . .
> *Then, in your kingdom freed from the corruption of sin and death, we shall sing your glory with every creature* through Christ our Lord, through whom you give us everything that is good.

In Eucharistic Prayer III the same note of anticipation in hope is sounded:

> *ready to greet him when he comes again* . . . *We hope to enjoy for ever the vision of your glory,* through Christ our Lord, from whom all good things come.

Because of Christ's gift of the Holy Spirit, who calls, inspires, and shows us *how* to approach God without fear but in confident love, we are fired with the desire to worship him with praise and thanksgiving.

Thanksgiving and Praise

The keynote of proclamation is *Eucharist* — thanksgiving and praise. This is the theme-song of the people of God and the heart of their worship and life. It takes us to the mind of Christ at the Last Supper. Thanksgiving sums up the Savior's constant attitude and relationship towards his Father — a relationship precisely expressed, for instance, in the famous *Hymn of Jubilation*:

> In that same hour he rejoiced in the Holy Spirit and said: "I bless [RSV = thank] you, Father, Lord of heaven and earth, for hiding these things from the learned and clever and revealing them to mere children. Yes, Father, for that is what it pleased you to do."[30]

If we wish to learn about relating to God, we cannot do better than turn to Jesus' attitude, best captured in the passages of the Gospel where he is at prayer. Here, we get a "cross-section," as it were, of "the mind [attitude] of Christ," the Incarnate Word of God. The whole of the seventeenth chapter of John introduces us into the finest catechesis of the Eucharistic mystery, prayer, and the Christian relationship of living *communion* (*koinonia*).

The Eucharist profoundly exemplifies catechesis through or at prayer. As noted above, it originates from the Jewish blessings or grace over the gifts of God shared at meals. This expressed Israel's deep awareness of its close relationship to God who is its Creator and Provider of all — *its giver of breath and bread*, in G.M. Hopkins' lovely phrase.[31] Historically this awareness came only after Israel discovered God as its Redeemer (*Go'el*) as Deutero-Isaiah illustrates. Thus, within this climate of grateful recognition of God's special salvific providence, in which his relationship to his chosen people was sealed, "Eucharist" comes to enjoy a very important role during the Jewish Passover celebrated annually. In this Passover context — leaving aside the question of whether the Last Supper was the Passover Meal

---

[30] Lk 10:21; Mt 11:25f.
[31] Cf. *The Wreck of the Deutschland* (opening stanza).

itself — Jesus gave the celebration a new significance and sense of direction as a sharing in the greatest and long-awaited "blessing of God," namely, his *presence* which brings liberation from the root of all oppression which is our habitual condition of unfreedom due to sinfulness. The Eucharist is in direct continuity with Israel's greatest boast: God's presence among his people. It is the sacramental manifestation of *Emmanuel — God with us*, as Pope Paul VI brings out very beautifully in linking Christ's Eucharistic presence, which extends after the celebration the grace of the Incarnation.[32]

Not only does the Church give thanks for God's infinite goodness in the history of salvation and especially for the culminating deed of all, his saving presence itself, the Gift of gifts, but it also recognizes that its very capacity to give thanks and praise is its privileged gift of grace. This is expressed in the liturgy — as in Eucharistic Prayer II:

> We thank you for counting us worthy to stand in your presence and serve you;

or in the Augustinian-inspired sentence in a weekday Preface:

> You have no need of our praise, yet our desire to thank you is itself your gift.

The Eucharistic Prayer most perfectly illustrates a phenomenon which studies in cultural anthropology have discovered, namely, the "logic or system of gifts," which is technically called *"potlatch."* What this means is that by means of the exchange of gifts persons are enabled to encounter one another and establish moral and spiritual ties or relationships between themselves.[33] The gift is the medium or "sacrament" enabling communication and also an external sign of inner, personal presence in relationship. With regard to the Eucharist, our absolute dependence and utter indebtedness to God become "relieved" by the fact that our only (and indeed best) gift in response consists in offering him the very gift we receive from him — *Eucharist*

---

[32] Cf. Encyclical Letter, *Mysterium Fidei*, (3 September 1967) n. 67; cf. Jn 1:14 and Dt 4:7.
[33] Cf. Mazza, op. cit., pp. 44-47.

being both God's gift to us of himself and our gratitude to him in response. This brings out the deep significance of Jesus' words to the Samaritan Woman at Jacob's well near Sichar: *"If you knew the gift of God."*[34]

The lesson of celebrating *Eucharist* is one for living in the presence of God constantly with an attitude of thanksgiving, appreciation, praise, and sense of devout dependency through petition. The experience of the Eucharistic Prayer leads, as St. Paul says, to a mentality of grateful praise in all that we think, say and do.[35] This quality of adoration and prayer — an awareness of deep awe, tender respect, and reverence for being — this praise and gratitude for being capable of such profundity of thought characterizes human life and communication with the new *God-ward* dignity of the children of the kingdom.

It is interesting to recall here that Martin Heidegger distinguishes this mode of creative thinking, which he calls *meditation*, from the calculated, technical pattern of pragmatic activity familiar to Western society. He shows how the former kind, the creative mode, is *thinking* in the strong sense of the word. The Anglo-Saxon and Germanic roots of this word (*thinking*) is related to our word for *thanking*. This bespeaks openness to Being-beyond-ourselves — with infinite possibilities![36]

St. Augustine, who eventually found himself in discovering the truth of God's beauty and truth in the Christian community's hymns, songs of praise, and joyous spiritual canticles celebrated especially at the Eucharist, confesses that the human heart experiences its true identity and worth in worship or praise of God:

> Man is one of your creatures, Lord, and his instinct is to praise you ... The thought of you stirs him so deeply that he cannot

---

[34] Jn 4:10.

[35] Cf. Col 3:15-17 — in which forms of the verb for thanksgiving/praise (*eucharist*) occur three times.

[36] Cf. *Discourse on Thinking* (1959), trans. by J.M. Anderson & E.H. Freund, Harper & Row, New York, 1966.

be content unless he praises you, because you made us for yourself and our hearts find no peace until they rest in you.[37]

On discovering the worth of acknowledging God with praise and thanksgiving — which for him was the essence of communication and the root meaning of *confession* — St. Augustine began his vast literary output and especially his life's work of tireless evangelization, catechesis and preaching.[38]

Thanksgiving or *Eucharist* is, thus, a characteristic Christian activity. It re-presents what Christ did and taught his faithful to carry out at the Last Supper as St. John Chrysostom says:

He gave thanks before giving [his body] to his disciples, in order that we too might give thanks. He gave thanks and then, after doing so, sang a hymn, in order that we might do likewise.[39]

The Christian community is truly *The Easter People* because *Alleluia* or "Praise of God" is the constant song at the heart of its journey in living. This community is indeed, if I may coin an expression, a *Eucharist-hearted* people — not only because the Eucharistic celebration is at the heart of their existence, but especially because Eucharist

---

[37] Cf. *Confessions*, I.1 — trans. by R.S. Pine-Coffin, Penguin Classics, 1970, p. 21. Cf. George Herbert's extended pun on the word "rest" (referring both to repose and the rest of God's gifts to human beings) in his poem *The Pulley*:
Yet let him keep the rest,
But keep them with repining restlesnesse:
Let him be rich and wearie, that at least,
If goodnesse leade him not, yet wearinesse
May tosse him to my breast.

[38] This meaning of the word *confession*, which is the leitmotif of his "theological autobiography," was already passing out of use, or rather, as St. Augustine notes with disappointment, it was employed by people more usually for confession of sins — e.g. cf. *Serm.* 29, 2, 2; *En. in Ps. 117*,1. The word (with its verbal form, *confitieri*) was richly resonant referring to praise (as especially in the psalms); profession of faith (hence, "confessors," those who were spared martyrdom); and admission of sinfulness. Cf. Christine Mohrmann, op. cit., p. 208ff. *Confessio* in this sense of praise is the Latin equivalent of the Hebrew *todah*, which was literally translated in the Greek Septuagint as *'eksomologeisthai*, to celebrate with praise and thanksgiving.

[39] Hom. 82.30 (PG 58, 740) — quoted by Mazza, *The Eucharistic Prayers*, op. cit., p. 5.

is their characteristic attitude, their joy in living Christ's Passover, and their very life.

Acclamation

Since the Eucharistic Prayer is the richest and most intense moment of the community's participation in the paschal mystery, the *"vox populi"* can hardly remain silent, but has its significant part to play in the *"acclamations"* during this Prayer. We may recall the words (attributed to St. Augustine) quoted by the Pope at Harlem and adopted by the Bishops of England and Wales in their Message at the end of the National Pastoral Congress of 1980:

> If we are silent about the joy which comes from knowing about Jesus, the very stones of our cities will cry out! For we are an Easter People and "Alleluia" is our song.[40]

The reform of the liturgy not only abolished the medieval aberration of the "silent canon," but also re-introduced the vital aspect of the people's part into the Eucharistic Prayer, principally at the *Sanctus, Eucharistic acclamation,* and the great *Amen* at the end of the Prayer.[41]

In Eucharistic Prayer I (or the "Roman Canon") there are various places where *Amen* may also be said by the people. This biblical word, which is a vestige of the Judeo-Christian liturgy, is richer in meaning than signifying simply affirmation. It is acknowledgement in praise, gratitude and worship. For pastoral reasons — not to detract from the importance of the final *Amen* —

---

[40] *The Easter People*, St. Paul Publications, 1980, n. 196, p. 67.

[41] The *Sanctus* was originally introduced into the liturgy not long before Pope Leo I (440-461) — cf. Mazza, op. cit., p. 47. St. Ambrose mentions that the people responded *"Amen"* after the words of Institution; his exhortation links this acclamation with the *"Amen"* they affirm on receiving the Sacrament — cf. *De Sacramentis*, IV.25. It is regrettable that occasionally one finds priests who for whatever well-intentioned but misguided reasons go ahead with the Eucharistic Prayer silently when the *Sanctus* is sung, as Charles Dilke, Congr. Orat., admits in his booklet *A History of the Roman Mass*, p. 5.

these are usually omitted. The Eucharistic Prayers for Masses with children interestingly employ the use of acclamations throughout, not only to hold their attention, but also so that they may learn implicitly that participation is of the essence in Christian worship.

To call these acclamations "dialogue" seems misleading since — unlike the exchanges between celebrant and people at the beginning of the Eucharistic Prayer as also at other places of the Mass — these acclamations are really part of the Church's whole prayer of praise. They in no way interrupt the flow of worship, but are integral to it. They express the Church's confident and enthusiastic realization that its worship is essentially communal, that its richest act of thanksgiving-praise is offered to God precisely because he wills and comes to save all people whom he transforms into a "chosen race, royal priesthood, holy nation."[42]

It is highly recommended to sing the acclamations since song more fully expresses the joy of "the heart in pilgrimage" (to borrow George Herbert's memorable description of prayer). It would be unthinkable that Jesus and his disciples did not sing at the first Eucharistic celebration. The great Hallel psalm is part of the Passover feast, which Jesus did not abolish but fulfilled:

Give thanks to the Lord, for he is good; his love is everlasting!

The words of the Sanctus (the *"Trisagion Hymn"*) are taken over from Isaiah 6:3-4, the Hallel psalm (117:25f.), and Luke 19:37-40.[43] They are full of a sense of joyous praise and lend themselves for singing. They should be sung by the whole congregation and never monopolized by the choir as a motet! The very nature of the *Memorial Acclamations* also demands that they should be sung as the people's affirmative proclamation of the Mystery of Faith.[44]

The *Amen* of the doxology at the end of the Eucharistic Prayer

---

[42] 1 P 2:9; cf. Ex 19:5-6. The Alexandrian Greek translation of the Hebrew text introduces the new idea of "royal priesthood/kingdom of priests" — cf. Rv 1:5, 8.

[43] Cf. also Rv 4:3.

[44] The official English translation provides two versions of the first of the three acclamations of the Latin text. The acclamations are modelled on those in the Eastern *anaphoras*, which however come after the *anamnesis* instead of before it as in our liturgy.

expresses the community's greatest affirmation of its part in proclaiming the Church's praise of God's glory. As in ancient times, this acclamation should be made in an impressive manner — singing (with repetition or harmonization) being the best way of all. It then fittingly signifies the congregation's firm and joyous response in faith to the celebrant's proclamation of the mystery of Christ in deed and word.[45] Furthermore, the eucharistic *Amen* may be understood as making explicit what is implicit in the baptismal act of faith in God's economy of salvation. The depth of this act of faith is particularly that of total personal commitment to God. It was St. Augustine who pointed out the significance of such total commitment as a return to love in commenting that we say: "I believe *in God*," rather than merely "I believe God" or "I believe that he exists."[46]

The significance of the acclamations is, most truly, that of participation in the glory of God. In the often-quoted phrase of St. Irenaeus of Lyons, "the glory of God is man fully alive."[47] The sacred liturgy particularly celebrates the revelation of *that Man* who is Christ; in him we not only behold the glory of God, but also become truly human by being united and, indeed, incorporated into him. At the Last Supper Jesus prayed that all called to the unity and love of his Mystical Body would participate in his and the Father's own glory.

---

[45] On this point Paul McPartlan notes the difference of approach between West and East in his recent comparative study of Henri de Lubac's and John Zizioulas' understanding of "the Eucharist makes the Church," in *The Eucharist Makes the Church,* p. 113f.: "The strong sense of a primary action of Christ himself into which others are subsequently drawn may be confirmed by comparing de Lubac's and Zizioulas' explanations of the eucharistic 'Amen.' De Lubac says that the people 'offer together with the priest,' manifesting by their 'Amen' that they 'agree with all that he does and all that he says.' However, this 'Amen' is but a response, by which the people associate themselves with the priest's action which has a certain self-sufficiency. It is not their own specific and necessary contribution to the eucharistic action itself, as it is for Zizioulas, whose conviction that when Christ is present so necessarily are his people in a corporate manifestation of the future Kingdom follows from his Pneumatological appreciation of Christ as a corporate personality. In the Eucharist, priest (or, rather, bishop) and people complementarily act, as we might say, *in persona Christi ecclesialis.*" (Quotation from de Lubac's *The Splendour of the Church*, Sheed & Ward, London 1956, p. 100.)

[46] Cf. *Serm. de Symbolo*, 1; *Serm. 94*, 2; *In Joh. Ev.*, 29, 6; *En. in Ps. 77*, 8. Cf. de Lubac, *Christian Faith*, Geoffrey Chapman, London, 1986, pp. 67; 70f.; 189 — cited by McPartlan, op. cit., p. 244f. Cf. Christine Mohrmann, op. cit., t.I, pp. 195-203.

[47] Cf. *Adversus Haereses*, IV.20.57.

Sharing in these acclamations of the great Prayer of the Eucharist manifests the fulness of human life, the wholeness/wholesomeness or salvation and holiness of becoming truly human in worship through, with, and in Christ, the Head of the Mystical Body. The Spirit of Jesus, who enables our access to the Father and Jesus as Lord,[48] binds us in that communion of love which is the glory of the Mystical Body of Christ. As St. Gregory of Nyssa says:

> The bond of this unity is glory, and that the Holy Spirit is called "glory" no sensible man will deny if he considers the Lord's words: "The glory which you have given me, I have given them." He truly gave such glory to his disciples, for he said to them: "Receive the Holy Spirit."[49]

No one better sums up Christian glory, however, than St. Irenaeus of Lyons, for whom Christ recapitulates (literally, "brings under his headship") all things. A great glory or "adornment" of the Catholic Church consists in its openness to all humanity — its evangelical proclamation of the universal call to all to become the people of God.[50] This important doctrine of recapitulation signifies, as the new *Catechism of the Catholic Church* states, that all creation finds in him "its transcendent fulfillment."[51] The Church stands for the sovereign and universal dominion of Christ the Lord, which it manifests through the Eucharist, the foretaste *par excellence* of the vision of God — that vision which is the fulness of human life. This splendid approach of Irenaeus is reflected and realized in the Eucharistic Prayer — particu-

---

[48] Cf. Rm 8:15; Gal 4:57; 1 Cor 12:3.

[49] Hom. 15 — cf. trans. in *The Divine Office*, III (Collins), p. 657.

[50] See n. 47 (*ut supra*) — "the life of man is the vision of God." The doctrine of recapitulation is derived from St. Paul — cf. Ep 1:3-10. This notion of recapitulation is explicitly included in the teaching of the Council when speaking of the universal call of all people to become part of the people of God — cf. L.G., n. 13, where reference is made to two texts in Irenaeus: *Ad. Haer.* III.16.6 and III.22.13.

[51] Cf. n. 668. Cf. also n. 518 where St. Irenaeus is quoted regarding the whole of Christ's life being a "mystery of recapitulation" (loc. cit., III.18.7; also III.18.1 and II.22.4). In n. 2854 on the last petition of the Lord's Prayer, the *Catechism* sees the words of the "embolism" ("Deliver us, Lord, from every evil past, present and to come . . .") as an expectation in the humility of faith for the realization of the final recapitulation of all in Christ when he returns.

larly in Eucharistic Prayer IV. The beauty of the whole community sharing in the acclamations of Eucharistic worship manifests the glory of unity, perfection, harmony, and communion between God and humanity. This beauty of participating in the divine communion is succinctly proclaimed in a Christmas Preface:

> Today in him a new light has dawned upon the world; God has become one with man, and man has become one again with God . . . So marvellous is this oneness between God and man that in Christ man restores to man the gift of everlasting life.[52]

Epiclesis or Invocation of the Holy Spirit

An unquestionable enrichment to our understanding of and approach to prayer in recent times has been the attention given to the Holy Spirit. In liturgical reform since the Second Vatican Council the role of the Holy Spirit in the history of salvation has once again been duly acknowledged and come into its own. The ancient tradition of invoking the action of the Spirit — a tradition never abandoned or lost in the liturgies of the Eastern Churches — has been restored in the new Eucharistic Prayers.

The question of the invocation of the Holy Spirit during the Eucharistic Prayer has been a vexed one for too long.[53] This is not the place to rehearse the intricacies of the arguments justifying the validity of the practice in the Western Church up to the reforms of the Second Vatican Council. It would be enough to refer to no less an authority than St. Ambrose in this regard. His view had an important influence on the approach of Western theology. According to this great bishop of Milan the words of Christ (that is, the "words of consecration" or Institution Narrative, as we shall see below) bring about the change of the bread and wine so that they become the Body

---

[52] Third Preface of Christmas — *Roman Missal*, Pr. 5.

[53] The language and tone of polemics is all too evident in that otherwise splendid eulogy of the rites of the liturgy by Schmemann, op. cit., pp. 160ff.

and Blood of Christ.[54] The Eastern Fathers, on the other hand, stress the necessity of the prayer of *epiclesis* or invocation for God to send the Holy Spirit to transform the gifts of bread and wine into Christ; some of them are evidently open, nonetheless, to recognize the power of the Institution Narrative, the Lord's word in the Gospel.[55]

However, even in the liturgy described by St. Ambrose there is a curious mention of a prayer for the elements to become the Body and Blood of Christ — a prayer which occurs before the Institution Narrative rather than after it, as in the Byzantine liturgy.[56] It is presumably to this prayer that St. Augustine, who from his conversion must have taken much from St. Ambrose's catechesis, refers in a beautiful passage of his great work on the Trinity regarding God's use of created realities to manifest his presence. This passage unambiguously attributes the consecration to the power of the Holy Spirit:

> The Apostle Paul [. . .] was able to preach the Lord Jesus Christ significantly, in one way by his tongue, in another by epistle, in another by the sacrament of His Body and Blood; now, we do not call either the tongue of the apostle, or the parchments, or the ink, or the significant sounds which his tongue uttered, or the alphabetical signs written on skins, the Body and Blood of Christ, but that only which we take of the fruits of the earth and consecrate by mystic prayer, and then receive duly to our spiritual health in memory of the passion of our Lord for us: and this, although it is brought by the hands of men to that visible form, yet is not sanctified to become so great a sacrament, except by the Spirit of God working invisibly [. . .].[57]

---

[54] Cf. *De Sacramentis*, IV.14-23. As Yarnold points out (*The Awe-inspiring Rites of Christian Initiation*, p. 42) there is an inconsistency between what Ambrose teaches here regarding the Eucharist and the consecration of the baptismal font which requires the invocation of the Holy Spirit.

[55] Cf. e.g., Nicolas Cabasilas, *Comm. on the Divine Liturgy*, 27-30. This author merits a mention in a footnote to LG n. 11, that important paragraph regarding the priestly community's life of worship and witness.

[56] *De Sacramentis*, IV.21.

[57] *De Trinitate*, III.iv.10; Arthur W. Haddan's translation (with slight modification) in *The Works of Aurelius Augustine*, Vol. VII on the Trinity, T. & T. Clark, Edinburgh, 1873, p. 87.

We must not linger here unduly over considering whether the *"mystic prayer,"* to which Augustine alludes, is the same as that referred to by the tradition of earlier Fathers of the Church,[58] whether it signifies the great prayer of thanksgiving, or whether he has in mind the invocation (*epiclesis*) of the Holy Spirit. It is very strange, however, that neither Augustine nor Ambrose in mentioning this prayer makes any reference to St. Paul's words in 1 Tm 4:4, which have a definite "Eucharistic" tonality, although they both quote from this Pastoral Epistle regarding Christ the unique Mediator between God and man (1 Tm 2:5), a text that is crucial to them.[59] The verse in St. Paul might very well have corroborated the "argument" used by both these Fathers regarding God's power to transform what already exists since it is "good," as shall be seen below:

> ... everything created by God is good, and nothing is to be rejected if it is received with thanksgiving, for then it is consecrated by the word of God and prayer.[60]

Nevertheless, what is important is that these Fathers clearly represent the Western tradition's unfailing faith in the necessity of the Holy Spirit to bring about and communicate so sublime and spiritual a reality as the Eucharistic Body and Blood of Christ — a necessity which is realized in the context of the prayer of the Church.

Though Eucharistic Prayer I (the "Roman Canon") makes no explicit mention of the Holy Spirit, except in the doxology, traces of an *epiclesis* may be detected in the prayer before the Institution Narrative (*Quam oblationem*); it is also implicit in the prayer for the consecrated Species to be borne to the heavenly altar (*Supplices*). The new Eucharistic Prayers, however, include a double *epiclesis* before

---

[58] Cf. e.g., Ignatius of Antioch, *Ep. to Smyrnaens*, vii; Justin, *Apol.*, I.56; Irenaeus, *Adv. Haer.*, IV.18.5.

[59] Wainwright says tersely that this scriptural text has been most helpful in understanding how the Eucharistic Prayer brings about our communion with Christ and pledge of our final salvation with the saints in the divine kingdom — cf. *Baptism and Eucharist: Ecumenical Convergence in Celebration*, op. cit., p. 102.

[60] The context of these words is the Apostle's warnings against various false teachings of a rigid nature reflecting dualistic tendencies which regarded matter as evil — abstention from certain foods, prohibition of marriage, etc. St. Paul clearly has in mind what is stated in the account of creation in first chapter of Genesis, often referred to by Ambrose and the Fathers.

and after the Institution Narrative. The first is for the faithful's offerings to be accepted by God and transformed into the sacramental Body and Blood of Christ; the other is for the transformation of those participating in the consecrated Gifts into Christ's Mystical Body. This double *epiclesis* is not unlike that found in the Alexandrian Liturgy of St. Mark. The importance of this prayer of invocation consists in the fact that it integrates the "offertory" rite into the action of the Eucharistic Prayer itself. The "offertory" rite is more correctly to be understood as the preparation of the gifts for the Eucharistic Prayer. In other words, the *epiclesis* brings out the true nature of the *"spiritual sacrifice/offering"* which is the specifically new quality of Christian worship as presented in the New Testament.[61]

---

[61] Cf. especially Rm 12:1ff.; 8:14-17; Jn 4:23f. The development of the notion of "sacrifice" in the Old and New Testaments from cultic to spiritual significance has been presented by Robert J. Daly S.J. in *The Origins of the Christian Doctrine of Sacrifice*, op. cit.; for the thorough background to this study cf. also the same author's *Christian Sacrifice: The Judaeo-Christian Background before Origen*, op. cit. Daly summarizes the contrasts in attitude between the ancient (O.T.) and modern (post-N.T.) concepts related to sacrifice thus (pp. 34):

	Ancient	**Modern**
Field of use	Wholly religious, never secular	Almost wholly secular; used religiously by transference
Purpose	Solely a cultic act	Never a cultic act
Size of the sacrifice	As large as possible	As small as possible
Recipient	Always offered to a god, thus indicating a recognition of superiority	Never offered to anyone
Performance and accompanying emotions	Always performed with joy; came to be identified with thanksgiving	Always performed with regret accompanied with sadness
Significant emphasis	Emphasis on giving and action. Deprivation, while a necessary fact, as with all giving, is never a constituent factor of the sacrifice	Emphasis always on giving up, and on deprivation
Death or destruction of the thing sacrificed	Wholly incidental and never with any inherent or significant meaning, a necessary factor in all sacrifice.	Signifies the "supreme sacrifice."

Building his researches on Daly's work, the Anglican theologian Kenneth Stevenson has made an important contribution to ecumenical dialogue in providing a valuable analysis of Eastern and Western eucharistic *anaphora*, in which the metaphor of sacrifice is expressed in a variety of ways — cf. *Eucharist and Offering*. He suggests that "the contemporary Western debate can only really progress if we develop a more imprecise (and Eastern) notion of eucharist as 'spiritual sacrifice,' indeed of *all* worship as sacrificial. Such a broad, ecclesial view of the sacrament of the Lord's Supper is both deeply traditional and startlingly contemporary" (ibid., p. ix).

The Holy Spirit is seen as enjoying the role of principal agent of God's love effecting the New Creation. Just as Jesus was raised up "by the power of the Spirit" to be the Risen Lord, so the hearts of his faithful who receive and share the gift of the Spirit's power to worship God are transformed and converted to him in a newness of being, attitude, and will to live the New Covenant in the *koinonia* or communion/fellowship of loving with "one mind and heart."[62]

The Institution Narrative

The words of the 1969 General Instruction on the New Order of the Mass sum up the whole perspective of the paschal mystery celebrated at the Eucharist. In citing the relevant paragraph of the ICEL translation it may be helpful to consider the complex statement of the text in four stages:[63]

(i)   The narrative of the institution: the Last Supper is made present ("re-presentatur") in the words and actions of Christ
(ii) when he instituted the sacrament of his passion and resurrection,
(iii) when under the appearances of bread and wine he gave his Apostles his body to eat and his blood to drink
(iv) and commanded them to carry on this mystery.

The most significant fact of the constant presence of an Institution Narrative in every Eucharistic liturgy is that the inspired word of God is recognized as being necessary to effect or bring about the Sacrament of the Eucharist — as it does the Church. Some of the Fathers of the Church explained in their catechetical homilies to the newly baptized adults the truth about the efficaciousness(!) or power of God's inspired or Spirit-filled word of the Gospel itself in bringing about the change in the bread and wine by recourse to Christ's role in recreating the world which he had made in the beginning. St.

---

[62] Cf. especially Ac 4:32; Jr 31:31ff.
[63] As suggested by Crichton, op. cit., p. 89. Cf. GIRM, n. 55d.

Ambrose, for instance, argues the "logic" of the Word's consecratory power this way: if he could create the world from nothing by his words: "Let it be . . . ," he could surely bring about the new creation from what already exists.[64]

Ever faithful to the word of God — especially to this *Narrative* of Christ's most treasured words and actions in instituting the sacred sign or sacrament of his paschal mystery[65] — the Church realizes the continuity of the mystery of God's saving presence revealed in its midst as if it is a "contemporary" of Christ. The Church, is more than this. Being the visible sacrament of his *Mystical Body* the Church is constantly attentive to the words of its Head, the Lord Jesus, who opens the living word of God while breaking the Bread for his pilgrim people, as he did once for the disciples on the road to Emmaus. In the sacramental "enactment" of the Institution Narrative we witness the fulness of the signs of Christ's real presence taught by the Council.[66] The Encyclical Letter of Pope Paul VI, *Mysterium Fidei*, merits close attention since it develops the Council's teaching about the "delightful truth" of the ways Christ is present in the Church. It offers a rich source of catechesis in fostering a religious awareness of the context of faith. Without such an awareness there can be little point in celebrating the Eucharist. Without a deepened sense of Christ's presence, the Eucharistic Prayer itself would become merely a sterile ritual and fail to be the vital proclamation of our access to God through our Lord's intimate communication — that communication of his living presence which invites and challenges us to live his sacrifice in love. Especially in the *Institution Narrative*, pronounced by the

---

[64] Cf. *De Sacramentis*, IV. 14ff. Apart from the passage cited above, St. Augustine frequently expresses the idea in his sermons by a terse formula: "When the Word is added . . . the sacrament comes about" — cf. *Sermo 227*.1; *Sermo Denis*, VI.1 & 3; *Sermo Guelf.*, VII.1, etc. Centuries later Baldwin of Canterbury would present an identical biblical approach at a time when treatises on the Eucharist abounded in rather arid philosophical categories — cf. *De Sacramento Altaris*, which deserves to be better known than it is!

[65] Re the "paschal" context, content and quality of the Institution Narrative in the Eucharistic Prayer cf. Augusto Bergamini, "Il Significato Pasquale del Racconto della Istituzione nella Preghiera Eucaristica" in *Mysterion*, op. cit., pp. 351-362.

[66] Cf. S.C. n. 7.

celebrant *in persona Christi (qua head)*,[67] we hear Christ himself, the New Adam, claiming humanity, us, as his own:

> This at last is bone of my bones and flesh of my flesh.[68]

This great mystery is contained in the sacramental proclamation of the Bread and Wine:

> This is my body which will be given up for you . . . This is the cup of my blood . . . shed for you and for all.

Because he communicates with us as the Head of the Mystical Body we are drawn in an "obedience of faith" to receive and realize the Reality of his transforming love. The words of Jesus in the *Institution Narrative* are crucial for appreciating how God discloses or reveals the real nature of all things — his *reality* permeating the stuff of our ordinary experience. For this very reason our familiar way of regarding the real presence, however, must not be restricted or taken in an exclusive sense "as though other forms of presence were not 'real,' but by reason of its excellence."[69] Because of the excellence of the Eucharistic presence, all else that is good or true or beautiful in human experience is revealed as charged with divine worth. Christ the Savior and Redeemer *proclaims this* in taking hold of *the fruits of the earth and the work of human hands*!

The Institution Narrative is no "magical" formula or ritual incantation in itself, no more than Christ's presence is some sort of potent talisman. But, the very fact of the community's receiving his

---

[67] It is not merely insofar as he acts "in the person or character of Christ," which pertains to all the Christian priestly people, but insofar as he represents Christ as *Head* or acts *in the person of Christ qua Head* that the celebrant realizes his ordained role as sacrament of Christ's priesthood. — cf. L.G. n. 10; P.O. n. 2; *Inter insigniores* (15 October 1976), n. 5; and various places in the teaching of Pope John Paul II, e.g. *Dominicae cenae* (24 February 1980), n. 8.

[68] Gn 2:23; cf. Ep 5:32. Cf. St. John Chrysostom's instruction to catechumens, which is included in the Office of Readings on Good Friday — D.O., II, op. cit., p. 297f., (Cat. 3:1319).

[69] *Mysterium Fidei*, n. 39. This sentence of Paul VI put pay to the anxiety lingering on from the time of the Council regarding any false interpretation of its teaching (cf. S.C. n. 7) to the belittling of Christ's Eucharistic manner of being present to his Church.

words in faith and rehearsing what he said and did — in fidelity to his request — manifests the *realization* of his multi-dimensional presence in the Church. Nicholas Lash puts this very well:

> . . . the fundamental form of the Christian interpretation of scripture is the life, activity and organization of the Christian community, construed as performance of the biblical text. The best illustration of what this might mean is, of course, the celebration of the Eucharist. Here, that interpretative performance in which all our life consists — all our suffering and care, compassion, celebration, struggle and obedience — is dramatically distilled, focused, concentrated, rendered explicit. In this context the principal forms of discourse are "practical": in praise, confession, petition, they seek to enact the meanings which they embody. And if, in the liturgy of the Word, the story is told, it is told not so that it may merely be relished or remembered, but that it may be performed, in the following of Christ.[70]

In other words, what is the point of this "performance" or "enacting" if it is not fidelity to Christ? This fidelity involves following him, most certainly! And following him means essentially a relationship — with the Father in the Spirit of Christ and through Christ among ourselves. The biblical scholar Xavier Léon-Dufour draws this conclusion from his analysis of the New Testament accounts of the Institution:

> The "words of consecration" are not isolated utterances dealing with an object in itself; they are part of an account which has a fundamental relational structure. [. . .] The words of Jesus do not simply assert the new state of the bread and wine. Their aim is to give rise to a dialogue, and they offer at the same time a food that is to be received and thereby lead to an existential commitment. I have therefore tried to bring out the intrinsic connection between the Eucharist and sharing.[71]

---

[70] *Theology on the Way to Emmaus*, op. cit., p. 45f.
[71] *Sharing the Eucharistic Bread*, op. cit., p. 282.

The context of the Narrative in the Eucharistic Prayer is drawn from the accounts of the New Testament sources.[72] While this is slightly varied from one Prayer to another, for pastoral reasons the words of Institution, however, have been kept uniform in all the Eucharistic Prayers. The variations of presentation help us to appreciate the depth of the Eucharistic mystery which is reflected in the different approaches and perspectives of both the Prayers and their sources.

Happily, the days of focusing narrowly on the precise moment of the change of the elements into the "real presence" of Christ's sacramental Body and Blood are past. We are beginning to discover afresh how to appreciate the manner in which the Church welcomes God's communication of his life through the progressive revelation of his word, action, and presence in the liturgy and life of the Christian community. Thus, no longer is the accent placed on the double "formula" of consecration, but on the Spirit-giving act of obedience in which we become faithful not only to carrying out ritually Christ's command at the Last Supper, but more importantly we become his faithful through obeying and imitating his own sacrifice of unswerving obedience to the saving will of his Father's love for the life of the world. This point is quite sensitively made in the Anglican-Roman Catholic International Commission's "Elucidation" on its Joint Statement on Eucharistic Doctrine:

> In the sacramental order the realities of faith become present in visible and tangible signs, enabling Christians to avail themselves of the fruits of the once-for-all redemption. In the Eucharist the human person encounters in faith the person of Christ in his sacramental body and blood. This is the sense in which the community, the body of Christ, by partaking of the sacramental body of the Risen Lord, grows into the unity God intends for his Church. The ultimate change intended by God is the transformation of human beings into the likeness of

---

[72] These accounts have been identified as: 1 Cor 11:23-25; Lk 22:19f.; Mk 14:22-24; Mt 26:26-28; and Jn 6:51c. — Cf. Joachim Jeremias, "The Words of Institution" in *Understanding the Eucharist*, op. cit.; cf. also the same author's major work: *The Eucharistic Words of Jesus*, op. cit., pp. 16-203. Apart from these N.T. sources, narratives in the Prayers also incorporate references to Mt 14:19; Jn 10:18 and 13:1ff.

Christ. The bread and wine become the sacramental body and blood of Christ in order that the Christian community may become more truly what it already is, the body of Christ.[73]

The Institution Narrative at the heart of the Eucharistic Prayer, therefore, can be regarding as proclaiming the purpose for which Christ is present in his community of disciples, that is, to bring about their relational being or holy communion among themselves and with the Father. It is to this end that sacramental communion and adoration of the Blessed Eucharist is ordered.[74] This understanding of the Institution Narrative, thus, can be seen as providing the basis of that ancient adage which became a key insight emphasized at the Second Vatican Council, thanks to the late Cardinal Henri de Lubac S.J. who was one of its great "architects":

> As the Church makes the Eucharist, so the Eucharist makes the Church.[75]

---

[73] *The Final Report*, CTS/SPCK, 1982, p. 21f.

[74] Cf. S.C. nn. 47 & 48; also cf. Instruction on the Eucharistic Mystery (*Eucharisticum mysterium*, 25 May 1967), n. 3a & f. Léon-Dufour's words, which at first might seem rather "shocking," express clearly the primary purpose or finality for which Christ intended the Eucharist and for which it exists: "My reading of the texts [of the N.T.] has brought out [. . .] that the Eucharist is part of the Church's cultic life and is basically a *community activity*. This reminder is especially necessary for those older readers who are used to liturgical practices that emphasize the close relation between the individual and the Eucharist; I am thinking of such practices as adoration of the Blessed Sacrament and visits to the Blessed Sacrament. The participation of each individual in this source of life is, of course, very important; the fact remains, however, that it is the congregation, the one Church, which celebrates the Eucharist, and that the Eucharist is directed to the congregation, the Church, in its entirety. The Lord is certainly present through the Eucharist, but he is present in the form of a gift to the Church as a whole" (loc. cit., p. 281f.). There is no question that Eucharistic adoration outside Mass, visits, etc. are to be belittled or neglected.

[75] Cf. L.G., n. 11; cf. also Pope John Paul II, *Redemptor Hominis*, n. 20; *Dominicae cenae*, n. 4; Henri de Lubac, *Meditation sur l'Église*, 2ieme ed., Paris, 1963, pp. 129-137. Cf. also the study by McPartlan, op. cit.

The Anamnesis or Memorial

The key to the doctrine of the Eucharist is the notion of sacramentality.[76] This is also the key to a sound catechesis of the Eucharistic Prayer. Thus, in regard to the Church's faith about the Mass being a true sacrifice the notion of sacramentality cannot be omitted. The vocabulary of sacramentality includes the notions signified by such words as *figura, imago, similitudo,* which in the very early Church meant the same as our *sacramentum.* But these terms, however, long ago lost their significance which is to some extent the reason underlying misunderstanding and disagreement regarding the Eucharist since the Reformation: for us — no less than at the time of the Reformation —they came to mean "merely a copy." They were originally used, however, in the rich context of the New Testament (especially Pauline) theology of imitation (*mimesis*) of the essence of the Lord Jesus' words and deed at the Last Supper. This imitation was considered as no "mere copy" or ritual observance, but pregnant with the power of obedience to the will of Christ ("Do this as my memorial"[77]), a power which is released in virtue of his own obedience to the Father's will in his sacrifice on Calvary.[78]

The action of the whole Eucharistic Prayer *sacramentally re-resents* the "once-for-all" gift of Christ on the cross by means of

---

[76] Cf. Dom Anscar Vonier, O.S.B., *A Key to the Doctrine of the Eucharist,* Burns, Oates & Washbourne Ltd., London, 1925, p. 76. In this classic work the author returns to the teaching of St. Thomas Aquinas (cf. S.T. III, q. 79, a. 5). St. Thomas bases his investigation largely on the insights of St. Augustine.

[77] This better translates St. Paul's repeated phrase [*eis ten emen anamnesin*] than "Do this in memory of me" — cf. Jeremias, op. cit.

[78] Cf. Mazza, *The Eucharistic Prayers of the Roman Rite,* op. cit., p. 69ff., where the successive stages are traced: from the early "imitation" theology through the Neo-Platonist Patristic interpretation of *"anamnesis"* or Memorial of the paschal mystery to our post-scholastic transubstantiation mentality. In summary:
— the early period — imitation (representation) of both the Last Supper and death and resurrection;
— Patristic period — bypasses the Last Supper and highlights the mystery of the death and resurrection;
— post-Scholastic period — bypasses both Last Supper and death and resurrection in focusing on the Real Presence of Christ.

In recent times attention has been directed to the whole paschal mystery as *re-presented in mystery,* that is sacramentally as the memorial/expectation of the Lord's presence indeed!

faithfully obeying his command to *re-present* sacramentally the essence of what he said and did at his Last Supper.[79] It is especially to the Eucharistic Prayer to which we should look regarding this unique sacrifice, which it represents in proclaiming the Lord's death until he return — rather than to the separated species, as was the preoccupation of many a theologian in the past! Proclamation is in the strongest sense re-presentation. The proclamation of the Eucharistic Prayer manifests what is ever present and unforgettable to the faith of the Church. Rather than being a mere symbol or subjective kind of "remembering," the Memorial of Christ's entire paschal mystery, just like the Jewish celebration of God's wonderful saving deeds, realizes this saving mystery as present to the Church, the community of the *Mystery of Faith*.[80] Authentic Christian faith is never subjective: it is the Church's faith in the presence of God who saves us from individualism, subjective or private interpretation, and sinful refusal to acknowledge that God calls us to acknowledge his saving love which leads us to the present opening the way to the future, or rather, to eternal life — his presence in the sacrament of his and the Church's sacrifice. This is what the *anamnesis* signifies in the Eucharistic Prayer, the text of which is understood in the context of the Church's intention to be faithful both to the Lord's command and his Holy Spirit's unfolding of revelation.[81]

Jesus' statements regarding his promise of the Holy Spirit cannot be restricted in meaning to liturgical "remembering" or *anamnesis*. But, with hindsight neither can an application of them to

---

[79] Cf. Council of Trent, Session XXII, Decree on the Sacrifice of the Mass, c. 1 (DS 1740) — where the word "re-present" is associated with that of "memorial." In fact, this concurs with the Jewish notion of *memorial*, which includes the dimension of sacrifice — cf. Nb 10:10 (LXX); Lv 24:7; Pss 37[38]; 69[70]; Lk 22:19. The idea was also familiar to the ancient Greeks — e.g. Plato, *Lys.*, 2.39: the gods are reminded of sacrifices offered. Cf. Liddell & Scott, *Greek-English Lexicon* (new 9th ed.) O.U.P., 1973.

[80] This is in complete accord with the Jewish idea of memorial, which was expressed by the word *"Zikkaron"* — cf. Max Thurian, *L'Eucharistie*, op. cit., ch. 1; cf. also Louis Bouyer, *The Eucharist*, op. cit., ch. 4 on the "Berakah" and B.S. Childs, *Memory and Tradition in Israel*, Naperville, Illinois (U.S.A.), 1962.

[81] Mazza puts it this way (op. cit., p. 75): "In the *anamnesis*, the Church tells God what it is doing, why it does it, and what the object is of its commemorative action. And in telling him all this, the Church itself becomes conscious of it. The *anamnesis* is the moment in which the Mass defines itself, and it does so through the text of the celebration."

our *memorial* offering of Christ's passover sacrifice be ruled out. For these statements of Jesus at the Last Supper certainly help to elucidate the spiritual sense of the Eucharistic Prayer, especially the significance of *epiclesis* and *anamnesis*. It is in this spiritual sense that Congar most beautifully says: "The apostolic Church was in fact a real and active 'concelebration' with the Holy Spirit."[82] What the apostolic Church was we continue in our Eucharistic celebration, thanks to the effective power of the Risen Lord's Spirit who breathes the prayerful truth of Love's sacrifice into us at the heart of our life of worship. Since the word of the Gospel resounding in the Christian community's heart constitutes the real *"anamnesis"* or "unforgetfulness" of all Christ's words, deed and gestures, so the presence of the *Word-made-flesh* in the Eucharistic Prayer proclaims constantly the heartening challenge of evangelization, which is the realization of God's blessings especially in Christ, who came to renew all human realities and who achieved this through his unique sacrifice.[83]

In the light of this we can understand better not only the significance of the *epiclesis* and *anamnesis*, but also that of the *intercessions* during the Eucharistic Prayer.[84] Christ did more than merely teach us to pray. He gave us his Spirit to pray in us and enlighten and lead us into all truth. May we not interpret the meaning of Jesus' discourse during the Last Supper, reported in the Fourth Gospel, as his own mystagogical catechesis of the Eucharist? Would it be too arbitrary, thus, to consider both the *epiclesis* and *anamnesis* as fulfilling his promise of the Spirit of truth? For here a form of the word anamnesis is used:

> These things I have spoken to you, while I am still with you. But the Counsellor, the Holy Spirit, whom the Father will send in my name, he will teach you all things, and bring to your remembrance ("hupomnései") all that I have said to you . . . When the Counsellor comes, whom I shall send to you

---

[82] Cf. *The Word and the Spirit*, Geoffrey Chapman, London, 1986.

[83] Cf. Cardinal Newman's fine sermon on "Christ Manifested in Remembrance" (*Parochial and Plain Sermons*, vol. IV, Longmans, Green & Co., London, 1897, p. 253ff.).

[84] As Msgr. Tena brought out in the conference referred to above cf. note 1.

from the Father, even the Spirit of truth, who proceeds from the Father, he will bear witness to me; and you also are witnesses, because you have been with me from the beginning.[85]

The context of these words is his encouragement to the disciples to believe in the effectiveness of their prayer and work — an effectiveness that continues the power of his prayer to the Father for them. The Christian community of discipleship continues Jesus' work of redemption by obeying his commands, especially his new command of fraternal love, which is *sacramentally* realized in "doing" the Eucharist.[86] This realization or "making real" goes further afield than the environment of liturgical ritual. It cannot be sufficiently emphasized that this realization spreads through and permeates the whole of living, which constitutes the worth of the Christian life of worship.

The conclusion that we can surely draw from this is that the meaning of *anamnesis* is an ecclesial reality. In other words, it pertains to the Church, under the guidance of the Holy Spirit, to recollect or call to mind, that is, make present the mystery of God's saving deeds of love. The Eucharistic Prayer, thus, like the Gospel words of the Institution Narrative, must be proclaimed with the living-giving breath or Spirit of God. Again, we are reminded of the new creation that comes about during the Church's Eucharistic Prayer. Though the Institution Narrative, as seen above, is itself the perfect expression of the *anamnesis*, all the Eucharistic Prayers extend the Church's praise and thanksgiving for God's saving action in recalling the whole movement of Christ's passover after the words of Institution have been pronounced.

For too long the significance of *anamnesis* or Memorial has been obscured by controversies concerning the sacrificial nature of

---

[85] Jn 14:25-26; 15:26-27. Wainwright coins the phrase "remembrancer of Christ" in regard to the Holy Spirit's role in the Church, especially at the Eucharist — cf. *Baptism and Eucharist,* op. cit., p. 106.

[86] Cf. Jn 14:12-17 — see the magistral three-volume work of Yves Congar O.P., *I Believe in the Holy Spirit*, Geoffrey Chapman, London, 1983. Cf. also Pope John Paul II, Encyclical Letter, *Dominum et Vivificantem* (18 May 1986) n. 62 where reference is made to the *epiclesis* of Eucharistic Prayer II in the context of commenting on the Johannine discourse.

the Mass. But, one of the most positive results of recent ecumenical discussions, prepared for by the liturgical movement and renewal of the Second Vatican Council, has been a rediscovery of our biblical and patristic heritage in the liturgy regarding this important notion of *anamnesis.* It would be ecumenically constructive, therefore, to include here the words of ARCIC on this subject:

> The Commission believes that the traditional understanding of sacramental reality, in which the once-for-all event of salvation becomes effective in the present through the action of the Holy Spirit, is well expressed by the word anamnesis. We accept this use of the word which seems to do full justice to the Semitic background. Furthermore, it enables us to affirm a strong conviction of sacramental realism and to reject mere symbolism.[87]

Offering

"Memorial," as the consensus of biblical and liturgical scholars has rediscovered, implies and also involves the dimension of sacrifice. The Basic Text of the International Eucharistic Congress of Seoul (October 1989) strongly stated this in unequivocal terms:

> While assuredly enjoining us to celebrate the Eucharist liturgically, does not this command tell us to "do" that very thing which Jesus himself did, namely, to give our own bodies, all of ourselves (1 Jn 3:16), as bread "for the life of the world" (Jn 6:51)? Are we not to "do" that same love? Yes, we are to "do this," the Eucharistic act, as the expression of a daily life of genuine self-giving "for all." Without it, the liturgy alone would become but gesture.

The Eucharistic sacrifice not only proclaims the Gospel without

---

[87] *The Final Report*, op. cit., p. 19f. Cf. also the "Lima Statement" for a similar convergence in faith about this notion: *Baptism, Eucharist and Ministry*, WCC, Geneva, 1982, p. 11.

compromise and challenges every fibre of commitment, but also provides us the needed grace of Christ's love to sacrifice ourselves.

For this needed grace, the sacrifice or offering of the Eucharist refers to the redemptive event of Christ's mystery of passover love not only as something of the past, but also as committing us to live fully in the present, and furthermore, as providing the pledge of our ultimate eschatological hope. This is beautifully expressed in that fine antiphon, attributed to St. Thomas Aquinas, which sets the theme for thanksgiving and praise during the *Magnificat* on the Solemnity of the Body and Blood of Christ (*Corpus Christi*):

> O sacred feast in which we partake of Christ: his sufferings are remembered, our minds are filled with his grace, and we receive a pledge of the glory that is to be ours.[88]

Christ's offering, sacramentally present in the Eucharist, gathers the whole of creation into the dynamic of his passover love — that overarching action, all-embracing and integrating movement — in the Spirit to the Father. Citing St. Paul's words, St. Augustine sums up the doctrine of the Eucharistic sacrifice:

> Thus a true sacrifice is every work done by which we may be united to God in holy fellowship; it refers to that supreme good and end wherein alone we can attain true beatitude . . . Such is the sacrifice of Christians: "We being many are one body in Christ." This is the sacrifice which the Church continually celebrates in the sacrament of the altar, known to the faithful. In it she teaches that she herself is offered in the offering she makes to God.[89]

In the Eucharistic Prayer the Church offers God the very gift which it has received from him. This gift, which is the perfect and once-for-all sacrifice or love-offering of Christ, the unique High Priest and Victim, is both the reason for the Memorial thanksgiving and praise

---

[88] *The Divine Office*, III (Collins), p. 40.
[89] *The City of God*, X.6. John Burnaby remarks that the Eucharist keeps the Church in mind of its sacrificial character — cf. *Amor Dei*, p. 124.

and also the reason for the community's hope. As Eucharistic Prayer IV puts it:

> Looking forward to his coming in glory, we offer you his body and blood, the acceptable sacrifice which brings salvation to the whole world.

Indeed, because of Christ, who calls, inspires, and shows us how to approach God without fear but in confident love, we are fired with the desire to worship him.

The Christian community's reality as communion has its basis in its communion or participation in Christ's sacrifice, which becomes the constant moral and spiritual challenge to our sinful egoism and its structures. The sacrifice of Christ transforms individuals into the new being of Christ's Mystical Body so that they become a community. Christ is the new identity experienced in the communion of his Mystical Body.[90] Christ not only restores us to right relationship with God, but also with our fellow human beings and the whole of creation by giving us access to his "at-one-ing" sacrifice in the Eucharistic mystery. Indeed, sacrifice imbued with love expresses the deepest and richest quality of human life. But, without Christ's love no sacrifice is really possible in an ungraced state of fallen nature. The notion of Christian sacrifice, thus, elevates our longing to love. Since one of the characteristic modes of being human is communication through language, the Eucharistic Prayer enjoys a unique place in expressing symbolically our essential relationship with God, fellow human beings and the created world. Such a relationship would be shallow and worthless without the realism of the dimension of sacrifice. Rather than viewing it primarily as a negative and morbid reality, however, we can regard Christian sacrifice as presenting a new creative thrust to our human potential and energies for integrating ourselves with the truth of our oneness with the world as intended by God in the beginning. For, the essence of Christian sacrifice is primarily not a fixation with the fear of a "God" who would only be appeased through our pain in the act of immolating or destroying part

---

[90] Cf. Gal 2:19-20.

of his creation — as once was thought in theories of sacrifice.[91] Its essence rather is to be seen as enshrined in Christ's revelation of atonement or reconciliation in love.[92]

Christ's love generously provides access both to God and all creation, empowering us to state our new creativity positively in the language of the Eucharistic Prayer. Communication/communion, which is the aim of any genuine sacrifice, is the very core and content of this Prayer of the Eucharistic sacrifice. Significantly the community is summoned to pray for its sacrifice to be "acceptable to God the Almighty Father," for it is profoundly true that "prayer and sacrifice are in the end indistinguishable when it comes to a consideration of their purpose," as Frances Young remarks.[93] Thus, for example, in the Roman Canon, after recalling the whole paschal mystery of Christ, the celebrant continues:

> ...from the many gifts you have given us we offer to you, God of glory and majesty, this holy and perfect sacrifice: the bread of life and the cup of eternal salvation ... Then, as we receive from this altar the sacred body and blood of your Son, let us be filled with every grace and blessing.

---

[91] Even the allegorical interpretation of the mystical separation of the elements of bread and wine as an image of the death of Christ is unacceptable today because, as Mazza states (*The Eucharistic Prayers*, op. cit., p. 273): "in the New Testament there is question not so much of the separation of the bread from the wine as of the distinction of two rites: the rite involving the bread as distinct from the rite involving the wine." Each rite shows in its own way the same reality, viz. the total self-giving of the Savior for the life of the world in fulfillment of the Father's will.

[92] Cf. Joseph Ratzinger, *Introduction to Christianity* (tr. by J.R. Foster) Burns & Oates, London, 1969, p. 218f.: "the nature of Christian worship does not consist in the surrender of things, nor in any kind of destruction, an idea that has continually recurred since the sixteenth century in theories of the sacrifice of the Mass. According to these theories God's overlordship of all had to be recognized in this fashion. All these laborious efforts of thought are simply overtaken by the event of Christ and its biblical explanation. Christian worship consists in the absoluteness of love, as it could only be poured out by the one in whom God's own love had become human love; and it consists in the new form of representation included in this love, namely that he stood for us and we let ourselves be taken over by him." Cf. also Masure, *The Christian Sacrifice*; also Daly, *Christian Sacrifice*; Young, *Sacrifice and the Death of Christ*. For an account of the various theories about the essence of Christian sacrifice see also Gustave Aulen's classic work, *Christus Victor* (tr. A.G. Hebert) London, 1931.

[93] Young, *Sacrifice and the Death of Christ*, p. 135f.

The idea expressed here and echoed in every Eucharistic Prayer fosters a sound appreciation of created realities. The divine economy of Love in addressing and handling the stuff of our everyday lives (food and drink) has profound implications regarding human ecology and the true sense of power to be discovered in distributing and sharing the world's resources and goods. Self consumerism can only be converted by a genuine spirit of sacrifice. It is this spirit of Christ which achieves the communion which the Eucharistic Prayer communicates. Here the language of sacrifice expresses the essential symbol of Christian relationship to God as the very word sacrifice itself means: to *make sacred/offer to God*. This has given the Eucharistic celebration one of its most ancient names as the *"anaphora"* or "sacrificial offering." This characteristic of offering in the Eucharistic Prayer holds the key for experiencing the joy of living, namely, recognizing how to offer, give, and share the things of this world by acknowledging God the Giver. It is the key unlocking the mystery of our part in shaping human history's ultimate meaning and purpose — a significance stamped not by material progress or temporal success, but sealed by the eternal glory of Love's mystery on the cross.

The language of offering — like the reality to which it points — is learnt in the school of prayer in the Upper Room of the Last Supper where the Lord showed his disciples by his words and example the gift of himself in self-sacrificing love to the Father's will for the life of the world. In prayer — the Eucharistic Prayer — the glory of the Lord is manifest. The Church as his Mystical Body participates in this glory as the sacrament of his love's sacrifice is appropriated by the gradual growth in consistency between what the Church *proclaims* in its Prayer and what it is in spirit and truth. Language and life merge together marvelously in the truth of sacrificial offering proclaimed in the liturgy of the Eucharistic Prayer. The General Instruction of the Roman Missal sums up well the significance of the function of the Eucharistic Prayer as *"oblation/offering"*:

> It is through this very memorial that the Church —in particular the Church here and now assembled —offers the immaculate Victim to God the Father in the Holy Spirit. The Church strives also that the faithful should not only offer the immaculate Victim but should learn to offer themselves; through

Christ their Mediator they should be drawn day by day into an ever more perfect union with God and with each other, so that finally God may be all in all.[94]

This striving in sincere imitation and assimilation of the grace of Christ's sacrifice is what is pointed to in the *Pastoral Constitution on the Church in the Modern World* with which the Bishops concluded the agenda of the Second Vatican Council. Here they called on all Christians to become committed to that kind of witness which puts prayer in self-sacrificing action at the service of humanity:

Christians can yearn for nothing more ardently than to serve the men of this age with an ever growing generosity and success... Not everyone who says "Lord, Lord," will enter the kingdom of heaven, but those who do the will of the Father, and who manfully put their hands to the task.

Intercession

Christian commitment to the suffering and struggle of people in the world finds a place in the element of *intercession* in the Eucharistic Prayer. This concern for commitment is raised to the power of Christ's infinite and constant pleading on behalf of his brethren in the world. Intercession implies the theological virtues of faith, hope and charity since these virtues or revealed attitudes stem from and are integrally linked with the gift of Christ's mediation as the unique Intercessor before the Father.[95]

The Eucharistic Prayer clearly expresses the faith of the Church regarding our solidarity in the "communion of saints," particularly in the two series of intercessions for the living and the dead — "who have gone before us marked with the sign of faith." The true significance of this expression, *"communion of saints,"* is implied in the intercessions. For the word "saints" (as in the New Testament usage)

---

[94] GIRM. n. 55(f); CTS Do455 p. 29.
[95] Cf. Rm 8:34; Heb 7:25; Rv 5:6 etc.

refers to all who share in or have communion fellowship with the "holy things," that is, the sacred gifts signifying God's love on the altar.[96]

The Christian community's hope likewise is here expressed most fittingly within the context of the Eucharistic Prayer in the presence of Christ's sacrifice, which pleads more incessantly than the blood of the just Abel. From the most ancient times there is ample witness to the confident hope of Christians in requesting God to bless and care for the living and the dead.[97] This hope which is expressed, however, is of a different order to wishful thinking or mere subjective longing! In the presence of the unique sacrifice of Christ, which has won God's acceptance and attention for his children's needs, the Eucharistic intercessions hold an especially powerful place not in changing God's will, but in changing our attitude and in providing us to live with confidence regarding the responsibilities for the future which we must take up.

The context of the intercessions during the Eucharistic Prayer is none other than that of charity in keeping with God's gift of his life of *koinonia* or communion. This is expressed in phrases like: "In union with the whole Church" (*"Communicantes"*). In this environment of love the Mystical Body of Christ fosters care, concern and communication with the Father for the deepest needs of our sisters and brothers. The approach of the whole Church at prayer thus manifests an atmosphere of loving respect for all — from our Blessed Lady Mary to the very least of us, who "though we are sinners" share in the great communion of saints. The Eucharistic Prayer expresses our true worth as being empowered to intercede for one another because of the gift of divine charity, the virtue or strength of God's Spirit in Christ.

In this perspective there is agreement among the Christian Churches about the catholic understanding of the Eucharist as

---

[96] Cf. J. Ratzinger, *Introduction to Christianity*, op. cit., p. 257; cf. also J.N.D. Kelly, *Early Christian Creeds*, Longman, 1972, p. 388ff.

[97] Cf. St. Cyril of Jerusalem, *Catecheses*, 23.8-18; St. Augustine also witnesses to the universal custom of offering prayers and sacrifices even for the dead — cf. *Confessions*, X. 12.32, where he most movingly speaks of remembering his mother at the altar.

"propitiatory sacrifice" shared in the communion of saints. As the Lima Statement of the World Council of Churches put it:

> The Church gratefully recalling God's mighty acts of redemption, beseeches God to give the benefits of these acts to every human being. In thanksgiving and intercession, the Church is united with the Son, its great High Priest and Intercessor ... The Eucharist is the sacrament of the unique sacrifice of Christ who ever lives to make intercession for us. It is the memorial of all that God has done for the salvation of the world. What it was God's will to accomplish in the incarnation, life, death, resurrection, and ascension of Christ, God does not repeat. These events are unique and can neither be repeated nor prolonged. In the memorial of the Eucharist, however, the Church offers its intercession in communion with Christ, our great High Priest.[98]

Intercession in the Eucharistic Prayer brings us back to basics —the theological quality of all life, that is, its God-centeredness. Not only is the power or virtue of faith, hope, and love revealed and given to us, but in the exercise of these gifts we discover familiarity with the nature of God's *koinonia* or communion of the Trinity of Persons revealed by Christ. Intercession brings us closer to one another because it draws us to and into God in humility while we patiently acknowledge our basic dependence on him and need for him who is love.

The Final Doxology

The Eucharistic Prayer, begun in praise and thanksgiving, is brought to a fitting finale in the *doxology*, which renders glory to the Triune God in the presence of the sacrament of the New Covenant. Gathered in that mystical at-one-ment of the Bread and Wine, the Church responds to God with confident affirmation of his grace: what

---

[98] *Baptism, Eucharist and Ministry*, op. cit., n. 8.

is Christ's is now the Church's, as his Bride. The Church draws into herself and makes her own the affirmation of the New Covenant which she enjoys as addressed and proclaimed to her in the real presence of the Word-made-flesh in the Eucharist:

> For the Son of God, Jesus Christ . . . was not Yes and No; but in him it is always Yes. For all the promises of God find their Yes in him. That is why we utter the Amen through him, to the glory of God.[99]

"Amen," however, is more than a word or mere agreement of affirmation. In the syntax of the Eucharistic Prayer it transcends natural, national, or cultural boundaries. It echoes the depth of prayerful faith. For it surges forth from the heart, soul, and spirit of religious experience, which has been once-for-all authenticated by the Word taking to himself the language of human nature. The great "Amen" of the Eucharistic Prayer responds to God's good pleasure over the creation of his love: "This is my body . . . this is my blood . . . It is good . . . it is very good!"

The "Amen" of the Eucharist responds directly to the Church's act of liturgical praise or *"doxology."*[100] The doxology concisely expresses the faith of the Church regarding the economy or arrangement of redemptive love in the ancient classical formula of praise: *to* the Father, *through* his Son Jesus Christ, *in* the Holy Spirit. This Prayer is the privileged context to learn about God — and also about how to relate to him and the world of his love in worship. We discover how to appreciate the movement of the Eucharistic Prayer as we grasp its trinitarian perspective. This perspective is especially dear to the Eastern Church, which expresses its faith and doctrine of God in this form. The Western tendency — with the exception of the Eucharistic doxology — has been to use the scheme: "Glory to the Father and to the Son and to the Holy Spirit." While both approaches are complementary, the dynamic Eastern approach, especially because enshrined at the end of every Eucharistic Prayer, has definite

---

[99] 2 Cor 2:19-20.
[100] Cf. Mohrmann, op. cit., t. I, pp. 277-286.

advantages. For it shows that: (i) dialogue with God, which is prayer, has its basis in the relations of the Divine Persons of the Trinity — that is, authentic prayer means entering into the silence of God's communion which reveals the communication of the Three Divine Persons' Being-in-Love; (ii) the spiritual and Christian life takes its origin and finds its fulness in the mystery of God; (iii) our unity in love — with God and among ourselves — is rooted in, grows from, flourishes and bears fruit when our center is the holiness of God's inner life of unity, harmony, or *koinonia*. Here in the mystery of God is authentic life — *"life in abundance"* — which the Father sent his beloved Son to reveal and which he communicates in the Holy Spirit.

The ancient practice of the congregation responding "Amen" after the double consecration is now superseded by our "acclamations." St. Ambrose mentions this and links it with the "Amen" affirmed by those communicating with the Gift of the altar as if it anticipates their at-one-ment with Christ's sacrifice.[101] Similarly, in a well-known passage in one of his sermons to the newly-baptized, who were admitted to communion for the first time on Easter night, St. Augustine expresses the direct and integral connection between what Christians receive at the Eucharistic celebration and who they are:

> If you wish to understand the body of Christ, listen to the words of the Apostle: "You are the Body of Christ" (1 Cor 12:27). If you are the body and members of Christ, your mystery is placed on the Lord's Table; you receive your mystery... For you hear "The Body of Christ" and you answer "Amen." Be a member of the Body of Christ, that your "Amen" may ring true.[102]

"Amen" is truly the word of Christ's faithful — their response to the proclamation of the Church's worship and their worth. It is, as the late Orthodox theologian Alexander Schmemann inspiringly put it:

---

[101] *De Sacramentis*, IV.25.
[102] Sermon 272.

Indeed one of the most important words in the world, for it expresses the agreement of the Church to follow Christ in his ascension to his Father, to make this ascension the destiny of man ... Upon this Amen the fate of the human race is decided. It reveals that the movement toward God has begun.[103]

Amen opens our hearts to all that the Church proclaims in the Eucharistic Prayer — the spiritual dynamic of Christ's *passover love*, the fountain of Christian spirituality and all holiness.

---

[103] Cited in *Sacred Symbols that Speak*, vol. 1, Light and Life Publ. Co., Minneapolis, Minnesota, 1985, p. 173f.

3

The Holy and Perfect Sacrifice of Praise
(The Roman Canon)

This canon was introduced into England during the seventh century [. . .] Thus the canon used by the Church of the city of Rome from the period between the fifth and seventh centuries (and possibly earlier), has been the only canon of the entire Western Church since the eleventh or twelfth century; in many countries it had already been adopted long before. This fact alone makes the suggestion that this canon should be simply abandoned a foolhardy one. [. . .] As distinct from all the other anaphora traditions, it is characteristic of the present Roman canon that [. . .] it is directed towards the offering of our gifts, their acceptance by God and their consecration. [. . .] The offering of bread and wine which we make to God in the Mass has, to put it briefly, a meaning that is at the same time cosmic, anthropological and sacramental. [. . .] In this offering we pray God to accept them, to bless them and transform them through his Spirit into the body and blood of Christ, asking him to give them back to us transformed in such a way that through them we may, in the Spirit, be united to Christ and to one another, sharing in fact in the divine nature. The very idea of sacrifice is seen against this background in the Roman canon. [. . .] It is basically the theme of the "sacrum commercium" [divine exchange] which is symbolized and made concrete in the offering of the gifts, at first unconsecrated and then consecrated which, after their consecration, we receive again in the communion, transformed into the body and blood of the Lord.[1]

---

[1] Vagaggini, *The Canon of the Mass*, p. 85, 87f.

This Prayer has withstood the test of time and the attempts of various liturgical reformers to discard or change it. If the hand of these reformers had not been stayed by the authority of Rome, the unhappy result would have been that Christian spirituality would have been deprived of the particularly rich contribution offered by what is called the "Roman Canon." This name, by which it has been known since the Middle Ages, comes from the rubric *"canon actionis"* which means the rule of what is *done* during the liturgy of the Eucharist. It has been truly remarked that the development in Rome of this Eucharistic Prayer is of great importance for the life of the Church in the West.[2] St. Ambrose in the fourth century bears witness to the existence of much of the wording and content of the Roman Canon. This fact presupposes that the Prayer had undergone a period of development and had supplanted the Greek text of the Prayer in use at the time of St. Hippolytus a century and a half earlier.

Our purpose here, however, is not to trace the history of the development of this Prayer, which has been thoroughly treated elsewhere.[3] Nor is it to examine its "merits" and "deficiencies" which Vagaggini has adequately dealt with in summing up the findings of the Committee for the reform of the liturgy after the Second Vatican Council.[4] Rather we shall direct our considerations to the chief characteristic features of this Prayer in order to pursue the overall intention in this book, namely, to show how the richness and essence of Christian spirituality is illustrated and stated in the Church at prayer.

The unity of this Prayer consists in the supreme action of the Church's offering to God the unique "holy and perfect sacrifice of praise" of Christ rather than in the unified structure of the text. Proclamation of the action of Christ's perfect sacrifice in praise of the Father's glory is itself the Church's principal action. This action, in fact, binds into a whole the text which is a compilation of various prayers arranged according to the Roman criterion of a perfect

---

[2] Cf. James T. O'Connor, *The Hidden Manna: A Theology of the Eucharist*, p. 175.

[3] Cf. Josef Jungmann, *The Mass of the Roman Rite*, I, op. cit.; Martimort, *The Church at Prayer: Eucharist*, vol. II; Mazza, *The Eucharistic Prayers*, op. cit., p. 49ff., etc.

[4] Cf. Vagaggini, loc. cit.; also Alan F. Detscher, "The Eucharistic Prayers of the Roman Catholic Church" in Senn (ed.) *New Eucharistic Prayers*, op. cit., pp. 25-27.

symmetrical pattern before and after the Institution Narrative. Thus, a series of commemorations for the Catholic or universal Church, the local church, the living, the Blessed Virgin Mary, apostles and early popes and Roman saints, is followed by a prayer for the Church's offering to be accepted by God the Father before the central memorial proclamation of the Institution. Balancing what precedes this there is again prayer for the offering to be accepted (recalling Israel's prophetic sacrifices) and a series of commemorations: of the dead and of the sacred ministers of the celebrating church to be admitted into the company of the apostles, martyrs and saints. The proclamation of the action of the sacrifice of praise concludes by being drawn up into the classical doxology or praise of the most Holy Trinity.

The title of this chapter, *The Holy and Perfect Sacrifice of Praise* has profoundly biblical roots.[5] Although it might justly be applied to any of the Eucharistic Prayers,[6] it seems apt to describe the Roman Canon whose main feature is a sense of the sacredness of sacrifice in the context of praise and thanksgiving for Christ's gift of himself. This feature implies the Church's involvement in the attitude of service which flows into intercessory prayer. The significance of the intrinsic bond between sacrifice and service needs to be rediscovered and reappraised in our contemporary experience of relating worship and living.[7] Although the language of the Roman Canon may sound strange to us and its stylistic rhythm seem rather stilted and formal,

---

[5] As Daly's extensive researches have brought out — cf. *Christian Sacrifice*, op. cit. As Stevenson points out (op. cit., p. 12), one would look in vain in the N.T., however, to find any trace of the Eucharist referred to in specifically sacrificial terms. The author of the Epistle to the Hebrews uses a technical term "sacrifice of praise" (cf. Heb 13:15) regarding liturgical worship as sacrificial because it implies authentic praise of God, that is, commitment to him. The sacrificial language is employed analogically because the quality of Jesus' sacrifice is unique and unrepeatable — cf. Rm 6:10; Heb 7:27; 1 P 3:8.

[6] Cf. Heb 13:15; Rm 12:1 — the phrase also occurs in Eucharistic Prayer IV and is the predominant aspect of the third Eucharistic Prayer of Masses with children. Cf. Mazza, op. cit., pp. 64 & 247.

[7] Mazza remarks on the theological status given to the sacredness of this Prayer's antiquity and immutability. He cites the words of the Council of Trent regarding this characteristic feature: "Holy things must be treated in a holy way and this sacrifice is the most holy of all things. And so, that this sacrifice might be worthily and reverently offered and received, the Catholic Church many centuries ago instituted the sacred Canon . . ." (DS 1745) cf. op. cit., p. 54.

we would be the losers if we dismissed this Prayer without some deeper reflection on the mystery of the sacredness of sacrifice and service which its words evoke. We would settle for superficial, makeshift meanings in expecting that words, especially those words forged in the fire of the experiences of the martyrs and saints, will readily yield up their religious significance. The mystery of God requires of us total abandonment; it cannot be encapsulated in words, though they serve to point in the direction of communication.[8] However, by considering this Prayer from different angles we hope to obtain a clearer appreciation of Christian sacrifice which the Eucharistic Memorial celebrates and which is an indispensable dimension for authentic human living.

The Church's Pure Offering

Christ's pure offering in communicating God's love fully reveals the new deeper reality of sacrifice. His pure offering becomes the Church's sacrifice of love. This dimension of love is what is wholly missing from the desire and endeavor to transcend the tragic aspects in human experience by relying solely on human resources. Christ's paschal mystery shows a living, joyous relationship to God as the Creator and Father of love; it transforms the meaning of sacrifice — simply speaking, an act bonded with death, fear, and destruction, which is implied in all merely human notions and ritual routines of sacrifice. In this mystery the inner pattern of all that exists is dis-

---

[8] T.S. Eliot reminds us of the need to *"be still"* since often our impatience to know all leads just as surely and quickly to superficiality. Depth of significance requires the silence of waiting for meaning to emerge out of the dark of mystery, for God to grace us with his gift realized in faith, hope, and love:

I said to my soul, be still, and let the dark come upon you
Which shall be the darkness of God. [. . .]
I said to my soul, be still, and wait without hope
For hope would be hope for the wrong thing; wait without love
For love would be love of the wrong thing; there is yet faith
But the faith and the love and the hope are all in the waiting.
Wait without thought, for you are not ready for thought;
So the darkness shall be the light, and the stillness the dancing.
(Four Quartets: East Coker III)

closed, namely, the structural dependence of *being* human on love. Love is the focus of sacrifice, as it is also its inspiration, source, and essence. Human dignity or worth finds its noblest expressions in that quality of love which is prepared to sacrifice all for the other as Christ's perfect self-offering reveals.[9] The Roman Canon expresses the transformation of our offering through Christ's action of making them holy by his sacrifice of love. This is evident in the contrast between the words for "offering" used in the post-Sanctus prayer and those in the prayer immediately after the Institution Narrative or "consecration" — a contrast, that is, which is clearer in the Latin text than in our ICEL translation. At the beginning of the Canon, the Church beseeches the Father to accept and bless what it brings to the altar, the bread and wine — which represent the fruits of the earth, the work of human hands and ourselves. In the Latin text three words are used for these offerings: *"dona, munera, sacrificia"* (which our English translates simply by *"gifts we offer you in sacrifice"*). After the "consecration" what is offered is expressed in a significantly different way:

Literal translation:	Latin:	ICEL:
from among the gifts you have bestowed on us, the pure victim, the holy victim, the all-perfect victim, the holy bread of eternal life and the chalice of everlasting salvation.	de tuis donis ac datis, hostiam puram, hostiam sanctam, hostiam immaculatam, Panem sanctum vitae aeternae, et Calicem salutis perpetuae.	from the many gifts you have given us [. . .] this holy and perfect sacrifice: the bread of life and the cup of eternal salvation.

We would miss the point if we were to focus merely on the "moment of consecration" as a great divide that transforms our gifts

---

[9] Pope John Paul II's words on the *human dimension* of the mystery of redemption offer a rich source of reflection — cf. his first Encyclical Letter, *Redemptor Hominis*, n. 10, which is based on the teaching of the Second Vatican Council especially in *Gaudium et Spes*. At the end of a crucial paragraph of this document on the transformation of the human heart and of the world, the Eucharist is presented as the foretaste of all things recapitualted in Christ who continues to employ and bring the elements of this world ("the fruits of the earth and work of human hands") to their fulfillment: *"A pledge of this hope, sustenance for this journey, our Lord left us in that sacrament of faith in which natural elements cultivated by men are turned into his glorious Body and Blood, the supper of fraternal communion, the foretaste of the heavenly banquet"* (G.S., n. 38).

into Christ's perfect and pure sacrifice. It is not the "moment" that is vital; but the mystery of transformation through the once-and-for-all action of Christ's proclamation of love of which the memorial proclamation of his words of Institution is the symbol. The proclamation — which is first of all Christ's and then the Church's — runs throughout the whole Eucharistic Prayer. It expresses the action of God's transforming our offerings and our lives as worthy of his love.[10]

The environment of Christ's *"holy and perfect sacrifice"* — the *divine milieu* of his proclamation in the words and gestures of the Last Supper which point to the supreme deed of his passover-love at Calvary manifests the deepest dimensions of our God-given capacity for the intimacy of dialogue. While all the Church's sacraments express facets of Christ's Paschal sacrifice, in the atmosphere of the Eucharist particularly we draw inspiration and strength from the grace of Christ's own presence in love to face the challenges of living as *spiritual*, that is, *relational* beings. The Eucharistic mystery of its very nature as communion in sacrifice attracts to itself, as it were, all the Church's sacramental actions and is the source and summit of the whole spiritual life of Christians.[11] In this way the Eucharist realizes the profound significance of Jesus' proclamation virtually on the eve of his passover:

I when I am lifted up from the earth will draw all to myself.[12]

---

[10] Gerald Vann, quoting H. Lucas and J. Jungman, puts it this way: "The unconsecrated bread and wine are called *dona* inasmuch as they are God's gifts to us, but *munera* because they are 'still ours to give back to him'; whereas the *Unde et memores* prayer after the consecration speaks of *dona* and *data*, God's gifts and presents to us: 'They are ours indeed, and they are offered once more; but they are no longer ours in the same sense . . . they are no longer in the nature of personal property which might have been otherwise disposed of. They have passed out of our control [. . .] Fr Jungmann sees in the three words an ascending gradation of meaning: *dona* are 'presents' in the ordinary colloquial sense; *munera* are rather an official 'presentation' (*munus* being equivalent of the Greek *leitourgia*, liturgy, a public office or duty whether sacred or profane); *sacrificia* are holy gifts or offerings, i.e. consecrated to God" (*The Paradise Tree*, Collins, London, 1959, p. 168).

[11] Cf. P.O., n. 5 which quotes St. Thomas Aquinas in a footnote: "The Eucharist is the final term of the spiritual life and all the other sacraments are ordered to it" — S.T., III. q. 73, a. 3c; cf. also III, q. 65, a. 3.

[12] Jn 12:32, which is cited in L.G. n. 3 regarding Christ's proclamation of *"the work of our redemption"* continued in the sacrifice of the altar; cf. also Jn 3:14; 8:28. There are two readings in the Greek manuscripts: *pantas* (all men) and *panta* (all things). The former is now accepted by most authorities, whereas the latter was adopted by many of the

To speak of spiritual relationship is to touch the heart of religion and, in particular, of Christian sacrifice. True religion as taught and lived by Jesus is essentially about relationship. Here the authentic meaning of "spiritual" is discovered as the reciprocal gift of self —that fulness of the truth in living to which Christ's Spirit leads in understanding the mystery of the passover sacrifice. Thus, it would be a travesty of this truth of love to interpret sacrifice and spiritual relationship as indicating a negation or belittling of the worth of the material world — as is the sad tendency in all dualistic approaches, which regard the material world as evil.[13] The art of God in revealing the true value of sacrifice draws out the inner worth of human living and of all creation. The movement of God's revelation in the mystery of the passover, which culminates in its greatest sign or sacrament, Christ's Eucharist, is proof positive of God's love for this world to the point that Christ identifies himself with it: he takes created realities such as bread and wine to himself as his Body and Blood to show us how the light of his loving presence permeates the reality of all things. In this way he offers us the finest clue to the spiritual life of God — eternal life which is utterly relational Being, Love's communion.

An example of this relational nature brought about by the Eucharistic sacrifice can be seen in the prayer of the Roman Canon called by its first two words in the Latin text *"Quam oblationem."* Since this prayer occurs just before the Institution Narrative (the "words of consecration") and since it is accompanied by the celebrant's gesture of extending his hands over the bread and wine, it is seen by some as a prayer of *"epiclesis,"* although there is no explicit invocation of the Holy Spirit. But without going into the complex history of this prayer or the controversy about it,[14] it is interesting to see this little prayer as a statement of the Church's faith regarding how God's acceptance

---

Fathers of the Church — e.g. St. Augustine, *In Joh. Evan.*, Tr. LII, 11. St. Augustine comments that not all have faith, but only those who are freed from "the Prince of this world" and predestined to salvation, that is, those who respond to the grace of Christ. This is not as "deterministic" as it appears, for, as the context of Augustine's words make clear, there is always the availability of grace and hence possibility of conversion and reconciliation for every person during life.

[13] See the positive, indeed, Christian doctrine of the Second Vatican Council, especially in the great document of the Church in the Modern World, *Gaudium et Spes.*

[14] Cf. Mazza, *The Eucharistic Prayers*, p. 68ff.

of the created realities of our experience — an acceptance which the Eucharistic Prayer proclaims with praise — is the necessary condition for them to become sacramental, that is, sacred signs relating us to God and also to the gifts of his world. This prayer illustrates the positive Christian notion of the nature of sacrifice in pleading for God's blessing and his acceptance of our offering.

This positive dimension is indicated particularly by the word *"rationabilem."* The ingenuity of liturgical scholars has been exercised in following St. Ambrose's explanation regarding the significance of *"rationabilem,"*[15] the most perplexing word in the string of five predicates. But, one thing is clear: the sense of this Latin word is somehow connected with sacrifice and would be best translated as "spiritual" (or, as the ICEL translators have rendered it, "in spirit and truth"). The Latin word *"rationabilis"* translates the Greek *"logikos,"* which the Christian vocabulary assimilated in translations of Rm 12:1 and 1 P 2:2. Here there is a clear allusion to Malachy's prophecy of a "pure oblation" (1:11). A transliteration of this word as "reasonable" (or worse, "rational"!) would, therefore, not only be unjustifiable, but also reduce its rich significance.[16] What is surely requested in this prayer, albeit *inter alia*, is a greatness of heart which comes from participation in Christ's sacrifice so that we may become capable of that spiritual or relational quality of being, which fittingly expresses our Christian identity according to the design of God and our Savior's manifest deep desire and example.

The spiritual "logic" of Christ's sacrifice

The Eucharistic Prayer is the greatest expression of humanity's imagination in expressing its heartfelt yearnings. And it is more than that! For through it we encounter God's great *desire* in Christ. Our mind's dullness is illumined by the light of Christ's pure oblation of love so that we may truly perceive communion coming about — that

---

[15] Cf. *De Sacramentis* IV.21.
[16] Cf. Mazza, op. cit., pp. 68ff., 300ff.; also Christine Mohrmann, op. cit., t. 1, pp. 179-187.

relationship in the mystery of God's intimate Being. In other words, only love which is the essence of sacrifice can bring about the relational-being of the Mystical Body.

Relationship understood merely as an abstract notion would be meaningless. It grows out of and requires existential expression, which implies both stability of union and permanent presence between persons. This is brought out in the Roman Canon proclaiming the bond between the community of the praying Church, which includes the Blessed Virgin and saints, and Christ in his act of sacrificial love. Referring to this intimate bond the Dogmatic Constitution on the Church states:

> It is especially in the sacred liturgy that our union with the heavenly Church is best realized; in the liturgy through the sacramental signs, the power of the Holy Spirit acts on us, and we celebrate together the joy of being a community in praising the divine majesty. [. . .] When we celebrate the Eucharistic sacrifice we are intimately united to the heavenly Church's worship as we express the fellowship of communion in honoring and remembering the glorious Mary ever Virgin, St. Joseph, the holy apostles, martyrs, and all the saints.[17]

Christians adore no idol; they make no idol of an ideal or idea. But as Christians we worship the living God who does not ask for a "victim" (such as in the burnt offering of dead animals or fruits), but the gift of our lives and free obedience, the gift of our faithfulness in the midst of weal and woe.

Living actions constitute the sacrifice of the Christ's New Covenant; they are given a new direction and become our share in Christ's sacrifice — sacrifice, the inner "logic" of which is the new

---

[17] L.G. n. 50. Note that the Vatican Council was speaking of the Roman Canon, which at that time was the only one in use in the Western liturgy. The name of St. Joseph was added by Pope John XXIII in his address at the end of the First Session of the Council on 8 December 1962, although the authoritative decree of the Congr. of Rites is dated 13 November 1962. Pope John XXIII's great devotion to St. Joseph (his baptismal name) moved him to place the Ecumenical Council under his patronage. The revision of the Canon permits a shortening of the list of saints, which is not suppressed and may be used in accordance with pastoral considerations.

sense of relationship and fellowship expressed in praise.[18] This Eucharistic Prayer speaks of our *"faith and devotion,"* recalling *"the sacrifice of Abraham,"* who is the Father of faith because of his fidelity when tested by God. This was likewise the quality of Abel, for which he received God's favor. All the prophets manifested this disposition in their denunciation of ritual formalism, which they sought to eradicate and which they recommended to be replaced by spiritual sacrifice — *"a sacrifice of praise."*

Christ's teaching and example enable us to recognize a spiritual "logic," as it were, both in the gifts of creation — in bread and wine as the symbols of God's will and ultimate generosity — and also in humanity's gradual coming to an awareness of how to relate all to the Father through him in the Holy Spirit. Taking into his hands this bread and this cup, the Lord expressed his intention to situate his sacrifice within the design of obedience to the Father. The Church's participation in this sacrifice realizes the same act of loving obedience in which its members share. Thus, from the beginning the Christian community has always proclaimed that its "unbloody sacrifice" or "clean oblation" is of a spiritual order in contrast to that of the Jewish or pagan world.

Christian sacrifice must always be gauged by fidelity and dedication to Christ, which the Church proclaims is known to God alone: *"You know our faith and devotion."* This disposition of dedication is the fruit of representing (*"being mindful of"*) Christ's sacrifice. Thus, Christian sacrifice, being utterly spiritual, transcends the offerings of Aaron's priesthood. It is linked rather with the sacrifice of Melchizedek, which possessed an unsurpassed degree of perfection and purity — particularly because it foreshadowed that of Christ, the unique Mediator. But, all the former "types" which foreshadowed Christ's perfect and pure self-offering can be seen and interpreted as such only by hindsight —in the light of the Church's reflection on Christ's proclamation of God's love which prepared the way gradually

---

[18] Cf. the discourse of St. Gregory of Nazianzen in the Office of Readings for Saturday of Week Five of Lent (D.O. II, p. 247): "Let us not sacrifice young calves or lambs [. . .] which are for the most part dead, insensate things. But let us offer a sacrifice of praise to God on the altar on high [. . .] To say something greater still, let us sacrifice ourselves to God; further, let us go on every day offering ourselves and all our activities [. . .] let us imitate the passion by our sufferings."

for his new and eternal covenant. The Roman Canon's recital of these names of Old Testament patriarchs and prophetic predecessors in true worship is thus no mere ritual cataloguing of a traditional faith, but, like the commemoration of Christian martyrs and saints, it proclaims a sense of solidarity or rather communal bonding in a procession, as it were, of living witnesses to love — a procession at whose Head is Christ. History is held in perspective and is given a sense of ultimate direction precisely because of Christ's paschal dynamism of worship. In other words, our temporal succession of events and endeavors towards authentic human existence has a *divine logic* the meaning of which is discerned in the light of Christ's revelation of spiritual worship.

Acceptance of Sacrifice

The Roman Canon's repeated prayers and requests for the Church's sacrifice to be accepted by God at first sight seems to raise a problem regarding the effectiveness of Christ's perfect sacrifice. We recall the Old Testament's description of the ritual sacrifice offered to God for sin.[19] This sacrifice was limited in its effectiveness, for it cancelled only sins committed through human error or weakness, not those of malice or full knowledge and ill-will which the Bible calls sins "with the raised hand."[20] The paschal lamb was also offered in sacrifice for sin.[21] But even this sacrifice was annually repeated. The idea that sacrifice offered in expiation for sin (*"kipper,"* sacrifice) did not imply, therefore, that it would be automatically accepted by God.[22] Another factor was required. It is that of integrity between ritual and way of life on the part of the offerer — that consistency for which the prophets were constantly calling. Jesus chose the paschal sacrifice as the type of his own — *"for you . . . for the remission of sins."*

---

[19] Cf. e.g. Lv 4.

[20] Cf. Nb 15:30-31.

[21] Cf. Ex 12:27; 34:25.

[22] Cf. Mazza's discussion of the two distinct though related notions of acceptance and expiation — op. cit., p. 72f.

His sacrifice exceeds the limited effectiveness of the ancient sacrifice; indeed, his unique and universal sacrifice was offered for the remission of all sin without distinction and without restriction as the Letter to the Hebrews emphasizes.[23] Hence the problem: if Christ's sacrifice is perfect in bringing about the remission of sin, why does the Roman Canon contain so many prayers for its acceptance by God? In particular, what is the significance especially of the *Hanc igitur* prayer? Clearly the same factor of integrity is required for us no less than it was for the people of the Old Testament, for it is no longer a question of merely carrying out an external ritual. Thus, what is the difference between Old Testament sacrifices and the uniqueness of Christ's perfect sacrifice which the Church offers sacramentally or in memorial? In offering Christ's unique sacrifice how is the Christian Church doing anything different from the repetitive rituals of Jews or pagans?

Attention to the content of the Church's prayer in the *Hanc igitur* provides the clue in resolving this dilemma. The key to understand this prayer consists in the idea of service in order to appreciate how we share in the renewal of the abundant life which Christ's perfect and pure sacrifice offers. For this service is the offering of the whole Church — that of Christ through whom his faithful can gladly join their own. It is an expression of the liberating power of the Christian sacrifice. Thus, it seems a pity that the ICEL does not translate the word "service" in this prayer since herein lies the key also to Christ's Gospel which challenges the Church to strive and work for justice that his peace may come about.

ICEL:	Literal translation:
Father, accept this offering	Therefore, we beseech you, Lord, to be pleased to accept this offering of our service
from your whole family.	and also that of your whole family;
Grant us your peace in this life,	put our days in order in your peace,
save us from final damnation,	grant that we be snatched from eternal damnation
and count us among those you have chosen.	and counted among the flock of your chosen ones.

---

[23] Cf. Heb 9:28; also Mt 26:28.

74

The tone of this prayer is clearly that of confidence in asking that in virtue of their service — being united with Christ's sacrifice — the offerers of the eucharistic sacrifice be granted both peace in this world and freedom from the fear of eternal torment. Sensitivity to the need to pray for peace is as urgent for us today as it was in the time of that great pope Gregory the Great, from whom it comes down to us — if not even more so.[24] Pope Gregory played his part in offering something nobler and more beautiful to civilization than the outworn *Pax Romana* could provide in sustaining the old order, which was collapsing both because of the threat of the Barbarians and its own decadence. He strove to inculcate the spirit of Christian worship which requires service and sacrifice — characteristic features of the Eucharist in the Roman Canon. Worship celebrates and brings about freedom from fear, peace and harmony. This great Pope taught Europe to look to God for true peace and to sing his praise as the Liberator of the whole world.[25]

Service of all people

The service of worship proclaimed in celebrating the Eucharistic mystery is related intrinsically to the value of working especially for justice and peace in this world with total dedication or self-

---

[24] Pope St. Gregory standardized the formula from the plethora of formulas expressing at times eccentric and private intentions in the most pejorative sense of the word. His wisdom shows itself here in the way he set the common good before private gain! Thus, this petition implicitly brings peace in the praying community itself. — Cf. Jungmann, op. cit., pp. 179-187. Maloney appositely (op. cit., p. 110) cites Pope Gregory's prophetic words: "Do not grieve yourselves over such evils, for those who live after us will see even worse times — so much so that, in comparison with their own age, they will think we have known happy days" (Ep 10, 15). In this prayer Gerald Vann catches the tone of the "Good Shepherd" psalm (23) and comments: "'Dispose our days in thy peace': that peace which the world cannot give, and cannot take away. But if that inner peace is a gift of God for which we can only pray, the 'bond of peace' which should unite the flock of Christ is something we have to strive to create, and which we can all too easily destory or harm" (*The Paradise Tree*, Collins, London, 1959, p. 179f.).

[25] The traditional chant of the Latin Church is known as Gregorian Chant, which takes its name from Pope Gregory though his part in its compilation is a matter of controversy. — Cf. *The Oxford Dictionary of the Christian Church* (Revised 2nd ed., F.L. Cross and E.A. Livingstone), O.U.P., 1983, p. 1099: article "Plainsong."

sacrifice.[26] Service of others in need is an imperative flowing from the Christian community's grasp of what it celebrates in Christ's sacrifice. As is evident in the second part of this prayer (the *Hanc igitur*), the quality and orientation of this service are shaped and broadened by the eternal perspective of the paschal mystery. Furthermore, the energy to undertake this service derives its unique strength from the liberating power and grace of Christ's unique sacrifice.[27] This kind of service which binds liturgy to living is what realizes that peace which is God's gift — a gift that can never be snatched away from Christian worshipers in this world or after their death.[28] Thus, in summary, what is brought out by this prayer is that — in virtue of its full confidence in the effectiveness of Christ's "at-one-ing" grace of sacrifice — the Church is empowered both to join its service and also to express its faith in God's acceptance.

Jesus proclaimed that he would die for all. His passover sacrifice realized this proclamation; it was the fulfillment of this proclamation, its perfection *in deed*. In recalling this deed the Church together with God's holy people offers the sacrifice of Christ's perfect obedience of love for the Father's will to save all humanity. Divine Service is the meaning of *liturgy*. It is the integration of life-service in love of one's neighbor with love of God. The Roman Canon's particular emphasis on sacrifice brings out the demanding nature of love, its far-

---

[26] Mazza sums up (op. cit., p. 73f.): "How could the memorial of Christ the Lord not be acceptable to God? And indeed, this memorial is, in itself, always acceptable. But it does not exist simply in itself or as such. It exists insofar as it is celebrated and it is inseparable from its celebrant. [. . .] The persistent emphasis on this theme in the Canon shows how concerned the Roman liturgy is, like men and women of today, with continuity and coherence between cult and life. The theological theme of the acceptability of sacrifice should also make us more sensitive to the criticisms of nonbelievers and non-practitioners who are scandalized when Christians do not carry over into their lives what they proclaim and celebrate in the eucharistic sacrifice. The discrepancy between liturgy and life is as much a cause of scandal to others as it is the reason why God does not 'accept' our sacrifices."

[27] At this point de Lubac's insight is especially relevant: "But if the sacrifice is accepted by God and the Church's prayer listened to, this is because the Eucharist, in its turn, makes the Church, in the strictest sense" (*The Splendour of the Church*, op. cit., p. 106 — cited by McPartlan, op. cit., p. xv).

[28] Peace is the direct effect of the sacrifice of the Paschal Lamb of God. It is thus the Risen Christ's first gift and greeting to his disciples (cf. Jn 20:19, 26), fulfilling his promise at the Last Supper (cf. Jn 14:27). The liturgy takes up this plea for peace, which is repeated through the Roman Canon, in the two prayers after the Lord's Prayer.

reaching implications, its costly responsibilities, and also its joy in proclaiming that Christ has liberated us to become capable of the greatest act of service — not only in unselfish generosity towards others, but also in praise of God. The service of God and humanity forms the focus of the sacrifice of the Mystical Body of Christ.[29] It is a truism to say that this service of love is essentially practical. The meaning of being a "practicing" Christian must not be measured merely in terms of fulfilling the minimum of Mass attendance and reception of the sacraments of reconciliation and communion at least once a year at Easter; but in exercising the essential practice of charity in the whole of living — practice which draws its vitality from the sacrifice of the Mystical Body of Christ. The hidden depths of God, which are revealed in the light of Christ's sacrament of sacrifice as love (charity), extend through the whole fabric of living. The practice of Christian charity in all its amplitude, thus, takes its "form," as Hans Urs von Balthasar brings this out splendidly, from the quality of grace realized in that special act of remembrance of Christ's sacrifice — a kind of remembering which coaxes us, as it were, to discover the paradox of life through death.[30] The closest relation exists between

---

[29] The one essential teaching of the Gospel can be summed up in the words of 1 Jn 4:19-20: "We love, because he first loved us. [. . .] This commandment we have from him, that he who loves God should love his brother also." — Cf. Jn 15:12ff., where Jesus transforms the nature of service to that of friendship with God precisely because he himself revealed perfect love and set the perfect example of service such as in washing the disciples' feet (Jn 13:2ff.).

[30] Cf. *Who is a Christian?* (Burns & Oates Ltd., London, 1968, p. 94f.): "For the Christian this neighbour who is always before him becomes the glass in which he can see the light of Christ. The other man seems faceless, a chip broken off from the universal mass, a cell in the same shapeless whole of which I myself am part. But if the encounter becomes a real meeting, this nonentity becomes a face in the crowd another person behind whom lies the freedom, dignity and uniqueness of the Quite-Other. Christ gives him a face, unlimited importance and superiority; and Christ presses me out of my own anonymity. [. . .] Behind my brother is God's commitment unto death, and for God my human brother actually has eternal value. As I look into my brother's face I look into the depths of the inconceivable. As I look, all aspects of revelation emerge, clearly delineated, real. They're no longer dry phrases, passages and verses in meaningless isolation: now they are necessary colours with which the painting is made complete. If Christ were not God, then his sacrifice wouldn't be exceptional and its fruit wouldn't be present to us. If he were not man, that mysterious representation could not take place that allows me to address my brother. [. . .] If Christ weren't present in the Sacrament, we wouldn't be joined to him in this indescribable way in which we seem knit together like parts of one body, in "remembrance" of him." Georges Rouault's many *Faces of Christ* reflect somehow the divine in human pain and anguish: it is the God who associated himself with publicans, prostitutes and sinners.

the cost of Christian living and "practicing" the mystery of sacrifice in the sacred liturgy:

> "Practicing" means going to church on Sunday. In the gospel and epistle at Mass we hear the word (and if what we hear then really isn't enough for us we're obliged to add to it by reading the Bible ourselves). Of course this hearing isn't done for its own sake, but implies our own activity — our own conversion so that when we're outside we can faithfully direct others to God. The Eucharist is the realization of Christ in the midst of the community and the congregation, and in the midst of every heart. It welds all hearts into one body, for no one is alone in his commitment but always has the whole community there to back him up. [. . .] The dual celebration —of word and sacrament — necessarily ends with the commission: "Ite, missa (missio) est." The man who has reached "maturity" through this celebration is sent out. He has heard the word from the cross and seen the body on the cross: he has received them. They are one; and so he has made them the form his life will take in the world, for the world.[31]

The sacrifice of the Mass, thus, provides the greatest service since it exercises us in discovering the deepest value of human existence — that value for which it is right and fitting to offer praise. As St. Augustine put it:

> . . . the price of my redemption is always before me. I eat it and drink it and pay it out [minister or serve it to others]; and as one of the poor I long to be filled with it, to be among those who "eat and have their fill and who, looking for the Lord, will cry out in praise of him" (Ps 21:27 [22:26]).[32]

This paradox, or rather, mystery of sacrifice which the Roman Canon focuses on in terms of service (*costing not less than everything*)[33] demands that Christ's faithful be prepared to go, if necessary,

---

[31] Ibid., p. 98f.

[32] *Confessions*, X.43; R.S. Pine-Coffin's translation in Penguin Books, 1961, p. 252 (slightly amended). Cf. also Augustine, Sermo 334.2.

[33] Cf. T.S. Eliot, *Four Quartets — Little Gidding V* (near the end).

to the extreme of dying for all — not merely for one's family, friends, or members of the same social class or system of beliefs and values.[34]

Communion in the Covenant Sacrifice

From the earliest Christian times the Jewish religious notions and insights especially regarding the essential bond between sacrifice and communion were incorporated and developed in the Church's worship, even if the particular ritual practices themselves were not strictly adhered to. The Jewish covenant sacrifice was offered in the context of the offerings made to establish peace as regulated by the Code of Leviticus.[35] It was a blood sacrifice, of which part of the victim was offered on the altar while the rest of it was shared in a sacred meal as was characteristic in peace-offerings. All shared in the sacred meal together — the priest, relatives, Levites, slaves, the poor and even

---

[34] Otherwise, as Albert Nolan highlights in his provocative meditation on reading the reality of Christ between the lines of the Gospel, our profession of being practicing Christians is a lie. — Cf. *Jesus Before Christianity: The Gospel of Liberation*, DLT, London, 1977 (reprinted 1980), p. 113f.: "There is a riddle about life and death which occurs in all the traditions, in several places in the gospels and in a variety of forms (Mk 8:35 parr.; Mt 10:39; Lk 14:26; Jn 12:25). It is, without doubt, based upon the words of Jesus himself. A careful comparison of each of the texts enables one to conclude that the original riddle or paradox must have been simply this: *The man who saves his life will lose it; the man who loses his life will save it.* One must remember that it is meant to be a riddle. To qualify it in such a way that it refers to losing one's life in this world to save it in the next world is to cease to treat it as a riddle. What then does it mean? To save one's life means to hold onto it, to love it and be attached to it and therefore to fear death. To lose one's life is to let go of it, to be detached from it and therefore to be willing to die. The paradox is that the man who fears death is already dead, whereas the man who has ceased to fear death has at that moment begun to live. A life that is genuine and worthwhile is only possible once one is willing to die. [. . .] Jesus did not die for a cause. As he understood it, one should be willing to give up one's life for exactly the same reason as one gives up possessions, prestige, family and power, namely for others. Compassion and love compel a man to do everything for others. But the man who says he lives for others but is not willing to suffer and die for them is a liar and he is dead. Jesus was fully alive because he was willing to suffer and die not for a cause but for people. [. . .] Jesus' willingness to die for all men is therefore a service just as everything else in his life is a service, a service rendered to all men. [. . .] 'For many' is a Hebrew and Aramaic expression which generally means 'for everyone.' Thus at the Last Supper, too, Jesus prefigured the offering of his blood 'for many' (Mk 14:24; Mt 26:28)."

[35] Cf. Lv 3.

strangers.[36] The flesh of the victim consumed here was sacred and thus required a state of ritual purity on the part of those eating it.[37] Jesus' sacrifice, on the other hand, is the sacrifice of the *new covenant*" because it is definitive, irrepeatable, permanent, eschatological and ultimate: it is *"blood of the new and eternal covenant,"* which was foreseen by the prophets.[38] Thus, the way to participate in the salvation-event which the celebration of the Eucharistic sacrifice re-presents is through sacramental communion in the gift of the Lord's Body and Blood. There can be no Mass without communion, which must always be presented in relation to the sacrifice being celebrated. Without communion our participation in the sacrifice of the Lord remains incomplete. Concern over the infrequency of the reception of communion in the Middle Ages led the Church to impose the famous *"Paschal Precept"* or the duty of annual confession and communion between Ash Wednesday and Trinity Sunday.[39] Furthermore, the reception of Holy Communion under both kinds is directly the fulfillment of the Lord's command: *"Take and eat . . . Take and drink."* Return to this practice is opportune for it best expresses the sacramental nature of participating in the Paschal Meal of Christ's unique sacrifice. This significance is brought out also by distributing particles of the bread consecrated at the same Mass.[40] Hans Urs von Balthasar incisively states the profound truth about the way the symbolism of Christian worship transforms ordinary human activities, whose sacramental meaning and purpose becomes thereby revealed:

> . . . the true sacramental sign in the Eucharist is the event of eating and drinking (which is the only thing that gives bread and wine their meaning as human symbols). What is important for the Church is not that something is to be found on the table of the altar, but that by consuming this nourishment the Church becomes what she can and ought to be. Mass without communion (something impossible for the celebrant as rep-

---

[36] Cf. Dt 12:18; 16:11, 14.
[37] Cf. Lv 7:19-21.
[38] Cf. Jr 31:31-34; Mt 26:28.
[39] Cf. Decree of the Fourth Lateran Council, *Unius utriusque sexus* (DS 812).
[40] Cf. S.C., n. 55; also G.I.R.M., nn. 48, 56(h); E.M., nn. 2, 5, etc.

resentative of the community) is impossible and meaningless for the Church as such; the concession extended in this respect to individual members of the community must, therefore, be made clear to them as such.[41]

The invocation *"Supplices"* of the Roman Canon fittingly sums up this intrinsic link of the fulness of participation (communion) in the sacramental covenant sacrifice:

> Almighty God, we beseech you that your Angel may take these things to your altar in heaven, in the sight of your divine majesty, so that all of us who receive from this altar the sacred Body and Blood of your Son may be filled with every heavenly blessing and grace.[42]

The meaning of the mystcrious sounding words of this prayer has long perplexed scholars and been the focus of debate — particularly regarding the identity of the "Angel."[43] Following the interpretation of it given by St. Thomas Aquinas,[44] that great Dominican Gerald Vann sees the symbolism of this prayer as expressing the mystical unity between what is realized sacramentally at the altar of the Mass ("these things," that is, "this sacrifice") and the eternal reality achieved on behalf of mankind through and with and in Christ, who is the "Angel of Great Counsel," that is, the Messenger mediating to humanity the great Good News of communion.[45] Vann sums up:

> As the priest says this prayer he bows before the altar and then kisses it — the kiss marking the identity of the two altars, in heaven and on earth — for the prayer expresses in terms

---

[41] *The Glory of the Lord*, Vol. I, op. cit., p. 573f.

[42] This translates the Latin more accurately than the ICEL.

[43] Cf. Mazza op. cit., p. 81f. — for discussion on the notion of the mediatorial function of angels in worship. While this notion may foster a sense of the transcendence of God (*vide infra*), it must be squared with the unique mediatorship of Christ through whom we have direct and confident access to the Father.

[44] Cf. *Sum. Theol.*, III.83.4 ad 9.

[45] This interpretation is obvious in the Latin (not ICEL) text in which "Angel" is given with a capital letter. Cf. Is 9:6. Cf. also Yarnold, *The Awe-inspiring Rites of Christian Initiation*, op. cit., p. 139, fn. 54.

of supplication what the Sursum corda expresses in terms of adjuration and challenge. Being now, as St. Paul says, risen with Christ, we must lift our thoughts above, where Christ now sits at the right hand of God; we must be "heavenly-minded not earthly-minded."[46]

The unity and utter identification between the Church's sacrifice and Christ's is also expressed in the words of the Institution Narrative, which, regrettably, is not evident in the ICEL translation of the original Latin text:

Literal translation:	Latin:	ICEL:
and taking *this* glorious chalice	accipiens et *hunc* praeclarum calicem	he took the cup

This identification in the Roman Canon quite specifically expresses the moment of cultic *anamnesis*. The significance of the demonstrative adjective ("this") cannot be missed: the chalice which is handled by the celebrant at Mass in the Church today is identical with the cup which Christ handed to his disciples to drink; by it Christ's faithful would remember his presence ever in their midst. This makes it clear that the Mass is the memorial of Christ's unique sacrifice and none other — nor a mere subjective recalling of a past event.[47] At the same time the meaning of this kind of act of remembering, in keeping with the usage of Semitic languages,[48] realizes the Church of Christ — that is, *makes real* or creates the new reality of the Body of Christ.

Service of Love . . . unto the end

The Church offers an incomparably valuable service in its proclamation of the unlimited extent of Christ's saving love in the Mystery of Faith. Its Eucharistic Prayer is the deepest profession of

---

[46] Op. cit., p. 237. Cf. Col 3:1-3.

[47] Cf. Mazza, op. cit., p. 252.

[48] Especially indicated by the Hebrew verb *zakar*, which means to realize or relive in the strong sense.

the Christian Faith; it celebrates the essential *kerygma* or announcement of the Gospel.[49] The salvific resonance of the proclamation of this loving service permeates all creation; it is heard throughout all regions of being: on earth as it is in heaven. From the depths of the underworld to the heights of heaven the division introduced into the world by sin (which is like a "general strike" of *non-service!*) is breached by Christ's *passover* love. The scope or extent of the effect of the proclamation of the Good News of this love is indicated in the Roman Canon's allusion to the ancient idea expressed in the Apostles' Creed regarding Christ's descent into hell by the phrase in Latin *"ab inferis resurrectionis,"* which is rather insipidly translated as "his resurrection from the dead."[50] The doctrine signified by the imagery imbedded in the phrase *"ab inferis"* ("from hell/the underworld") is not only worth recalling, but also an integral part of faith in the mystery of God's love revealed by Christ. Despite the fact that, as we must admit, it seems bizarre to us today, we would be amiss not to try to penetrate the significance of this essential article of faith.[51] Our endeavor to come to terms with this mystery will yield a deeper appreciation of the Savior's sacrifice of service and of Christian spirituality which is integrally bonded with proclaiming the whole paschal mystery.

This is an instance of the Judeo-Christian community's attempt to represent its faith in the great mystery of the resurrection as

---

[49] The Canon adds the Ascension to the content of the early *kerygma* or preaching of the apostles recorded in the Acts: he became man, suffered, died, rose . . .

[50] Cf. also Eucharistic Prayer IV: "we recall [. . .] his descent among the dead" for *"eiusque descensum ad inferos recolimus."*

[51] Cf. Ratzinger, *Introduction to Christianity*, op. cit., p. 223f.: "Possibly no article of the Creed is so far from present-day attitudes of mind as this one. Together with the belief in the birth of Jesus from the Virgin Mary and that in the Ascension of the Lord, it seems to call most of all for 'demythologization,' a process which looks devoid of danger and unlikely to provoke opposition. The few places where Scripture seems to say anything about this matter [. . .] are so difficult to understand that they can easily be expounded in many different ways. Thus if in the end one eliminates the statement altogether one seems to have the advantage of getting rid of a curious idea, and one difficult to harmonize with our own modes of thought, without making oneself guilty of a particularly disloyal act. But is anything really gained by this? Or has one simply evaded the difficulty and obscurity of reality? One can try to deal with problems either by denying their existence or by facing up to them. The first method is the more comfortable one, but only the second leads anywhere."

transforming that existential fear peculiar to humanity of death and loneliness. Though this mystery defies description, it can somehow be depicted in imagery, through which we reach into and glimpse divine revelation.[52] In the West the mystery is represented as the empty tomb or appearances to Mary Magdalene, the holy women or disciples, whereas the rich imagery of Eastern icons of the Descent into Hell is drawn from the Judeo-Christian tradition — a tradition which relies on 2 P 3:19f. and Ac 2:31.[53] The early Judeo-Christian Church presented the Christ's descent into hell as an integral component of its vision of evangelization:[54] redemption and the proclamation of salvation were perceived strictly in terms of Christology, that is, as the work of Christ the Word who saves and calls all to salvation.[55] The meaning of Christ's descent into hell, thus, is first of all to proclaim the Good News of salvation and, secondly, to call all to conversion, awakening by his light those who sleep in death due to sin in order to lead those who accept and follow him to his Father.[56] This imagery found its way also into medieval poems about Christ's "Harrowing of Hell." It dramatically depicts Christ's complete victory over evil and its effects: Christ the Light overcomes the dark abyss of sin; with his cross he pries open what is closed and despoils hell of its prisoners.

---

[52] John Baggley finely remarks in *Doors of Perception — Icons and Their Spiritual Significance*, Mowbray, London & Oxford, 1987, p. 42: "Verbal and visual imagery co-exist in our consciousness, and in the language by which the Church articulates the revelation given in Jesus Christ."

[53] Cf. also 2 P 4:6; Ep 4:9; Rm 10:7; Mt 12:40. Apart from these N.T. texts and the use of St. Paul's doctrine of Christ as the Second Adam, "the imagery used in icons and liturgical texts [of the East] is coloured by material from the second century apocryphal Gospel of Nicodemus," as John Baggley says in his splendid book *Doors of Perception,* p. 41.

[54] The new *Catechism of the Catholic Church* (n. 634) says that Christ's descent marks the "last phase of Jesus' messianic mission; through this his proclaiming the Good News of the resurrection is not restricted only to those who were dead at the historical moment of his own death or from the Jewish nation, but extends to people of all ages and from all nations.

[55] Cf. Jean Danielou, *The Theology of Jewish Christianity*, (translated by John A. Uaker), DLT, London, 1964, pp. 233-248: "The Descent into Hell."

[56] Cf. Mt 27:52 — the sense of this text must not be confused with what is stated in 1 P 3:18-20 (Christ's preaching to the "spirits in prison"), which refers to his triumph on the cross over the demons whose "prison" was understood as being the air, as in Col 2:15; cf. Lk 1:78f. — Cf. Danielou, ibid., p. 234f.

This allusion in the Roman Canon to Christ's descent to hell holds in focus the whole passover mystery which cannot exclude what the liturgy of Holy Saturday commemorates.[57] The mystery of Holy Saturday cannot be left out of Christian contemplation or spirituality would be impoverished — and indeed lacking in integrity of vision — if it were directed solely to what is clear, coherent, and easily understandable. The Eucharist Prayer stretches our human capacity and exercises us in celebrating what we profess in the Symbol of the Christian Faith: *We believe in [. . .] the Creator of all things visible and invisible.* The intelligibility of Christ's sacrifice (with its mind-stretching effects!) plunges us into the ultimate mystery of the cross being the supreme moment of the revelation of God's glory. Here we are confronted, as Christ himself was as man, with the mystery of God's silence. For the rhythm of Christian practice includes both action and contemplation, in which Christ's faithful offer a spiritual sacrifice, that is the surrender of mind and heart.[58] In the contemplation, which the liturgy provokes in confronting human reason with the supreme moment of the paschal mystery, that is, the

---

[57] Cf. the text from an ancient homily given in the Office of Readings for Holy Saturday (D.O., II, p. 320f.; PG 43, 439, 451 — cited in the *Catechism of the Catholic Church*, n. 635): "Truly he goes to seek out our first parent like a lost sheep; he wishes to visit those who sit in darkness and in the shadow of death. He goes to free the prisoner Adam and his fellow-prisoner Eve from their pains, he who is God, and Adam's son. The Lord goes in to them holding his victorious weapon, his cross. When Adam, the first created man, sees him, he strikes his breast in terror and calls out to all: 'My Lord be with you all.' And Christ in reply says to Adam: 'And with your spirit.' And grasping his hand he raises him up, saying: 'Awake, O sleeper, and arise from the dead, and Christ shall give you light' [Ep 5:14]." De Lubac explains the patristic insistence on the salvation of Adam: "If several of them [the Fathers] held so strongly . . . that Adam was saved, one of the reasons for this was undoubtedly that they saw the salvation of its head as the necessary condition of the salvation of the human race" (*Catholicism*, Burns & Oates, London, 1962, p. 2 — cited by McPartlan, op. cit., p. 295). However, McPartlan, taking up Zizioulas' challenging approach, adds: "The human race holds together not in Adam, from the past, but in Christ, from the future. Adam himself becomes a corporate personality only in Christ. [. . .] The Christian is a microcosm, not of that which encounters Christ, but of Christ. Outside of Christ, humanity and the Church are scattered individuals" (p. 296).

[58] Cf. Rm 12:1. Cf. also St. Ignatius of Antioch on the crucial challenge of reckoning with the silence of God if one is to gain mastery of proclaiming the word of God — e.g. *Epist. to the Ephesians*, 15:1 —"Indeed, it is better to remain silent and be, than to not to be what one professes with eloquence . . ."; ibid., 19.1; *Epist. to the Magnesians*, 8.2. This problem of the "hiddenness~ of God is most profoundly treated by Joseph Ratzinger — cf. loc. cit.

mysterium crucis, Christ's faithful have to wrestle with God's seeming absence — indeed, the *death of God!*[59]

Only the presence of the loving Savior can reunite earth to heaven, from which sin had torn it asunder; only his presence in the "underworld" (the region of the dead) could make it accessible to the prayer of the Mystical Body; and, only his sacramental presence on earth itself could heal the division resulting from sin, which makes nations hostile to one another, persons alienated from one another, brother turned against brother. The passover mystery of Christ's presence-in-love involved the radical descent of the Word of God to our dire level of hopelessness — that movement of descent, or *"kenosis"* ("emptying") as St. Paul called it,[60] which was required so that his Good News might be announced to all by none other than him who is the Good News of salvation. The depths of passover love to which Christ was prepared to go is succinctly expressed at the beginning of the Beloved Disciple's account of the Last Supper:

> Now before the feast of the Passover, when Jesus knew that his hour had come to depart out of this world to the Father, having loved his own who were in the world, he loved them unto the end.[61]

The full depth of the paschal mystery of Christ's sacrifice, which is not lacking in drama (in its radical sense as being the ultimate "action") is situated or presented in terms not just of his death, but of his glorious resurrection and ascension as well. Perhaps this imagery seems too vivid or not according to our taste today when talk of hell

---

[59] In a sense this experience of the hiddenness of God was what the disciples too had to share, as von Balthasar says in citing Martin Luther (*The Glory of the Lord,* op. cit., Vol. I, p. 47): "All the disciples betrayed their crucified Lord, and on the day of Easter 'they all sit together as if in hell, with an evil conscience and great fear . . . Then Christ the Lord comes to them in his love as if he were coming into hell, and says: You are my brothers! . . . Our hearts cannot comprehend this' (*Sermon on Easter Wednesday,* Wittenberg, 1531)."

[60] Cf. Ph 2:7 and Ep 4:8f.

[61] Jn 13:1; cf. also Lk 22:14-15: "When the hour came he sat at table with the apostles. He said to them: I have earnestly desired [Vulgate: *desiderio desideravi;* Greek: *'epithumia 'epethumesa*] to eat this passover with you before I suffer." — cf. Lk 12:50.

has become unfashionable and the very notion of it (together with the devil) has been "exorcised" from some approaches to modern catechesis.[62] It is nevertheless an integral part of the scenario of Christian Faith's realism, which is paradoxically more supportive of hope than what a shallow "demythologised Christianity" diluted with a materialistic rationalism has to offer.[63] The Church's sacramental realism provides the only adequate response to that yearning for authentic spirituality which is experienced among many people today.[64] This sacramental realism opens the human heart to the mystery of God's transcendence which Christ's passover revealed as imminent.

Glory and Holiness

The Roman Canon expresses in various ways the transcendence of God's glory — that transcendence which promotes, rather than diminishes or demeans, our human worth and joy in celebrating

---

[62] T.S. Eliot puts his finger on the pulse of fear under our rationalistic tendency, which tries to escape confronting the mystery of suffering and death: *"human kind/ Cannot bear very much reality"* — *Four Quartets* — *Burnt Norton I.* He repeats this statement also in *Murder in the Cathedral*, Part II (Thomas a Becket's speech on being "at peace with your thoughts and visions"). Echoing the "negative theology" of the mystics, Eliot advocates a surrender of this tendency to "the darkness of God":

> *Wait without thought, for you are not ready for thought:*
> *So the darkness shall be the light, and the stillness the dancing* (Ibid., *East Coker III*).

[63] One recalls here St. Bonaventure's warning of the danger of pouring "so much water of merely human thinking into the wine of Holy Scripture that it becomes watery" — *Collationes in Hexaemeron*, visio 3, coll. 7, n. 14 (Ed. Delorme F., Quaracchi 1934, 217).

[64] Without digressing it may be just worth suggesting that the imagery of the descent into hell could be reconsidered (and further developed in another place) in the light of the explorations of "depth psychology" which reveals the anguish of the human heart disorientated by rationalism from its "instinct" for mystery and faith in God. As Victor White put it: "Depth-psychologists themselves have convinced us that a dream, or a spontaneous, dreamy phantasy, can tell us more of what is happening below the surface of the human mind than any amount of intellectual analyses or statistics" (*God and the Unconscious: An Encounter Between Psychology and Religion*, Collins Fontana Books, p. 38). The imagery of hell has been shaped in human consciousness not merely by moralism, but also by the very structure of sin which is rebellion against a metaphysical perspective of being. This imagery is powerfully illustrated in poetry — for instance, in Dante's *L'Inferno*, Milton's *Paradise Lost*, Rimbaud's *Une saison en enfer*.

worship and sacrifice.[65] The use of the formal language and rhetoric of "beseeching" is no mere empty formalism of hieratic ritual. The Church pleads before God's divine majesty or, rather, expresses on behalf of all creation the awe of worship in the presence of the utter splendor of divine beauty.[66] This act of pleading is no grovelling, unworthy of the dignity of human beings before God their Father, but an essential condition of allowing our minds and hearts to be raised and transformed by the grace of the mystery of Christ's sacrifice. It implicitly acknowledges with praise and thanksgiving that this sacrifice has wondrously bridged the infinite gap between Creator and creation — an abyss widened (if the "infinite" can be split!) by sin, that is, human rebellion against its creaturely condition. The language of the Roman Canon, thus, prevents us forgetting that the re-presentation of Christ's sacrifice draws us into that "awesome exchange" (*"sacrum commercium"*) through which the Church's offering itself, as a symbol of ourselves, becomes valid and worthwhile.[67]

As Creator of the world God provides not only the *"the many gifts you have given us"* to offer back in recognition of his supreme dominion, but also brings the natural order, which human selfishness defaced, to completion:

---

[65] Cf. Vann, op. cit., p. 260ff. regarding the joyful gestures which the celebrant formerly used to make since the Middle Ages over the chalice with the host during the Great Doxology; these gestures, as it were, "signed" the Offering with five swift movements in the form of a cross, and suggested the symbolism of David dancing before the ark of the covenant.

[66] Cf. von Balthasar's penetrating analysis of the necessity of a sense of awe to pierce through the crust of our commonplace experiences, as it were, in order to behold the true "form" of reality —being-in-God — Cf. *The Glory of the Lord*, op. cit., Vol. I, p. 18: "Beauty is the last thing which the thinking intellect dares to approach [. . .] Our situation today shows that beauty demands for itself at least as much courage and decision as do truth and goodness, and she will not allow herself to be separated and banned from her two sisters without taking them along with herself in an act of mysterious vengence. We can be sure that whoever sneers at her name as if she were the ornament of a bourgeois past — whether he admits it or not — can no longer pray and soon will no longer be able to love."

[67] Re *"Sacrum /admirabilel commercium"* — see the text from Vagaggini cited at the being of this chapter. It is a poignant phrase which often occurs in the liturgy and is drawn from the Fathers of the Church — Cf. von Balthasar, *New Elucidations*, Ignatius Press, San Francisco, 1986, p. 129.

Through Christ our Lord you give us all these gifts. You fill
them with life and goodness, you bless them and make them
holy.[68]

This is because what is specifically offered to God from among the
best of created realities is that with which Christ has utterly identified
himself and which he has transformed into *"this holy and perfect
sacrifice: the bread of life and the cup of eternal salvation."*[69] What is of
utmost importance here is the fact that through his identification with
and transformation of these common created realities, Christ has
given us the means of offering perfect worship worthy of the all-holy
God. At the same time the transcendent dynamism of the Church's
sacrifice of praise on earth is kept clearly in focus. For, alluding to a
reference in the Book of Revelation,[70] the Canon brings out the
eschatological orientation of the Church's life and sacrifice, which is
identified with what is offered on the *"altar in heaven,"* as was seen
above.

The perspective of the Canon's proclamation in praise for the
redemptive paschal mystery is drawn from that of the New Testament
regarding the notion of God's glory being manifest through Christ
crucified.[71] This notion, which develops the theme of "glory" in the

---

[68] The ICEL translation unhappily breaks the flow of the single sentence in the Latin text
by dividing it into two sentences. Thus it does not appear so clearly that the Father
achieves everything through Christ:
> *Per Christum Dominum nostrum, per quem haec omnia, Domine,
> semper bona creas, santificas, vivificas, benedicis, et praestas nobis.*
> (Through Christ our Lord, you are always creating all good things,
> making them holy, enlivening them, blessing them and bestowing
> them on us.)

[69] The resonance of the rich Latin rhetoric certainly presents a challenge to any
translator!
> *de tuis donis ac datis hostiam puram, hostiam sanctam, hostiam immaculatam, Panem
> sanctum vitae aeternae et Calicem salutis perpetuae.*

But, why did the ICEL translators not respect the use of capital letters for "Bread" and
"Cup"?

[70] Cf. Rv 4:8.

[71] Especially in St. Paul — cf. 1 Cor 1:18-28; Col 1:14-15; and in St. John — cf. 12:23; 13:31;
17:1ff.

Old Testament,[72] becomes a familiar one in tradition, and can be summed up for example in Origen's statement:[73]

> His glory is [. . .] the suffering of the Cross. He was glorified when he came to the Cross and suffered death.

The same idea is taken up by and frequently expressed in the liturgy, as for instance in the Mass and Office of the Exaltation of the Holy Cross.[74] Indeed, glory is the very life of God insofar as it is both transcendent and mysteriously imminent, that is, sacramentally communicated through *"grace and blessing,"* as the Canon says.

The notion of glory cannot be separated from that of holiness. Both these notions are complementary and spring from and reflect the same source, namely, the intrinsic reality of God's transcendence. The transcendent *"otherness"* of God's holiness and glory, however, is charged with the vitality of communicability since God is the ultimate and perfect *Holy Communion* in the Three Divine Persons. This Canon, like every Eucharistic *anaphora*, therefore, takes up the theme of the Trisagion hymn ("the *Sanctus*") in addressing God as "Holy" and brings out how Christ above all communicates the glory of divine holiness: his Ascension is accomplished *"in glory"*; his hands are *"venerable"*; the eucharistic sacrament comprises *"the glorious chalice," "the holy mystery of the body and blood," "the holy victim."* In

---

[72] The O.T. often speaks of "glory" as belonging to God's essential nature. It is difficult to translate the notion expressed in the Hebrew words *"kabod Yahweh,"* which imply the sense of "majesty, glory, light." In 1927 C.A.A. Scott, while commenting on Paul's Christology, remarked that the "history of the word *Glory* in the Bible has yet to be written." A recent study by Carey C. Newman provides a most useful service towards filling this lacuna — cf. *Paul's Glory-Christology*, 1991 (ISBN:90-04-09463-6). By employing the methodological tools developed by semantics, semiotics, and — more generally — literary theory, Newman examines the origin and rhethoric of Paul's approach. The investigation involves three distinct tasks: (1) to plot the tradition-history of "glory" forming part of Paul's linguistic world; (2) to examine Paul's letters in the light of the reconstructed tradition-history of this word and notion; and, (3) to map out the implications of such an identification of the Apostle's rhetorical strategy for his theological perspective.

[73] *In Exod. Hom.* 6 [PG 12, 332]. For other texts of the Fathers —cf. S. Tromp, *Mystici Corporis*, #25, Pont. Univ. Gregoriana, Rome, 1943, p. 79f.

[74] Cf. also the hymn *Vexilla Regis* of Good Friday.

sharing the sacrament which saves all humanity, the whole world itself becomes radiant with the glory of the Lord's holiness. For the sacrament of the eucharistic sacrifice, as the extension of Christ's Word become flesh, is the privileged luminous point of humanity's encounter with the transcendent holiness of God.[75] The mystery of sanctification is thus proclaimed with praise and communicated lovingly as his *"holy and perfect sacrifice."*

---

[75] Cf. von Balthasar, *The Glory of the Lord*, Vol. I, op. cit., p. 29: "In fact, God's Incarnation perfects the whole ontology and aesthetics of created Being. The Incarnation uses created Being at a new depth as a language and a means of expression for the divine Being and essence. Although ever since Luther we have become accustomed to call the Bible 'God's Word,' it is not Sacred Scripture which is God's original language and self-expression, but rather Jesus Christ."

4

Gift of Liberation
(Eucharistic Prayer II)

Human beings are totally free only when they are completely themselves, in the fullness of their rights and duties. The same can be said about society as a whole. The principal obstacle to be overcome on the way to authentic liberation is sin and the structures produced by sin as it multiplies and spreads. The freedom with which Christ has set us free (cf. Gal 5:1) encourages us to become the servants of all. Thus the process of development and liberation takes concrete shape in the exercise of solidarity, that is to say, in the love and service of neighbor, especially of the poorest: "For where truth and love are missing, the process of liberation results in the death of a freedom which will have lost all support."[1]

The Second Eucharistic Prayer is substantially based on the text of one of the earliest known examples of eucharistic prayers. It is adapted from a Eucharistic Prayer or *anaphora* presented by Hippolytus in the *Apostolic Tradition*, which was composed about 215-220.[2] It is helpful at this point to have before us synoptically the new Eucharistic Prayer and Hippolytus' *anaphora*.

---

[1] S.R.S., n. 46; translation in *Briefing '88*, Vol. 18, No. 5, p. 111f. The Pope cites the *Instruction on Christian Freedom and Liberation* (22 March 1986), n. 24.

[2] Hippolytus was a Syrian migrant to Rome where he taught as a philosopher and theologian. His teaching on the Trinity led to controversy with Popes Zephyrinus and Callistus. This could explain why his writings were better known outside Rome. Two texts of Hippolytus are important for understanding the early history of the liturgy: an episcopal ordination prayer and an *anaphora* suggested by him. The latter is the model for Eucharistic Prayer II. It influenced liturgies in the East; the Ethiopian Church has always used a version of this *anaphora*. Cf. Mazza, op. cit., p. 90ff.; also *Essays on Hippolytus* (edited by Geoffrey J. Cuming) Grove Books, Bramcote, Notts., 1978, and *Hippolytus: A Text for Students*, Grove Books Ltd., Bramcote, Notts., 1987.

Father, it is our duty and our salvation, always and everywhere to give you thanks through your beloved Son, Jesus Christ.

He is the Word through whom you made the universe, the Savior you sent to redeem us. By the power of the Holy Spirit he took flesh and was born of the Virgin Mary.

For our sake he opened his arms on the cross; he put an end to death and revealed the resurrection. In this he fulfilled your will and won for you a holy people. And so we join the angels and saints in proclaiming your glory as we say:

Holy, Holy, Holy Lord, God of power and might, heaven and earth are full of your glory. Hosanna in the highest. Blessed is he who comes in the name of the lord. Hosanna in the highest.

Lord, you are holy indeed, the fountain of all holiness. Let your Spirit come upon these gifts to make them holy, so that they may become for us the body and blood of our Lord, Jesus Christ.

Before he was given up to death, a death he freely accepted, he took bread and gave you thanks. He broke the bread, gave it to his disciples, and said: Take this, all of you, and eat it: this is my body which will be given up for you.

When supper was ended, he took the cup. Again he gave you thanks and praise, gave the cup to his disciples, and said:

Vere dignum et iustum est, aequum et salutare, nos tibi, Sancte Pater, semper et ubique gratias agere per Fiiium dilectionis tuae Iesum Christum.

Verbum tuum per quod cuncta fecisti: quem misisti nobis Salvatorem et Redemptorem, incarnatum de Spiritu Sancto et ex Virgine natum.

Qui voluntatem tuam adimplens et populum tibi sanctum acquirens extendit manus cum pateretur, ut mortem solveret et resurrectionem manifestaret.

Et ideo cum Angelis et omnibus Sanctis gloriam tuam praedicamus, una voce dicentes: Sanctus, Sanctus, Sanctus Dominus Deus Sabaoth. Pleni sunt caeli et terra gloria tua. Hosanna in excelsis. Benedictus qui venit in nomine Domini. Hosanna in excelsis.

Vere Sanctus es, Domine, fons omnis sanctitatis. Haec ergo dona, quaesumus, Spiritus tui rore sanctifica, ut nobis Corpus et Sanguis fiant Domini nostri Iesu Christi.

Qui cum Passioni voluntarie traderetur, accepit panem et gratias agens fregit deditque discipulis suis, dicens:

ACCIPITE ET MANDUCATE EX HOC OMNES: HOC EST ENIM CORPUS MEUM, QUOD PRO VOBIS TRADETUR. Simili modo, postquam cenatum est, accipiens et calicem, iterum gratias agens dedit discipulis dicens:

ACCIPITE ET BIBITE EX E0 OMNES: HIC EST ENIM CALIX

We render thanks to you, O God, through your beloved Boy [pais], Jesus Christ,

whom in the last times you sent to us as Savior and Redeemer and Angel of your will; who is your inseparable Word, through whom you made all things, and in whom you were well pleased.

You sent him from heaven into the Virgin's womb; and conceived in the womb he was made flesh and manifested as your Son, being born of the Holy Spirit and the Virgin.

Fulfilling your will and gaining for you a holy people, he stretched out his hands when he should suffer, that he might release from suffering those who have believed in you.

And when he was betrayed to voluntary suffering that he might destroy death, and break the bonds of the devil, and tread down hell, and shine upon the righteous, and fix a term, and manifest the resurrection, he took bread and gave thanks to you, saying,

Take this, all of you,and drink from it: this is the cup of my blood of the new and everlasting covenant. It will be shed for you and for all so that sins may be forgiven. Do this in memory of me.

[Let us proclaim the mystery of faith . . .]

In memory of his death and resurrection, we offer you, Father, this life-giving bread, this saving cup.

We thank you for counting us worthy to stand in your presence and serve you.

May all of us who share in the body and blood of Christ be brought together in unity by the Holy Spirit.

Lord, remember your Church throughout the world; make us grow in love, together with N. our Pope, N. our bishop, and all the clergy.

Remember our brothers and sisters who have gone to their rest in the hope of rising again; bring them and all the departed into the light of your presence.

Have mercy on us all; make us worthy to share eternal life with Mary, the Virgin Mother of God, with the apostles, and with all the saints who have done your will throughout the ages. May we praise you in union with them, and give you glory through your Son, Jesus Christ.

Through him, with him, in him, in the unity of the Holy Spirit, all glory and honor is yours, almighty Father, for ever and ever. AMEN.

SANGUINIS MEI NOVI ET AETERNI TESTAMENTI, QUI PRO VOBIS ET PRO MULTIS EFFUNDETUR IN REMISSIONEM PECCATORUM. HOC FACITE IN MEAM COMMEMORATIONEM.

[Mysterium Fidei . . .]

Memores igitur mortis et resurrectionis eius, tibi, Domine, panem vitae et calicem salutis offerimus, gratias agentes, quia nos dignos habuisti astare coram te et tibi ministrare.

Et supplices deprecamur, ut Corporis et Sanguinis Christi participes a Spiritu Sancto congregemur in unum.

Recordare, Domine, Ecclesiae tuae toto orbe diffusae, ut eam in caritate perficias una cum Papa nostro N. et Episcopo nostro N. et universo clero.

Memento etiam fratrum nostrorum, qui in spe resurrectionis dormierunt, et eos in lumen vultus tui admitte.

Omnium nostrum, quaesumus, miserere, ut cum beata Dei Genetrice Virgine Maria, beatis Apostolis et omnibus Sanctis, qui tibi a saeculo placuerunt, aeternae vitae mereamur esse consortes, et te laudemus et glorificemus per Filium tuum Iesum Christum.

Per ipsum, et cum ipso, et in ipso, est tibi Deo Patri omnipotenti, in unitate Spiritus Sancti, omnis honor et gloria per omnia saecula saeculorum. AMEN.

"Take, eat; this is my body, which shall be broken for you."

Likewise also the cup, saying,

"This is my blood, which is shed for you; when you do this, you make my remembrance."

Remembering therefore his death and resurrection, we offer to you the bread and the cup, giving thanks because you have held us worthy to stand before you and minister to you.

And we ask that you would send your holy Spirit upon the offering of your holy Church; that gathering (her) into one, you would grant to all who partake of the holy things (to partake) for the fullness of the holy Spirit for the strengthening of faith in truth,

that we may praise and glorify you through your Boy [*pais*] Jesus Christ,

through whom be glory and honor to you, with the holy Spirit, in your holy Church, both now and to the ages of ages.

AMEN.

Eucharistic Prayer II presents the simplicity of the most ancient sources of the eucharistic liturgy, while the purity of its structure and style has much to teach us concerning the essential form of the Church's central act of worship. It provides an exemplary illustration of what was seen above when considering the nature of the Eucharistic Prayer in general. In spite of its simplicity — or rather, because of this — this Prayer offers a rich source for reflection on the doctrine and spiritual significance celebrated in Christian worship.

We shall first of all consider this prayer in relation to Hippolytus' text and to its Jewish models of "table prayers" of thanksgiving or *"berakoth."* Then we shall examine the main points of doctrine embodied in its structure and content. Lastly, from this cursory study, it will be fitting to draw out some of the features of Christian spirituality as proclaimed in this Prayer in order to understand how the Eucharist empowers us to live Christ's gift of freedom and peace.

From Jewish blessings to Christian thanksgiving

Eucharistic Prayer II clearly exemplifies what was discussed earlier regarding the way the Christian community gave a distinctive character and shape to the *"table prayers"* of blessing which were familiar to those of its members from a Jewish background. Since this distinctive character was assimilated and transformed by the Christian community it can be quite rightly regarded and called "Christian" both because of the motive and manner of "giving thanks."

Throughout this Prayer, which is the most Christological of the Eucharistic Prayers, the motive for offering thanksgiving or "eucharist" to God the Father is unmistakably because his Son was sent into the world to show us the art of thanksgiving in the Christian act of eucharistic worship and throughout Christian living. The whole of this Prayer is framed, as it were, by a phrase which occurs near the beginning and end: *"through your Son, Jesus Christ."* The slight variation occurring in the first appearance of the phrase only adds emphasis to the motive for thanksgiving: it focuses on the special quality of *this Son* — his unique qualification to teach thanksgiving for being related to God as Father, whose "beloved Son" he is. Later in this chapter we must look more closely at the biblical significance of this phrase. Here it is sufficient, however, simply to note this point regarding both the Jewish roots of the Christian attitude of thanksgiving and also how Christian prayer enhanced the Jewish notion of *"berakoth"* — or, for that matter, every other human kind of relationship of gratitude to God. The motive of thanksgiving for the gift of God's own Son, Jesus Christ, bestows on the life of worship a new direction and empowers it with a new dynamism. We recognize this new direction and dynamism in the Trinitarian manner of giving thanks, which, though adapted from the Jewish style of "table prayers," goes utterly beyond what a strictly orthodox monotheistic approach of faith could allow or even envisage.

We can discern in Eucharistic Prayer II (and especially in its source, Hippolytus' *anaphora*) the ancient threefold temporal structure familiar to Jewish "blessings after meals." This structure presented a pattern for giving thanks for God's gifts enjoyed in the present, recalling as ever-present his great deeds of deliverance in the past, and petitionary prayer for fulfillment of his design in the future. However, what distinguishes this Prayer from its Jewish background is the manner this pattern is adapted and developed to express the revelation of the Triune God as taught by Christ, who is the Incarnate Word and personal "deed" of God's love. Praise is offered now to the Father who sends his Son as the Savior; thanksgiving for the story of salvation of the past is summed up in the sacrament of the Son's incarnation, death, and resurrection; and prayer is expressed for the Holy Spirit to guarantee the fulness of unity in the body of Christ in the future.

God's gracious good will

A closer examination of this prayer in comparison with its source in Hippolytus helps us to appreciate its profound significance for our life of worship.

In examining this prayer we cannot ignore the fact that it really begins with the preface as we saw above.[3] The Trisagion Hymn or

---

[3] Cf. *supra* Chapter II.

"Sanctus" is absent in Hippolytus' text in which the praise of God flows uninterruptedly in the Institution Narrative and *anamnesis*. The vocabulary employed in the "preface" of this prayer lends support to the choice of *liberation* as the salient theme of this prayer.[4] This is only strengthened especially when we consider the rich biblical background of each phrase and notion implicit in the *anaphora*.[5]

Praise and thanksgiving are addressed to the Father as in every Eucharistic Prayer. It is he who sent his Son and Word to proclaim and communicate most fully his will to save humanity; it is he who actually bestows his Holy Spirit to accomplish his will to transform, restore, and unite humanity with all creation. It is the Father's will that we realize our true worth as being made capable and empowered to offer him the honor and glory of worship. The Father's gracious good will is really what is praised in the mission or sending of his Son and gift of the Spirit.

Fountain of all holiness

All this is signified by the lovely metaphor of the *Fountain of all holiness*. This figure — so rich in the flavor of oriental exuberance and biblical imagery — is suggestive of the awesome source and support of all living beings, while likewise implying the flowing ease, grace, and beauty of freedom. God's holiness pertains both to the awesome, utterly ineffable and unique simplicity of the reality of being, and yet it is also somehow communicated. This is the paradox or, rather, the mystery of God's intrinsic freedom to communicate the mystery of his *holy communion*. For this especially we praise and thank God.

The Eucharistic Prayer is neither a treatise in morality nor in metaphysics! It is as direct and concrete in expression as the Scrip-

---

[4] Cf. the meticulous study of the sources of the Roman Missal by Anthony Ward and Cuthbert Johnson in *Notitiae* 252-4, Vol. 24 (1987), nn. 79, p. [267] 675. They list the following words as forming the principal vocabulary of the "preface" of this *anaphora*: *dilectio verbum cunctus facio mito salvator redemptor incarno virgo nascor voluntas adimpleo populus acquiro extendo manus patior mors solvo resurrectio manifestus.*

[5] Cf. ibid., p. [265-267] 673-675.

tures, from which it borrows the metaphor *"fountain."* The richly ambivalent symbol, water, signifies both that which threatens destruction (as in the Flood, the Red Sea, etc.) and also that which offers hope, refreshment, purification and, above all, communication of God's life. The Christian liturgy, therefore, frequently employs this evocative symbol for the unspeakable gift or grace of God's Spirit in expressing the truth that his eternal life requires the relinquishing and being freed from what is ephemeral and, indeed, mortal.[6] Since the Spirit of God is the source of all vital power, inspiring both religious awe and confident hope, the image of the *fountain* points us to God's act of communicating his vitality through the outpouring of Christ's Spirit.[7]

The metaphor, *fountain of all holiness*, which applies properly to the Father since he is the Source of all that is authentically holy and worthwhile, can have an extended application here regarding the Son's inner freedom and eternal gift of himself in love, which the Sacrament manifests. The Institution Narrative of this Prayer brings out clearly the full extent of what he embraced — *"he opened his arms on the cross . . . in this he fulfilled your will"*[8] — and offers in the Eucharistic sacrifice: a death he freely accepted. Jesus' prophecy to the Samaritan woman about genuine worship finds its fulfillment in this free gift of God, the well of his love in the eucharistic outpouring. Though the circumstances of time and place are different, the encounter is eternally the same.[9] Only the Son can lead humanity to

---

[6] Cf. Jean Danielou, *The Bible and the Liturgy*, DLT, London, 1964, pp. 6f., 71, 195.

[7] In many places in the Fourth Gospel especially reference is made to water as the sign of Christ's life: cf. Jn 1:19-24; 2:1-11; 3:1ff.; 4:14; 5:1ff; 6:1, 16f., 25 (Jesus crosses the sea of Galilee to the other side to interpret the sign of the miracle of the loaves, to bring out the life-giving, spiritual sense of his deeds and words — 6:63); 7:37-39 — St. John explains that Jesus' words about quenching our hearts' thirst for living water referred to the Spirit which he would give — cf. Jn 19:30, 34-35. Cf. also 1 Cor. 12:13: *For by one Spirit we were all baptized into one body — Jews or Greeks, slaves or free — and all were made to drink of one Spirit.*

[8] The Latin suggests embracing the Father's will — *adimplens.*

[9] Cf. the poem of Karol Wojtyla, "The Samaritan Woman Meditates" in *Easter Vigil* (translated by Jerzy Peterkiewicz). Arrow Book, London, 1980, pp. 20-22. Cf. also St. Columbanus' beautiful explanation of Christ "who is bread and fountain" — *Instruct.* 13, 12 in *The Divine Office*, Vol. III, op. cit., p. 469.

experience the tender intimacy of loving worship of the Father. Here the Fountain is seen to flow![10]

Through your Beloved Son

Jesus Christ is called the Father's "beloved Son" precisely because he perfectly fulfils his will not only in proclaiming it in creation as its inner principle of being and "logic" or Word, but especially by communicating to human beings the Father's design to save them through the paschal mystery of his death and resurrection.[11] As the Father's Word, Jesus intimately shares in his gracious good-will. Our English version regrettably loses the tone of intimacy somewhat by leaving untranslated the word "your," rendering the Latin rather flatly: "He is the Word through whom you made the universe . . ." The Latin is closer to the text of Hippolytus which describes the relationship of the Son to the Father even more

---

[10] *Vide* the mystical allusion to the gift of God's self in love (in the Eucharist) in the poems of St. John of the Cross — e.g.:

> *How well I know that fountain's rushing flow*
> *Although by night . . .*
> *The eternal source hides in the Living Bread*
> *That we with life eternal may be fed*
> *Though it be night . . .*
> *This living fount which is to me so dear*
> *Within the bread of life I see it clear*
> *Though it be night.*
>
> [Trans. by Roy Campbell]

There is the medieval Eucharistic "acclamation," *Ave Verum* (attributed to Pope Innocent VI, +1362), in which reference is made directly to Jn 19:34: *fluxit aqua et sanguine.* Cf. Julian of Norwich, *Revelations of Divine Love*, c. 60. Also, Pope Pius XII's Encyclical Letter *Haurietis Aquas* (*Acta Apostolica Sedis*, Vol. 23, 1956).

[11] Cf. Gn 1:1; Jn 1:1-14, Heb 1:1-4; 1 Jn 1:1-4. The Greek Fathers especially relished the theme of the creative Word, which they understood as the principle and inner structure of all things — cf. e.g. St. Justin, *Apologia* II, xiii; extending this creative meaning of the Word, Justin speaks of the consecrated Elements as "eucharistized food," literally food over which the word of thanks/praise has been spoken: "through the word of prayer which we have from him" (*Apol.*, I, lxv). From the Greek Fathers the notion of the consecratory power of the Word passed over to the Latin Fathers in the West — cf. esp. St. Ambrose, *De Mysteriis*, 54 and *De Sacramentis* IV, 14-15.

emphatically: "your inseparable Word." The enigmatic and almost mystical phrase "Angel of your will" is completely omitted.[12]

As the *"beloved"* of the Father, his Son Jesus Christ enjoys the fulness of freedom. He fully manifests the mystery of freedom, in him *"the fulness of grace and truth"* appears, as St. John bears witness at the end of the Prologue of his Gospel. For only what is conceived and formed in love can act in perfect freedom. The expression *"beloved Son"* is so pregnant with meaning that it demands closer examination in the light of its biblical background and significance.

In the ICEL the phrase *through your beloved Son* translates the Latin for "through the Son of your love" (*per Filium dilectionis tuae*). It would be pedantic to insist here on a more literal translation, which in fact is also quite unnecessary since "beloved Son" is the equivalent in meaning to the more poetic Hebrew expression followed in the Latin text. Recourse to the Latin original of this *anaphora*, however, is useful (indeed essential!) if we are to penetrate its rich content and gain some deeper insight into the Church's mystery of faith expressed in prayer.

Rather than referring to the theophanies in the Synoptic Gospels, where the divine identity of the *"beloved Son"* is proclaimed,[13] the Latin text of the Eucharistic Prayer clearly seems to allude to a verse in the Apostle Paul's "Christological Hymn":

> He has delivered us from the dominion of darkness and transferred us to the kingdom of his beloved Son.[14]

The context here is St. Paul's hymn of praise to the Father for the excellence of Christ who is the icon or image uniquely capable of manifesting the "invisible God."[15] Christ makes *Love* visible espe-

---

[12] This phrase, whose meaning seems obscure to us now, was not uncommon among the early Christians for whom it referred (probably) to Jesus, the messenger *par excellence* of the Father — cf. Josef Jungmann, *The Mass of the Roman Rite: Its Origins and Development* (*Missarum Sollemnia*), Vol. II, op. cit., p. 231ff.

[13] Re the Baptism of Jesus: cf. Mt 3:17; Mk 1:11; Lk 3:22 (which all cite Is 42:1, whereas Jn 1:29-34 makes no mention of the verse from Isaiah). Re the Transfiguration: cf. Mt 17:5; Mk 9:7; Lk 9:35; cf. also 1 P 1:17 — John does not mention this event, although perhaps an allusion to so important an event is implied in the Johannine statement of the Incarnation: *"we have beheld his glory, glory as of the only Son from the Father"* (Jn 1:14).

[14] Col 1:13 — literally: *"Son of his love."*

[15] Col 1:15 — a favorite Johannine theme, cf. Jn 1:13 (Ex 33:20); 3:11; 6:46; 1 Jn 4:12.

cially because he perfectly resembles and truthfully communicates the nature of his Origin, who is Charity unlimited. This is the kernel of the New Testament witness to the Good News of Jesus Christ.[16] His *being* is from or of "your love" (*dilectionis tuae*), as the Latin has it, echoing St. Paul. The *anaphora* goes on to thank and praise the Father for sending such a Son who is uniquely able to extend love in creation, especially through the sacrament of his sacrifice. *Being free* in love, Christ is *free* to communicate and give love. As the Institution Narrative puts it:

> Before he was given up to death, a death he freely accepted.

True liberation of the world from the opposite of love, namely the sin of pride's selfishness, is born from the limitless freedom in the heart of Jesus' loving obedience to the Father's will. He manifests the genuine nature both of love and also of liberation in his will to Love, that is, his "godly will," or that quality of his inner dynamism to seek always the sovereign good and worth of the Father's will.

As mentioned above, the expression *"beloved Son,"* which occurs twice in this *anaphora* (near the beginning and at the end), would seem also to refer indirectly to those passages in the New Testament where the first Song of the Suffering Servant is quoted from Deutero-Isaiah to establish Jesus' identity of divine sonship. These passages relate two mysterious theophanies: at Jesus' Baptism and at his Transfiguration. The word for "son" is identical in all versions of the Greek and Latin-Vulgate texts of the New Testament — namely, *"huios"* and *"filius"* respectively. Thus, Eucharistic Prayer II would apparently seem to be alluding to these passages in speaking of the *"beloved Son."* However, the *anaphora* of Hippolytus does not give *"huios/filius"* at the corresponding verse, but uses another word altogether: *"pais"* (Greek) or *"puer"* (Latin). This is translated as *"boy/ child/servant."* What is most interesting about this is that Hippolytus would clearly seem to be referring or alluding not to the theophanies of Jesus' Baptism or Transfiguration, but to another theophany which is reported only in Mt 12:18. In this verse Matthew quotes the same passage from Deutero-Isaiah's first Song of the Suffering Servant, but

---

[16] Cf. 1 Jn 4:16ff.; 1 Cor 13:1-13, etc.

instead of "son" has "boy/child/servant," a word possessing far richer overtones and significance than the usual word *"son,"* since it is one of those *"primordial words"* of language.[17]

The deliberate option for *"Son"* in preference to Hippolytus' evocative word *"boy/child/servant"* may clarify and strengthen the Christological statement of faith in our modern version of the *anaphora*, but in doing so something is sacrificed, namely the power of poetic beauty present in the ancient praise-singer.

Another slight difference between our English text and the Latin is also worth noticing. If we compare the three texts of the Eucharistic Prayer above, it is evident that our English text states simply that in fulfilling the Father's will, Christ's dying "put an end to death and revealed the resurrection." The Latin, however, is here, as elsewhere, more faithful to Hippolytus' *anaphora*; it expresses the idea that Christ's obedience to death is *in order to fulfill* the will of his Father, that is, to achieve the final liberation from death and to manifest the resurrection. In other words, whereas the English version has the simple indicative mood in making a statement, the Latin more finely indicates consequence and purpose by employing the subjunctive mood.

The Savior you sent to redeem us

However, one difference which is an improvement between our English version and the Latin is found in the translation of *misisti nobis Salvatorem et Redemptorem* by *the Savior you sent to redeem us*. The improvement consists in the succinct way two ideas are linked. There is certainly more than a shade of difference in meaning between these two words *"savior,"* and *"redeemer"*: the former refers

---

[17] It is worth recalling here Karl Rahner's words regarding the irreplaceable quality of certain "premordial words":

Blossom, night, star and day, root and source, wind and laughter, rose, blood and earth, boy, smoke, word, kiss, lightning, breath, stillness: these and thousands of other words of genuine thinkers and poets are primordial words. They are deeper and truer than the worn-down verbal coins of daily intellectual intercourse, which one often likes to call "clear ideas" because habit dispenses one from thinking anything at all in their use. —
Theological Investigations, Vol. 3, DLT, London, 1967, p. 298.

to one who saves, that is, preserves, keeps safe, rescues; the latter signifies one who redeems, that is, frees or liberates another from hardship or bondage which results from oppression. A redeemer pays something costly to bring about the salvation or rescue of another person. Both words (*savior/redeemer* and their corresponding verbal forms) were salvaged from ordinary secular usage and acquired a religious significance as God's people learned to interpret their socio-political experience in the light of their growing faith-awareness of the hand which God took in their history. Both words in this *anaphora* thus crystallize the socio-religious experience of gratitude and praise for God's deliverance of his people from all forms of tyranny and oppression — political, social, and at root, moral and spiritual.

Because of the direct allusions to the first Song of the Suffering Servant in this *anaphora*, the word "redeemer" has a very special ring to it. For, in Deutero-Isaiah the promise of a redeemer (*Go'el* in Hebrew) sustained the people's hope for liberation and prepared the way for the One whom God would send *"in the last times"* (as the ancient *anaphora* adds). This promise was indeed faithfully fulfilled by the Redeemer who delivered himself up freely *"for our sake!"* The lovely personal (Christian!) name of this Redeemer is *"Jesus"* — a name which itself means *Savior*.

The compilers of this Prayer omit the dramatic way in which Hippolytus presented Christ's act of redeeming and delivering humanity from the power of evil — breaking the devil's chains, the hallowing of hell, etc. This archaic imagery is rather obscure and would be lost on us today, whereas in Hippolytus' day it expressed a need to present Christology in relation not only to popular superstitious beliefs and practices, but also to the demonology and Gnostic cosmologies confronting Christianity (cf., e.g., Col 2:15ff.). It is a *martyr's* Song of certainty of resurrection through imitation of what is celebrated in the sacrifice of Christ the Redeemer and, as such, it has little in common with that preoccupation with the gruesome aspects of the sufferings of the passion as later came about during the gothic Middle Ages.[18] However, it seems a missed opportunity that the

---

[18] An example of this in art is Matthias Grünewald's altarpiece triptych of the crucifixion in Esenheim, Colmar.

compilers of our modern version did not transpose into a new key, that is, the language of liberation and solidarity, what Hippolytus expressed in terms of the Christ's triumph over the powers of evil.

These words, *Savior/Redeemer* (and the notions they signified), formed part of a vocabulary descriptive primarily of a profound religious experience before they passed into the technical language of doctrine, theology and dogma. The language of this Eucharistic Prayer, which is derived from and close to the well-spring of the Christian tradition of worship, is a far cry from the complicated theories and debates, theological wrangling and methodological precisions concerning redemption which the late medieval Schoolmen spun around, like the tops school boys once used in competing to affirm dubious superiority.[19] As legitimate as reflection upon faith may be and as imperative as it is in a responsible use of the precious gift of intelligence, there can be no substitute ultimately for the living expression of faith's best exponent, namely, the living worship of the Church.

It cannot be sufficiently emphasized that these words refer first and foremost to the experience of the presence of God's loving will, which is communicated in the Body of Christ. Encounter with this Body liberates humanity from all that threatens and thwarts the Father's design to share his own inner life of love, joy, peace and freedom with his children. In this Eucharistic Prayer, thus, the words *"Savior"* and *"Redeemer"* form part of a statement that is primarily of faith in the mystery of Jesus. That is, they confess and acknowledge gratefully the revealed reality of Christ's union and relationship with the Father and also the revealed *Good News* of his real, sacramental, mystical relationship with his Bride the Church in the nuptial Banquet of his Flesh and Blood, in which genuine liberation is experienced. For through and in Christ's mystical Body we know the freedom of God's children — that state of spiritual or *related being.*

---

[19] Cf. Gustaf Aulen, *Christus Victor*, S.P.G.K., London, 1970. One of the clearest medieval exponents of the doctrine of atonement/redemption is St. Anselm of Canterbury, who preserves a personal and religious tone through his writings — cf. *Trinity, Incarnation, and Redemption*, Harper Torchbooks (Harper & Row), N.Y. and London, 1970; *Cur Deus Homo*, John Grant, Edinburgh, 1909.

The dew of the Holy Spirit

The "consecratory" *epiclesis*, which has been added in our modern Eucharistic Prayer II to Hippolytus' *anaphora*, expresses a prayer for refreshing continuity in the flow of God's liberating holiness by his gift anew of the Holy Spirit to sanctify the bread and wine presented.[20] Though mention of the Holy Spirit is brief in Hippolytus' *anaphora*, it is nevertheless highly significant and important as one of the earliest witnesses expressing the Church's faith regarding the real continuation of the liberation Christ revealed — a continuation which the Holy Spirit guarantees and manifests in our eucharistic celebration.

The "second" *epiclesis* in our modern text parallels Hippolytus' petition for the outpouring of the Holy Spirit to make the Church as a credible sign or witness to Christ's sacramental Body and Blood, in which it participates. The implication of this prayer is a cry for the Spirit of truth to consecrate the Christian community and to guarantee both its authenticity of love and its consistency in living out what it expresses and handles in worship. Comparison of our text (in both the original Latin and English version) with that of Hippolytus shows that, while there is a general parallel of meaning between them, our version has altered fairly radically the syntax of its ancient model. For Hippolytus introduces the prayer for the Holy Spirit after the Institution Narrative, succinctly integrating in this prayer the request for God's power to consecrate and transform both the gifts offered by his people and the people themselves who participate in the "holy things" of the Eucharist.

The English translation changes the sentence structure even further. For it places the direct request for the Holy Spirit of the ancient *anaphora* as a subsidiary phrase and omits altogether to translate the words *"supplices deprecamur"* ("humbly we beg"). This results in the fine balance with the previous sentence of the *anamnesis* being broken: *"Memores . . . offerimus. . . supplices deprecamur"* ("Remembering . . . we offer . . . humbly we beg"). This seems

---

[20] The ICEL translation misses out altogether the lovely traditional metaphor of the dew of the Holy Spirit given in the Latin. This rich image, which is borrowed from ancient Eastern sources, finely complements the image of the Father's *fountain of all holiness*.
— cf. Mazza, *The Eucharistic Prayers*, op. cit., p. 147 n. 87.

anything but an improvement![21] For it changes the emphasis entirely from the active transforming power of the Holy Spirit to accentuate our growth in love, which the Latin places as the object of God's gift in the *epiclesis*. In other words, the primacy of grace is hardly given due recognition.

The Spirit of priestly service

This Eucharistic Prayer highlights the tender and delicate relationship of communion between the Son and the Father. In celebrating the filial obedience of Christ to the Father's will — an obedience which *"destroys death and proclaims the resurrection"*—the Church not only focuses on a program of morality, but takes up the Son's dialogue with the Father on behalf of all creation. This dialogue of thanksgiving and praise in the living Word, through whom the Father *"has created all things,"* enables the Church to fulfill its vocation as a priestly people: *"we thank you for counting us worthy to stand in your presence and serve you."* The verb in the Latin text (*ministrare*) richly points to the priestly nature of the Christian vocation of service. Realization of this vocation entails calling confidently on the Father to send the Spirit to transform both the gifts presented and also the members of the Christian community. This is done in the double prayer of *epiclesis*—before and after the Institution Narrative. The invocation is made on behalf of the community by the Church's ordained minister, who also pronounces it in the name of Christ (*in persona Christi*). For this sacramental act of the sacred ministry expresses the Church's share in the Beloved Son's intimate dialogue with the Father.

The notion of service, which originates in a liturgical context as is evident from various passages in the Old Testament,[22] is transformed by Christ who follows the great prophets in denouncing the arid formalism and empty rituals of religion separated from living. Worship, the primary vocation and responsibility of the Christian

---

[21] As Maloney claims — cf. *The Eucharistic Prayers in Worship, Preaching and Study*, op. cit., p. 54.

[22] Cf. Jos 24:14-24 — people must serve God by cultic worship.

priestly people, means more than cultic ritual.[23] The message had to be hammered home that God is not served by the offering of material gifts unless these *"fruits of the earth and work of human hands"* represent hearts devoted to seeking to serve him as well as one's neighbor for the love of him. The new *priestly people* is drawn from those whose service of God is consistent with lives dedicated to seeing that justice is done especially to the poor and in striving to be peacemakers. In other words, consistency between liturgy and life is of the essence of divine service. What the prophets proclaimed, Christ uniquely realized, for he fulfilled their prophecies regarding the *faithful Remnant of Israel*.[24] By his faithful obedience to the Father unto giving up his own life for all as their Redeemer, this *Beloved Son* of the Father embraces in his arms outstretched on the cross the people whom he wins over to the holiness of his priesthood of love.

Intercession — Christian service of love

This service of love has its first expression in intercessory prayer during the very act of worshipping God. For it would be unthinkable that those who have received the same Spirit of sonship as that which revealed the *Beloved Son* at his Baptism did not unite with him in praying for his brethren. In fact, the teaching that Christian baptism consecrates believers as worshipers[25] would be quite devoid of meaning (apart from leading to ritual formalism!) if it did not deeply signify both that Christians are united to Christ in his prayer as the *Beloved Son* and also that they become ever more deeply united to their brethren in and through intercession. In this sense, we may say that baptismal consecration is directly related to the Christ-revealing action of the Spirit of service and love among the priestly people.

---

[23] The Second Vatican Council in dealing with the ministerial priesthood thus insists that the sense and exercise of its service is not restricted to cultic worship in offering the eucharistic sacrifice (which remains their principal duty — *munus precipuum*), but includes the essential responsibilities of evangelization (proclaiming the Word of God) and wise ordering of the faithful — cf. L.G., n. 2t; P.O., nn. 46.

[24] Cf. Jr 17:13-18; 15:10-21; and especially the "Servant Songs" in Deutero-Isaiah — 42:14; 49:1-7; 50:4-11; 52:13ff.

[25] Cf. L.G., n. 12.

Intercession for the members of the Church — living and dead — is the strongest expression of unity and fraternal belonging to the one family of God the Father. The invocation of *epiclesis* includes a heartfelt cry especially for the unity of the Church so that the Father may make it whole in charity. This echoes the ardent desire of the *Beloved Son* during his "high priestly prayer" during the Last Supper: "Holy Father, keep those whom you have given me in your name that they may be one, even as we are one" (Jn 17:11f.). This is the Christian sign challenging the world to believe in his love — the double sign, that Christians both pray together and are together at-one.

As in the other Eucharistic Prayers, the intercessions here bring before God persons who exercise various ministries — the pope, whose ministry is especially to be a sign of unity in the universal Church, the bishop, and the clergy, who serve to build up the local church in love particularly by nourishing it on the word of God and the sacraments. It is noteworthy that specific intercessions did not form part of the source from which this Eucharistic Prayer is drawn. Was this addition in order to maintain a uniformity of style with our other Prayers? Or rather, to express an enriched awareness and development in our sense of the spirituality of Christian prayer — namely, a spirituality that is specific and incarnational? In no way is it being suggested that intercessory prayer was unknown to the early Church, but that it is inseparable, though distinct, from praise and thanksgiving to God. Christian worship manifests the primacy of loving service; it expresses best the wholeness of our communion with God and humanity, Father and his children.

The sobriety of style of this intercession contrasts with the more expansive prayer for those who have died — not only deceased brethren, whose faith is the basis of hope, but also who rely on the merciful love of the Father. This intercession for the dead requests that all may share in the joy of the Beatific Vision: *"may they rejoice in the light of your presence."*[26] This prayer, which is made in the

---

[26] Allusion is made to Ps 26:8ff., which expresses in concrete terms the desire of those who walk along the path of hope. This intercession may also be focused more specifically on occasions when the community gathers to offer Christ's sacrifice for deceased members, who by baptism have been united in the paschal mystery of Christ's death and resurrection — cf. Rm 6.

sacramental presence of God's Beloved Son, implies the most intimate and intrinsic connection between the *Mystery of Faith* and the reality of God who communicates and gives himself through Christ's sacrament of eternal life. It also recalls Jesus' reply to Philip during the Last Supper: "He who has seen me has seen the Father" (Jn 14:9).

Before concluding this Eucharistic Prayer with the doxology, which returns to the primary act of praising and thanking God, we pray that in his mercy the Father will enable all those taking part in it to deepen their possession of the gift of faith and worth in sharing the firm and eternal life enjoyed by the Blessed Virgin Mary, apostles and saints and all God's pilgrim people.[27] The last phrase of the intercession — *"who have done your will throughout the ages"* — brings out the true nature of liberation, which consists in responding to God's gracious good will. It recalls both the Blessed Virgin's surrender of herself to become the servant of the Word of God announced to her by the angel Gabriel and also Jesus' high praise for those *"who hear the word of God and keep it"* — words which implicitly also recognize the glory of his mother while pointing to the Church (the community of disciples faithful to the Word) as greater than her.[28] The communion of saints finds it best expression in the eucharistic celebration precisely because the Holy Spirit enables us to share sacramentally in communion with the Author or *Fountain of all holiness.*

The glory of the Blessed Virgin Mary and all the saints is that through the grace of Christ the Redeemer, their and our Savior, they share his condition of sinlessness — or, to put it positively, they share his state of love, the Blessed Vision of God's Beauty, full communion with God, whose life is pure love. We, who are called by God to this communion and who are given a taste for it in eucharistic worship, deepen our grasp of it through prayer, which is essentially an encounter with the transforming power of love. The difference between the glorious state of Christ and the Church Triumphant and our state of being *"Christ's faithful,"* is that they "are not able to sin" whereas we are "enabled not to sin." This distinction, which we owe to the Doctor

---

[27] This petition, which is absent in Hippolytus' *anaphora*, is a definite enrichment.
[28] Cf. Lk 1:38; 11:28; 8:15, 21.

of grace, St. Augustine,[29] is no mere clever play on words. It brings out
the true nature of the freedom of the children of God, which all who
are in Christ's Mystical Body of love share. It positively states that in
the freedom of love there is no sin, that is, there is no place for
selfishness, materialism, or pride. However, it realistically recognizes a difference between those confirmed and stable in God's love
and those who are still pilgrims of love. While thanks to Christ's grace
we are "enabled not to sin," nevertheless, we are still pilgrims subject
to the vicissitudes of our present unstable condition of life and, more
to the point, we have much to learn about loving and God who is love.
Hence springs our dire need of prayer — such as here in eucharistic
worship where we acknowledge the worth of the love-bond of prayer
between Christ's members in the communion of saints. Prayer —
especially the perfect prayer of the whole Mystical Body united with
Christ, its Head — restores and ennobles our freedom.[30]

Prayer — especially that of eucharistic worship — introduces
us to the mind, that is, inner attitude of Christ, the Father's *Beloved
Son*. This is the real revolution or "conversion" and renewal of our
hearts, which St. Paul frequently urges.[31] In the "preface" of this
Eucharistic Prayer the disposition or "posture" of Christ is symbolized as extending his arms. This not only represents, as noted above,
his embracing of the Father's will and all humanity in love, but also
recalls the traditional Jewish gesture of prayers ("Orantes") adopted
by the early Christians and the celebrant now. It richly signifies also
hands open to give generously to others, especially those in need and
who suffer, what we have received in prayer.

---

[29] For St. Augustine's distinction (*non posse peccare/posse non peccare*) — cf. *De Natura et
Gratia*, XII.33 (PL 44, 936); *De peccatorum meritis et remissione*, II.vii.2; xvii.3; xviiii;
xx.4. Cf. also Mary T. Clark, *Augustine: Philosopher of Freedom*, Desclée Co., New York,
1958.

[30] Cf. St. Augustine, *Ad Simplicianum*, I q. 1.14. His well-known prayer — "Give what you
command, [then] command whatever you wish" (*Da quod iubes, jube quod uis*) in
Confessions X.29 — is said to have stirred up a hostile reaction in Pelagius' circle in
Rome. It illustrates well the conviction that grace given in answer to earnest prayer
enables us to accomplish all things even the breaking of the most inveterate habits, the
conquering of human weakness, and the keeping of the most difficult commandments,
such as that of chastity.

[31] Cf. Rm 12:2; Ph 2:5ff.; Ep 4:22f.; 5:10; cf. also Mk 1:15, etc.

This Eucharistic Prayer, in which the theme of liberation is intrinsically linked with the gift of God's holiness in worship, celebrates the delight of joining the angels and saints in praising the all-holy Name of God.[32] As a proclamation of our worth (*worthy to stand in your presence*), this Prayer is a forthright affirmation of the truth which St. Augustine realized: that the gift of the Holy Spirit not only assists us to avoid sin, but that his grace makes the avoidance of sin a delight:

> We delight in not sinning thanks to the Holy Spirit, whose gift makes us justified. This is freedom! Without the Spirit, our delight is in sin. And that is slavery![33]

Freedom to proclaim God's glory and bear Christian witness

While everything good and worthwhile results from God's presence in our hearts by grace (including the gift of freedom!), we are inspired and empowered by the Eucharistic Prayer to imitate (and not merely admire and honor) the cooperation of the Blessed Virgin Mary and the saints in the work of redemption, the Father's offer of holiness. For what good is any gift unless it is appreciated in use! Not forgetting that this Prayer is based on one which comes from the Church of the Martyrs, we can take heart from the fact that our freedom to celebrate the Eucharist is a grace won by the saints and *martyrs* or heroic witnesses even today in the Church of silence. The words of one such witness within living memory poignantly testify to the *fountain of all holiness* refreshing, strengthening and building up Christ's Mystical Body:

---

[32] Eucharistic Prayer II adds the word "saints" to "angels" in the introduction to the Trisagion Hymn or *Sanctus*. This has now been followed also in some of the new Prefaces.

[33] Cf. *De Spiritu et littera*, 16 (PL 44.218). Grace in no way destroys or even diminishes freedom; on the contrary, it enhances true freedom — cf. St. Augustine, *De Natura et Gratia*, XXXII.36; cf. also the whole of *De gratia et libero arbitrio* (On grace and free will).

The Church was born in Christ's regenerative Blood on the cross, just as every one of God's children enters into the world. The child is healthy when his blood flows; a blood clot is dangerous for the human body. In the same way, stagnant blood is dangerous for the Mystical Body of Christ. It must always flow somewhere, not only in chalices at Mass but also in the living chalices of human souls. The bleeding of the Church must take place somewhere, so that it may remain in good health, filled with vigor and strength. And that is why the Church is forever bleeding, in the endless persecutions ever present in the history of the Church.[34]

The Freedom of Holiness

The Second Vatican Council took a bold step forward in proclaiming Jesus' universal call to holiness through which true freedom is discovered. Quoting St. Paul's words, it makes clear the centuries' old debate about the essential Christian vocation to holiness:

All in the Church, whether they belong to the hierarchy or are cared for by it, are called to holiness, according to the apostle's saying: "For this is the will of God, your sanctification" (1 Th 4:3; cf. Ep 1:4). This holiness of the Church is constantly shown forth in the fruits of grace which the Spirit produces in the faithful and so it must be; it is expressed in many ways by the individuals who, each in his own state of life, tend to the perfection of love, thus sanctifying others; it appears in a certain way of its own in the practice of the counsels which have been usually called "evangelical."[35]

In the Eucharist, in which the whole priestly people prays, the deep significance of the Holy Trinity's liberating gift of the paschal mystery can be realized as the *Fountain of all holiness*.

---

[34] *A Freedom Within — The Prison Notes of Stefan Cardinal Wyszynski*, Aid to the Church in Need, Harcourt Bruce Jovanovich Inc., 1985, p. 267.

[35] L.G., n. 39 — the whole of Chapter 5 is devoted to this crucial question.

Genuine Liberation through the Church's Prayer

The theme of liberation has been singled out as the key to Eucharistic Prayer II not merely because it is one that features in the forefront of contemporary theological thinking and language in response to the urgent needs today, but because it undergirds the content and thrust of this prayer. We discover that far from being an arbitrary choice of theme from among others, which are certainly also present, liberation is the pattern that emerges from the various threads intricately woven into the fabric of this expression of praise-thanksgiving — the threads of salvation, redemption, fidelity of the Beloved Son to the Father's gracious good will, and the outpouring of the Spirit of holiness through which all Christ's faithful are freed to pray and serve. Liberation, in fact, is the gift or grace of God's free-will manifest in Jesus Christ and communicated by the power of his Holy Spirit in the Eucharist.

Particularly during the second half of this century much attention has been paid to the moral and social implications of the Eucharist. Thanks to prophetically spirited voices, Eucharistic theology has made significant advances in taking to heart the Gospel-values of social justice and, especially the paradoxes of Jesus called the *Beatitudes*, which would remain a dead letter until experienced as the *praxis* of Christian living.[36] While this can be seen as a definite development in faith seeking to understand how its privileged expression in the eucharistic liturgy relates to life, the tendency to present the Gospel in a merely humanist fashion and Eucharist as an *ideological tool* is tantamount to a denial of the intrinsic divine power of the Eucharist itself as the sacrament *par excellence* in communicating and bringing about unity and integrity.[37] An ideology — no matter how noble, such as that presented by certain liberation theologians or

---

[36] Cf. Instruction II on Christian Freedom and Liberation, n. 62; also n. 52ff. where the experiential aspect of grace in the sacraments, etc., is positively presented as empowering the realization of Christ's teaching.

[37] Aidan Nichols, O.P., points out the shortcomings of "Liberation Theology" regarding the Eucharist — cf. *The Holy Eucharist: From the New Testament to Pope John Paul II*, Oscott 6, Veritas, Dublin, 1991, p. 117ff.

even the highest-minded thinkers[38] — can never be a substitute for the *Mystery of Faith* which the Church proclaims in the Eucharistic Prayer. This prayer gives concrete expression to the Bread of God's word in the Gospel, especially, as we have seen in Eucharistic Prayer II, in articulating everything that Jesus, the Beloved Son, expressed in his life: "My meat is to do the will of the Father." The sacrament of Christ's Paschal Mystery challenges us to acknowledge the transcendent sense of "Bread" while celebrating the imminent presence of God the Giver himself. The Church cherishes the truth of this Bread at the heart of its life of solidarity with and preferential option for the world's poor. This truth about *the Bread of Life* is the fundamental principle undergirding the Church's dialogue with anyone who wishes to reshape the proclamation of the Gospel. Thus, the first Instruction on Liberation Theology states:

> Faced with the urgency of sharing bread, some are tempted to put evangelization into parenthesis, as it were, and postpone it until tomorrow; first the bread, then the Word of the Lord. It is a fatal error to separate these two and even worse to oppose the one to the other. In fact, the Christian perspective naturally shows they have a great deal to do with one another.[39]

This statement echoes the Church's commitment to human development and genuine liberation which was clearly spelled out at the

---

[38] Simone Weil, that brilliant and holy French Jewess, penetrated the difference between true faith in God's providence and its counterpart, faith in humanity — cf. "Forms of the Implicit Love of God" in *Waiting on God*, Collins, Fontana, 1971, p. 150f.: *"The trap of traps, the almost inevitable trap, is the social one. Everywhere, always, in everything, the social feeling produces a perfect imitation of faith, that is to say perfectly deceptive. This imitation has the great advantage of satisfying every part of the soul. That which longs for goodness believes it is fed. That which is mediocre is not hurt by the light; it is quite at its ease. Thus everyone is in agreement. The soul is at peace. But Christ said that he did not come to bring peace. He brought a sword [. . .] It is almost impossible to distinguish faith from its social imitation. All the more but not quite impossible. Under the present circumstances, it is perhaps a question of life or death for faith that the social imitation should be repudiated."*

[39] Instruction on Certain Aspects of the "Theology of Liberation," VI.3 (Vatican City, 1984, p. 15)

Second Vatican Council.[40] All are urged to promote both the advance of this world and the kingdom of Christ.

This is more than an ideal.[41] It is the new Testament or Will to live the life of the Spirit, the source and fountain of spirituality. The Spirit of God continues to form and shape, revive and refresh Christian awareness, however, to realize that celebration of the Eucharist means not only a looking forward to individual well-being and otherworldly, *eschatological* object of salvation, but that this is *the* Sacrament of hope for the transformation of this world here and now. This eucharistic hope is the particular kind of nourishment needed for our journey in faith and love today. Without this kind of hope which is deepened through prayer — particularly the Eucharistic Prayer — we remain either imprisoned in a frustrated time-bound and materialistic vision of human development or bound to a romantic escapist kind of false spirituality. In either case there is no true development or liberation because there is really no realization of the fundamental option which Christ the Savior-Redeemer uniquely offers.

In the light of the Eucharist the parable of the Sower offers a rich source of reflection when seen in relation to many other passages in the Gospel. In the Eucharist we realize in a new way the mystery of the kingdom of God, which is contained in the parable of the Sower. The Eucharist is itself both the parable *par excellence* of the kingdom and the mystery or sacrament of the kingdom of God/heaven in our midst. Just as the living Word germinates and becomes fruitful in the good soil[42] of the Virgin Mary, who in receiving God's Word is not

---

[40] Cf. e.g., G.S., nn. 38-39; and more recently by John Paul II, Encyclical Letter, *Sollicitudo Rei Socialis.*

[41] Simone Weil describes it in terms of contemplative looking, loving attention which is the "soul's looking." She was opposed to a voluntarism or "muscular' type of morality — cf. loc. cit., p. 145f.: "One of the principal truths of Christianity, a truth which goes almost unrecognized today, is that the looking is what saves us. The bronze serpent was lifted up so that those who lay maimed in the depths of degradation should be saved by looking upon it. [. . .] The effort which brings a soul to salvation is like the effort of looking or of listening; it is the kind of effort by which a fiancée accepts her lover. It is an act of attention and consent; whereas what language designates as will is something suggestive of muscular effort."

[42] It is interesting to notice that whereas our English translation gives various words ("earth," "ground," "soil"), the same word is used in the Greek and Latin texts (*ge/terra*) of the Lord's Prayer as in the various other places as well; cf. Mt 6:10; 13:1-23; Jn 12:24, 36-41; Is 55:10-11; Pss 8:1; 19:1, etc.

above or greater than the Church but its Prototype and Model in faith,[43] so Christ, who is himself the Gospel or fulness of Good News, evangelizes the Church's community of faith gathered together in his presence at the Eucharist and through his Spirit effectively produces the abundant fruit of love as intended by and worthy of the Father.

The faithfuls' *Amen* to the final doxology of this Prayer proclaims their assent to the grammar of life in the *Mystery of Faith*. In a word, this *Amen* signifies the realization and willingness on the part of the Church, the community of Christ's disciples, to live what the Beloved Son teaches it by his Spirit in prayer: *Thy will be done on earth as it is in heaven.*

---

[43] Cf. L.G., nn. 55-59 — Her receptivity and willingness to cooperate in the work of redemption exemplifies the "obedience of faith" which is fruitful for salvation; cf. Rm 1:5; 16:26; 2 Cor 10:5-6.

5

Sacrament of Unity
(Eucharistic Prayer III)

Guided by the Holy Spirit, the Church from the beginning expressed and confirmed her identity through the Eucharist. And so it has always been, in every Christian generation, down to our own time, down to this present period when we await the end of the second Christian Millennium. Of course, we unfortunately have to acknowledge the fact that the Millennium which is about to end is the one in which there have occurred the great separations between Christians. All believers in Christ, therefore, following the example of the Apostles, must fervently strive to conform their thinking and action to the will of the Holy Spirit, "the principle of the Church's unity," so that all who have been baptized in the one Spirit in order to make up one body may be brethren joined in the celebration of the same Eucharist, "a sacrament of love, a sign of unity, a bond of charity"![1]

Eucharistic Prayer III is considered representative of the Church's contemporary understanding of the theology of the Eucharist and characteristic of its approach to spirituality. For among all the new Eucharistic Prayers it was the composition of this which most occupied the devoted attention of the team of various experts (*Coetus X*), among whom Dom Cipriano Vagaggini's influence in the reform of the liturgy after the Council was most notable. This Prayer is some-

---

[1] Pope John Paul II, Encyclical Letter *Dominum et Vivificantem —The Holy Spirit in the Life of the Church and the World* — (18 May 1986), n. 62; Catholic Media Office, London, p. 38f. The Pope cites the Decree on Ecumenism (U.R.) n. 2; St. Augustine, *In Joh. Evan.*, Tr. xxvi.13 which is referred to in the Constitution on the Sacred Liturgy, S.C., n. 47.

times referred to as the Eucharistic Prayer of Paul VI insofar as before its definitive promulgation it underwent much revision in which the Pope himself took no little interest. It reflects the genius of the Roman Western liturgical tradition for its conciseness, while having its roots in the Syrian Antiochian Liturgy.[2]

The New Creation of the Holy Trinity

The dominant theme of this Prayer is the proclamation of the work of the Holy Trinity in the mystery of salvation. Despite, or rather, because of the absence of a proper preface (as was composed for each of the other new Eucharistic Prayers), maximum flexibility is provided in the use of this *anaphora* especially on Sundays and Feasts during which the Church celebrates different aspects of the Holy Trinity's action in regard to humanity. Thus, far from seeming to be "mutilated" due to not having its proper preface, Eucharistic Prayer III is by no means lacking in motives for remembering or recalling God's saving operation, but rather, because of its adaptability it opens up a vast and rich theological and spiritual perspective regarding the Church's special quality as the sacrament or visible sign of the mystery of the Holy Trinity's saving design and action in revealing and communicating its inner life of union or communion. The Second Vatican Council sought to describe the nature of the Church in terms of the key biblical and patristic ideas of mystery, communion and mission. Referring to this teaching the recent Roman Synods of bishops pointed out that the identity and mission of all Christ's faithful is discovered when rooted in the mystery of the Blessed Trinity's communion, which is celebrated at the Church's celebration of Christ's Paschal mystery.[3]

Since Eucharistic Prayer III particularly features this dimension of unity, it merits attention from this point of view. In focusing on

---

[2] Cf. Mazza, *The Eucharistic Prayers*, op. cit., pp. 125; 167f.: Vagaggini's proposed draft was considerably changed . . . Pope Paul VI himself took a hand in reworking what was presented after the committee stage.

[3] Cf. L.G., nn. 3-6; C.L., n. 8 (re identity of all); P.D.V., n. 12 (regarding "the priest's identity").

this dimension we shall be enabled to understand better Christian Eucharistic worship, the nature of belonging to the Church, and our urgent responsibility to work and pray for unity among Christians. For such is the intrinsic nature of the Eucharistic Prayer that, as our celebration of the New Covenant of God's love, in expressing the consecration of Christ's faithful to God, it also manifests their commitment to one another unless their worship, words and deeds are to fall apart and become a lie — that is, unfaithful and untrue to the Gift of God's truth of love.

An expression of the dominant theme of the Trinity's work of redemption is quite clearly that of unity.[4] This is the context in which the Lord Jesus prayed at the Last Supper when, at the same moment, he manifested his desire that his essential multidimensional action of giving himself for the life of the world be commemorated by his disciples. This theme of unity, as the supreme work of the Holy Trinity, is certainly not absent from the other Eucharistic Prayers, as, for instance, in the *epiclesis* after the Institution Narrative in the new Eucharistic Prayers II and IV:

> May all of us who share in the body and blood of Christ, be brought together in unity by the Holy Spirit;
>
> . . . by your Holy Spirit gather all who share in this bread and wine into the one body of Christ, a living sacrifice of praise.

It is also unmistakably evident in the Roman Canon:

> grant it [the Church] peace and unity . . . Grant us your peace in this life . . .

---

[4] The ancient expression *"the work of our redemption"* might be understood as *"the liturgy of our redemption."* This richly significant expression occurred in the "secret prayer" (the Prayer over the Gifts) of the 9th Sunday after Pentecost which the Constitution on the Sacred Liturgy quotes: "Through the liturgy, most of all through the Eucharist, *the work of our redemption is accomplished [opus nostrae Redemptionis exercetur]"* (S.C., n. 2). — On the meaning of *"exercetur"* ("is accomplished/effected/performed/brought about/realized") cf. also E. Denys Rutledge, O.S.B., "Thoughts on an ancient 'Secret' Prayer" in *Priests & People*, Vol. 2 No. 1 (Feb. 1988), pp. 34-36. The closely related idea that the Eucharist is the fruit of redemption in the Church's life is expressed in other texts of the Roman Missal to which the Council refers: post-communion of the Easter Vigil (S.C., n. 10); prayer of Easter Tuesday (S.C., n. 10); prayer over the gifts of Whit Monday (S.C., n. 12).

In fact, the *epiclesis* after the Institution Narrative is a prayer for the Holy Spirit to consecrate and transform into unity all members of the Mystical Body, especially those sharing in the Eucharistic celebration. The particular object of the request in the second *epiclesis* of Eucharistic Prayer III is for the Father to bring about a transformation of the celebrating community so that it may discover itself as one body and one spirit in Christ. This is the single purpose of this request clearly stated in the Latin text, whereas our ICEL version distracts from this in requesting also that we "may be filled with his Holy Spirit." The Latin text presents the condition or qualifying basis for becoming (or being found — *"inveniamur"*) one in Christ: participation in sacramental communion, and being filled with Christ's Spirit. Indeed, the two go together, for it is the Spirit that brings about real communion — that is, without spiritual reception of the sacrament there is no discernment of Christ's presence as Lord or real communion with him. This spiritual communion, however, is the basis for confidence in requesting the Father to bring about the transformation of the Church into the Mystical Body of Christ (*"ut . . . unum corpus et unus spiritus inveniamur in Christo"*).

> May he [Christ] make us an everlasting gift to you and enable us to share in the intercession of your saints, with Mary . . .

In this way Christ's faithful glorify God's inner unity in the final doxology — that unity (*"in the unity of the Holy Spirit"*) which the Eucharistic community receives and which it manifests or witnesses in the world.

The Church gathers to praise and thank the Holy Trinity for having chosen it from the whole of humanity and for forming it into that community in which an adequate faith-response is offered for the saving action of God's revelation. It discovers and realizes the mystery of this reality particularly as it stands before God and proclaims before the world the great Prayer of the Eucharist. This is the privileged moment or opportunity for discernment of how God accomplishes his great design and fills his people with his choicest gifts through and in Christ working by the Holy Spirit so that they may enter fully into the *divine milieu* of the awareness of Love.

Proclamation of Divine Life — Unity made visible

This "environment" of grace becomes available through the sacramental nature of the Church's mystery especially at the Eucharistic celebration, as the Second Vatican Council amply brought out while complementing the First Vatican Council's rather incomplete description of it in terms of hierarchical institution and "perfect society."[5] The teaching of Vatican II is unequivocal regarding the spiritual dimension of the Church being *"as if (*veluti*) a sacrament and instrumental sign of intimate union with God and of unity for the whole human race."*[6] This teaching, which is rooted deeply in what the liturgy realizes, would be inconceivable without an appreciation of the Eucharist as the Sacrifice for and Sacrament of Unity. For in the strong sense of the word, the Eucharist is the Sacrament of the Church's inner unity and cohesive identity.

In referring to the Church's (Eucharistic) Prayer and the working of the Holy Spirit, what was said above regarding the *epiclesis* and *Institution Narrative* must be recalled.[7] For there an important point was brought out regarding Christian spirituality flowing from Eucharistic worship in such a way that it cannot be considered apart from this kind of worship. It would be true to say that the Church's Prayer and the working of the Holy Spirit are not two separable

---

[5] It is well-known that the draft of the original schema presented to the Council which followed the lines of Vatican I was rejected and another more biblical and patristic approach was adopted and developed into the great Dogmatic Constitution on the Church, *Lumen Gentium*. The eloquent words of Cardinal Wyszynski, who had come through the Stalinist regime of persecution and spoke for the "Church of silence," no doubt played no little part in persuading the Council Fathers of *"the Council's duty to reveal to God's people the Church of Christ in its interior dimensions, that is, its supernatural quality, which we call the Mystical Body of Christ"* (reported in *La Documentation Catholique*, 17 novembre 1963, n. 1412, col. 1505).

[6] L.G., n. 1; This is emphatically clarified by Pope John Paul II in the Encyclical cited at the beginning of this chapter (n. 64, loc. cit., p. 37): *"When we use the word 'sacrament' in reference to the Church, we must bear in mind that in the texts of the Council the sacramentality of the Church appears as distinct from the sacramentality that is proper, in the strict sense, to the Sacraments. Thus we read: 'The Church is . . . in the nature of a sacrament — a sign and instrument of communion with God.' But what matters and what emerges from the analogical sense in which the word is used in the two cases is the relationship which the Church has with the power of the Holy Spirit, who alone gives life: the Church is the sign and instrument of the presence and action of the life-giving Spirit."*

[7] *Vide supra*, p. 35ff.

actions, but one dynamic action. For the Church cannot pray without the inspiration and life-giving breath of the Spirit.[8] And, likewise, the Spirit (though "breathing where he wills") does not force entry, so to speak, but respects and operates through the freedom of the children of God, whom he makes free to be Christ's faithful, that is, worshipers whom the Father seeks. This is certainly the motive for praising God in the opening words of this Prayer. Thus, it is clear from the start of this *anaphora* that unity is not so much "some thing" or some quality prayed for as it is the dynamic divine reality being celebrated in the action of the Eucharistic Prayer.

The "visibility" of Christ's grace, which manifests and communicates the life of God's inner unity, is proclaimed in the Church's Eucharistic Prayer and brought about through its special ministry of reconciliation by cooperating with the working of the Holy Spirit. Reconciliation and unity among Christians is a much-needed sign to the world of the Church's credibility![9]

Eucharistic Prayer — sign of visible unity

What the Spirit makes visible — namely, the Church united in prayer (and the deeds of love flowing from prayer in a consistent way with what is celebrated) — would be shallow without the inner dimension of the grace of unity and without the inner dynamic of the Spirit of truth, the Gift from the Father and the Son. That is, it would be a grievous mistake to reduce the Sacrament of Unity to the ordinariness of human "sociability" and to blur its Mystery of the eternal *Agape* of the kingdom of God with an impoverished meal of human meanings or makeshift subjective "feelings" of cosy togetherness! The unity of the Church, as Eucharistic Prayer III finely proclaims, is not primarily a matter of our deepened social awareness or sensibility regarding solidarity, but of the *spiritual* communion of God's people becoming Christ's faithful in the Mystical Body. The ecclesiology of this Prayer expresses sound Christology and theol-

---

[8] Cf. L.G., n. 50 (towards the end).

[9] This question will be treated further in dealing with the Eucharistic Prayers for Reconciliation — *vide infra*, Chapter VII.

ogy of the Spirit.[10] Without this basis both ecclesiology and prayer would founder in a sea of subjectivity and human feelings.

The opening paragraph of the Prayer — the *"post sanctus"* — must be taken together with the Preface employed. It forms the *anamnesis* part of the literary structure. Its source has been identified as derived from the so-called Mozarabic or Spanish liturgy.[11] Our ICEL translation seems not only flaccid, but it fails to convey the full force and sense expressed in the Latin original, which in a single sentence splendidly affirms the dynamic action of the three Divine Persons through the revelation of their presence in creation and sanctification. In breaking up the text into two sentences and suppressing the word "because" (*quia*) our translation does not present the "logic" of the Blessed Trinity's salvifically re-creative action and art. This is clear in comparing the ICEL and a literal translation of original text:

ICEL:	LITERAL TRANSLATION:
Father, you are holy indeed and all creation rightly gives you praise. All life, all holiness comes from you through your Son, Jesus Christ our Lord, by the working of the Holy Spirit. From age to age you gather a people to yourself, so that from east to west a perfect offering may be made to the glory of your name.	Lord you are holy indeed and every creature rightly praises you, because through your Son, our Lord Jesus Christ, by the power of the Holy Spirit, you enliven and sanctify all things, and you do not cease to gather a people to yourself so that from the rising of the sun to its setting a pure sacrifice may be offered to your Name.

The differences in translation indicate not merely a break in the flow of language and thought of the Latin, but also a shift in emphasis and theological perspective: from a proclamation of praise of the

---

[10] Cf. Cardinal Josef Ratzinger, *The Ratzinger Report*, Fowler Wright Books Ltd., 1985, p. 47: *"Behind the concept of the Church as the People of God, which has been so exclusively thrust into the foreground today, hide influences to ecclesiologies which* de facto *revert to the Old Testament; and perhaps also political, partisan and collectivist influences. In reality, there is no truly New Testament, Catholic concept of Church without a direct and vital relation not only with sociology but first of all with Christology. The Church does not exhaust herself in the 'collective' of the believers; being the 'Body of Christ' she is much more than the simple sum of her members."*

[11] Cf. Della Torre, op. cit., p. 85.

revelation of God's work of holiness in unity to three rather flat-sounding statements about (i) creation praising God; (ii) life and holiness coming from the divine Persons; and, (iii) God gathering a worshiping people from all over the world.

Similarly in the *epiclesis*, the two distinct sentences of ICEL change the unified perspective of the Latin original. Furthermore, the emphasis is placed (i) on our prayer for the Holy Spirit's action; (ii) our preparation of gifts for consecration, which effects the real Offering; (iii) substitution of "eucharist" for "mysteries" weakens the meaning considerably by reducing it to our human action rather than the saving action of God.

ICEL:	LITERAL TRANSLATION:
And so, Father we bring you these gifts. We ask you to make them holy by the power of your Spirit, that they may become the body and blood of your Son, our Lord Jesus Christ, at whose command we celebrate this Eucharist.	Therefore we humbly pray you, Lord, to sanctify by that same Spirit these gifts which we have brought you to be consecrated, that they may become the body and blood of your Son, our Lord Jesus Christ, at whose command we celebrate these mysteries.

The expression *"at whose command"* is not merely a neat stylistic way of introducing the Institution Narrative, but, in fact, it sets the theological basis of liturgical obedience to the pattern given by our Lord at the Last Supper. This basis is the approach adopted by St. Paul in recalling the Lord's Supper to the Corinthian community as the norm for their conduct. Confirmation of this Pauline perspective is found in the introductory words to the Institution Narrative: "On the night on which he was betrayed."[12] The whole context of this passage in First Corinthians brings out how St. Paul not only put his finger on the Corinthians' failure in lack of unity, but also touched most accurately the essential relation between Eucharist and Church. While the Eucharist sets the standard for the lives of the Christian community it also provides and is the remedy. United in obedience to

---

[12] Cf. 1 Cor 11:23-25; cf. Mazza, ibid., p. 130 re the three liturgical formulas: Roman ("Who, on the day before"); Alexandrian ("Because he himself, the Lord"); and Antiochean/Pauline (as here in EP III).

the Lord's command to enact the sacrament of the New Covenant, the Church presses forward to fulfil the supreme law of love. Obedience in faith and love fosters the unity among Christians.

Communion — the very life of the Three Divine Persons (*koinonia*), as this Prayer so splendidly celebrates — is more than mere "sharing." It expresses entire oneness with the divine. St. John Chrysostom commenting on 1 Cor 10:16 brings this out most clearly in sensitively reading the distinction which exists in the language of the Apostle:

> "The bread which we break — is it not the community of the body of Christ?" Why then does he not say "sharing" (metoche)? Because he wanted to reveal still more and show us a deeper bond (sunatheia). For we are in community (koinonoumen) not merely by sharing (metechein) and participating (metalambanein) but by becoming one with him ('enousthai).[13]

---

[13] *Hom.* 24.2; PG 61.200. One is reminded of T.S. Eliot's description of the sad state of modern society ("Chorus from 'The Rock'", *Collected Poems 1909-1962* (Faber & Faber, London, 1963, pp. 168; 170f.):

> *What life have you if you have not life together?*
> *There is no life that is not in community,*
> *And no community not lived in praise of GOD.*
> *Even the anchorite who meditates alone,*
> *For whom the days and nights repeat the praise of GOD*
> *Prays for the Church, the Body of Christ incarnate.*
> *And now you live dispersed on ribbon roads,*
> *And no man knows or cares who is his neighbour*
> *Unless his neighbour makes too much disturbance,*
> *But all dash to and fro in motor cars,*
> *Familiar with the roads and settled nowhere.*
> *Nor does the family even move about together,*
> *But every son would have his motor cycle,*
> *And daughters ride away on casual pillions. [. . .]*
> *Where there is no temple there shall be no homes,*
> *Though you have shelters and institutions,*
> *Precarious lodgings while the rent is paid,*
> *Subsiding basements where the rat breeds*
> *Or sanitary dwellings with numbered doors*
> *Or a house a little better than your neighbour's;*
> *When the Stranger says: 'What is the meaning of this city?'*
> *Do you huddle close together because you love each other?*
> *What will you answer? 'We all dwell together*
> *To make money from each other'? or 'This is a community'?*
> *And the Stranger will depart and return to the desert.*
> *O my soul, be prepared for the coming of the Stranger,*
> *Be prepared for him who knows how to ask questions.*

The Communion of and with the Holy Trinity is the reality at the heart of the Church — that sacramental reality whose dynamism Eucharistic Prayer III celebrates. This dynamism is creative of the Church which, as an "icon" or image, as it were, points to the relations of the Persons of Trinity.

Sacrifice at the heart of the Church's intercession

The *intercessions* in Eucharistic Prayer III flow on directly from the second *epiclesis* after the consecratory Institution Narrative of Christ's passover sacrifice of love. Whereas intercession is presented in Eucharistic Prayer II as a simple request for (and expression of) deeper communion in the Mystical Body of the Son, it is linked here to the theme of sacrifice — in particular, to Christ's passover sacrifice celebrated in the Eucharistic Prayer. It is useful to refer to the phrase used in Latin, which indicates more clearly the object of the request made. Thus, *"perficiat munus aeternum"* is richer in overtones of sacrifice than what we have in the vernacular: *"May he* [i.e. Christ] *make us an everlasting gift to you."* The request is for Christ to bring this about completely and thoroughly (which is better expressed in the Latin *"perficiat,"* than our limp word, "make"!). The word "gift" takes the bite out of the sense of the language of sacrifice used throughout after the consecratory Institution Narrative: "holy and living sacrifice," "Church's offering" (*oblationem*), "Victim" (*Hostiam*), etc. For what is being precisely asked is that the members of the Church may be united with Christ in this context of offering his unique sacrifice that it may be offered with him.[14] This adds a new

---

[14] Maloney (op. cit., p. 126 ff.) rightly observes that our ICEL translators are reluctant to convey exactly the "propitiatory character" of the Eucharistic celebration as expressed in the Latin text. He cites the classic text of St. John Chrysostom (PG 63, 131) regarding the identity of the sacrifice of the cross with what is celebrated in the Mass. Maloney's concluding comment is worth recalling: *"the propitiatory nature of Christ's oblation on the cross is an intrinsic part of our tradition from the New Testament on (Rm 3:25; Heb 9:1ff.; 1 Jn 2:2), and so it is part of that in which the Eucharist shares, given the identity of victim in the Mass and on the cross. Atonement is one of those primordial realities which people grasp without being able to put into words. It is one of the basic needs of religious man, and the Church has always pointed to the Eucharist as a part-fulfillment of that need. It is significant that it continues to do so at the heart of the most contemporary of our prayers. The official German version preserves the idea neatly by introducing a reference here to the lamb that takes our sins away"* (p. 128).

dimension to the element of intercession in the Eucharistic Prayer. Not only is the assembly the "offerers," but also what is "offered" with and through Christ's gift of self. The bread and wine is a sign of ourselves which we ask God to accept.[15] The Eucharistic sacrifice makes us the Church at-one with the Body of Christ. The real "matter" of the sacrifice is ourselves with Christ; the bread and wine is the sign of this sacrifice.[16] In keeping with our Lord's teaching in the Gospel, unless we become reconciled with our brethren, all our prayers or sacrifices are lip-service and sham. The force of this request, thus, implies that on becoming reconciled we realize more deeply our unity in vocation as intercessors with Christ (the First Intercessor) and the Blessed Virgin and the saints.

The prayer of intercession continues with confidence, since sharing in Christ's sacrifice has brought about our reconciliation (*reconciliationis* — rather than "peace"!). The responsibility of intercession extends us to pray for others. The offerers and sharers in Christ's sacrifice exercise their role of intercessors as a holy and priestly people in pleading for "the peace and salvation of all the world." The role of intercession in the local church makes it ever mindful of the wider Church universal. The importance of this responsibility of intercession is expressed within the Second Vatican Council's perspective of the pilgrim people of God. Intercession for leadership within the hierarchical nature of the Church is not separated from "the entire people" whom Christ won by his sacrifice for God's kingdom. This intercession is expressed as much in union with the ministry of the pope and bishops as for them, as was seen above in regard to the Roman Canon. Prayer for the bishops and pope cannot be gainsaid, since the Eucharistic "Mystery of Faith" is their special responsibility to oversee and guarantee.[17] This is a serious responsibility, which should be carried out not as a matter of routine

---

[15] Cf. Heb 10:5-10.

[16] Cf. Jn 4:21-24; Ph 2:17; 1 Tm 4:6.

[17] The teaching of the martyr-bishop St. Ignatius of Antioch on the closest bond between the bishop and the Eucharistic community was recalled by Vatican II — cf. S.C., n. 41 (*Epist. Ad Magn.*, 7; *Ad Phil.*, 4; *Ad Smyrn.*, 8); also L.G., n. 13 (*Ad Rom. praef.*); n. 20 (*Ad Phil.* 1.1; *Ad Magn.*, 6.1). Cf. O'Connor, *The Hidden Manna*, op. cit., in which the author splendidly shows the link between the Petrine ministry in guarding the authentic teaching of the Holy Eucharist, which, in Pope Paul VI's memorable phrase, is "the treasure of the Church."

or grudgingly but joyously. Our Lord himself set the example of praying that Peter's faith may not fail in order that he might serve and strengthen his brethren. In this way, that is, especially through intercession at the Eucharist, the Church goes on its pilgrim way from strength to strength in faith and charity.

The Eucharistic Prayer then manifests the Christian *heart in pilgrimage* in fulfilling its duty to intercede for those members of God's family who have gone ahead to be admitted into the Beatific Vision of God's glory, for which the focus of the Church's eschatological hope and desire is especially sharpened by the Holy Eucharist. On occasion of funerals or special Masses for particular members of the faithful departed an extended intercession may be used.[18] With remarkable conciseness this intercession alludes to four texts of the New Testament which form the basis of the Christian doctrine of hope in the resurrection of the dead: that through baptism, which unites us with Christ's passover mystery, we share in his resurrection (Rm 6:5); that our mortal bodies will become transformed into the image of Christ's glorious body (Ph 3:21); that God will wipe away every tear from our eyes (Rv 21:4); and, that we shall become like God because we shall behold him as he is (1 Jn 3:2). Thus, from beginning to end, this Prayer celebrates the rich biblical tradition of faith in the trinitarian work of redemption.

The Mystery of Faith — challenge of Christian Unity

One of the most urgent motives for intercession must surely be that of praying for unity among all members of Christ's Mystical Body — that is, visible unity of all who are baptized in Christ.[19] In view of the strong emphasis in Eucharistic Prayer III on the unity of the Church, we may legitimately ask: what of Christian unity in sharing fully in Eucharistic worship — *"communicatio in sacris"* (that is ministers of other Christian denominations sharing in the Mass) —

---

[18] As likewise a special insertion for Sundays or on occasions of baptisms, confirmation, weddings enriches the quality of this Prayer.
[19] Cf. L.G., n. 15; U.R., n. 3.

and the passionate issue of "intercommunion"? The answer given by Rome is that the Eucharist is not only the source or means to build up unity among Christians, but it also signifies and contains the summit in expressing unity in full faith among Christ's faithful.[20] Crucial to this wholeness of faith is recognition of unity with the See of Peter. This may at first look like insistence on juridical form and seem like Roman "legalism." But, there is more to it than that. If we consider the Eucharist as the *Word-made-sacrament* — the Word of Truth, guaranteeing and pledging the Father's design to call all to *real visible unity* — then, to engage in intercommunion or, *a fortiori*, in *"communicatio in sacris"* would be tantamount to enacting a lie. It would be performing, pretending, and "making believe" that we are fully united, whereas — insofar as only aspects of full faith and the discipline flowing from it are present — this is sadly and manifestly just not the case. The argument that the world cannot believe in Christ as long as Christians remain disunited cannot be used to force the issue of intercommunion at any price. Such an argument just does not work since nonbelievers would be skeptical and, perhaps even, suspicious — and rightly so! — at such a "show" or "play" at unity. Serious minded seekers for truth and for its authentic manifestation cannot be duped into accepting this kind of duplicity which only highlights the dichotomy between the words and lives of Christians who claim and boast to belong to the one authentic revealed religion.

More is needed than a shallow-minded and sentimental approach that this sort of argument imposes. For "feelings" of being "at-one" or "in solidarity" with others on certain occasions are not enough if in other respects or areas of our lives we are poles apart. Such "feelings" may certainly move us — and ought to challenge us — to work the harder and especially to pray the more earnestly to be converted to seek with generosity to listen to and learn from others'

---

[20] This was acknowledged in the Final Report of the Joint Roman Catholic-Lutheran Commission in 1978: *"The Eucharist is thus at once the source and climax of the church's life. Without the eucharistic community there is no full ecclesial community, and without the ecclesial community there is no real eucharistic community"* — cf. *Growth in Agreement: Reports and Agreed Statements of Ecumenical Conversations on a World Level*, Ed. by Harding Meyer and Lukas Vischer, Paulist Press, New York/ World Council of Churches, Geneva, 1984, p. 198. Cf. also the Letter of the Sacred Congregation for the Doctrine of the Faith (15 June 1992), *Communionis Notitio*, n. 11.

experience, understanding, appreciation, traditions, and insights of the Gospel and of the Mystery of Faith.[21]

In this *decade of evangelization* nothing is more urgently required than that we learn that "speaking the truth in love"[22] is not an easy matter of instant change of our outward conduct or ritual, but a work of immense patience which is that love assuring genuine growth in the Mystical Body of Christ. The dialogue of Christian Unity has moved beyond the narrow perspective of requiring *uniformity* of all Christians in conforming to one external form of ritual. It consists in helping us to grow to appreciate the richness of different traditions of Christian worship and challenges us to recognize the diversity of God's gifts in an authentic living of the Gospel of Christ's love.[23]

The question is not whether we must surrender what is essential for fulness of faith — the revealed truths guaranteeing authentic unity — but whether we are prepared to abandon ourselves to search

---

[21] Cf. Timothy Radcliffe, "The demands of the Mass" in *The Tablet*, 1 December 1990, p. 154ff., where further light is thrown on the Catholic hesitations regarding intercommunion. The author focuses on the Last Supper as "a curious gathering" which "embraced and included everything that could possibly destroy human communion." He reminds us that the sacraments "spring from an older and more incarnational sense of being human" than the post-Cartesian and post-Romantic approach to meaning of *being human* — an approach which turns us inward to regard humaneness as "thinking beings . . . as feeling beings." In the sacraments we are truly liberated insofar as we encounter the living Christ, who by entering our "fundamental human and bodily dramas" of struggle for survival consecrates them so that our perspectives are transformed to realize in faith, hope, and love a sense of communion inaccessible to a merely human sense or feeling of solidarity.

[22] Cf. Ep 4:15f.

[23] The Dutch Dominican Edward Schillebeeckx expressed the growing desire for Christian Unity this way:

Since World War II the idea that non-Catholic communities might be recognized as Churches has been gaining ground among Catholics, and the view was confirmed by the Second Vatican Council. This has served to point up in a particularly painful way the abnormality of the situation in which Christianity has been placed by the divisions in the one Church of Christ. But at the same time it has contained for Catholic theologians the implication that Christian experience outside the Catholic Church is also a locus theologicus *a place which provides material for theology. The Protestant experience of the Eucharist must therefore be taken into consideration by Catholic theologians. It is only in dialogue with Protestants that a truly Catholic interpretation of this datum of faith is completely meaningful. All Christians have to learn from each other it is no longer possible for one Christian community to exclude another a* priori. (*The Eucharist*, op. cit., p. 105). Cf. also the ecumenical studies presented by Senn (ed.), op. cit., and Thurian/Wainwright (eds.), op. cit.

for the truth of manifesting Christ's presence in and to the world. The Eucharist as the Mystery of Faith is especially the test and challenge of our times. At every celebration we pray, as Christ did at the Last Supper, for the communion of Christ's faithful and for the unity of the world. To neglect to do this — or to do so without yearning for it and living it in the spirit of genuine acceptance of others — would be to forsake the divinely revealed truth of the Mystery of Communion. Ecumenism — or rather, commitment to pray and work for Christian unity — is not an optional extra! It is of the very fibre of the Gospel proclamation and the extension of the sacrifice we celebrate in the Mystery of Faith. In the words of St. Cyprian of Carthage, whose attitude was exemplary in his struggle for the unity of the Church against the divisive rigorism of the Donatists in the third century:

> The God of peace, the teacher of harmony, who taught unity, willed that each should pray for all, according as he carried us all in himself.[24]

The Eucharistic Prayer which, as we have seen above, proclaims our union with Christ in his sacrifice for the "peace and unity" of the world, enables us to meet the challenge facing us to sacrifice ourselves for Christian unity.[25] There is no doubt that our inability (for sound theological reasons) to share the gift of Christ's Body and Blood continues to be a source of deep pain. If it is not so it is a matter

---

[24] D.O,, III, p. 193.

[25] The Bishops of England and Wales declared in 1980: *"We feel able to remark that, although we are still divided, although we have not achieved that unity for which Christ prayed the night before he died, we are becoming almost imperceptibly one community in process of reconciliation: we have achieved albeit with the reservation that our common sinfulness and blurred vision imposes on such an affirmation — a reconciliation in charity"* (*The Easter People*, n. 70; op. cit., p. 27). Cardinal Basil Hume's decisive intervention at the Ecumenical Conference at Swanwick, Derbyshire in 1987 merits being recalled: *"I hope that our Roman Catholic delegates at this Conference will recommend to members of our Church that we move now quite deliberately from a situation of cooperation to one of commitment to each other. By 'commitment to each other' I mean that we commit ourselves to praying and working together for Church unity, and to acting together, both nationally and locally, for evangelization and mission. [. . .] This will be in response to a gospel imperative, and, in our case, following a clear directive from the Second Vatican Council. [. . .] Christian unity is a gift from God."*

of concern and, indeed, we are the less truly Christ-like in our sensitivity![26] Entering into the spirit of Christ's sacrifice for unity does not take away the heart-searching pain which comes from not being able yet to participate fully in communion in Christ's passover love, but it does give us the grace to bear this suffering generously in confident hope that some day what should be "*our* daily bread" will be accessible to all Christians every time they celebrate the memorial sacrifice of the Lord's passover sacrament. The Bread of the Eucharistic Sacrifice of Praise already gives us a taste of what we pray at the end of the Eucharistic Prayer: "*all good things,*" which come through Christ — especially Christian unity, the visible expression of the Holy Communion with the Blessed Trinity.

---

[26] Cf. Rosemary Goldie's talk to the National Delegates preparing for the 44th International Eucharistic Congress in Seoul (*The International Eucharistic Congresses for a New Evangelization*, op. cit., pp. 109-119). She quotes the words of Cardinal Willebrand's homily at the I.E.C. of Nairobi (August 1985):

It is a tragedy that on the occasion of this Congress to thank God for the gift of the Holy Eucharist, we are still unable to share together at the Lord's Table, that we still lack that oneness in faith, that unity in apostolic order which is necessary to give the Eucharist its integrity. This must be a burden of suffering which keeps alive in our hearts a determination to persevere in every effort that can bring us nearer to the full profession of a common faith that would enable us to gather about one altar (ibid., p. 118).

6

In the Light of Salvation History
(Eucharistic Prayer IV)

[We] do not forget even for a moment that it was Jesus Christ, the Son of the living God, who became our reconciliation with the Father (Rm 5:11; Col 1:20). He it was and he alone, who satisfied the Father's eternal love, that fatherhood that from the beginning found expression in creating the world, giving human beings all the riches of creation, and making them "little less than God" (Ps 8:6), in that they were created "in the image and likeness of God" (cf. Gn 1:26). He and he alone also satisfied that fatherhood of God and that love which human beings rejected by breaking the first covenant (cf. Gn 3:6-13) and the later covenants that God "again and again offered to them" (cf. Eucharistic Prayer IV). The redemption of the world — this tremendous mystery of love in which creation is renewed (cf. G.S., n. 37; L.G., n. 48) — is, at its deepest root, the fullness of justice in a human Heart — the Heart of the Firstborn Son — in order that it may become justice in the hearts of many human beings, predestined from eternity in the Firstborn Son to be children of God (cf. Rm 8:29-30; Ep 1:8) and called to grace, called to love. The Cross on Calvary, through which Jesus Christ — a Man, the Son of the Virgin Mary, thought to be the son of Joseph of Nazareth — "leaves" this world, is also a fresh manifestation of the eternal fatherhood of God, who in him draws near again to humanity, to each human being, to whom he bestows the thrice holy "Spirit of truth" (cf. Jn 16:13). This revelation of the Father and outpouring of the Holy Spirit, which stamp an indelible seal on the mystery of the Redemption, explain the meaning of the Cross and death of Christ.[1]

---

[1] Pope John Paul II, Encyclical Letter *Redemptor Hominis* [R.H.], n. 9; translation in Ed. Ancora, Milano, p. 18f. (amended).

Eucharistic Prayer IV differs from the others not only because of its length, but also because of the rich variety of themes woven around the central motif of the history of salvation. In structure too this *anaphora* differs since it presents a continuation of the proclamation of praise after the *Sanctus*. Whereas the main verbs in the pre-*Sanctus* are related to thanking and glorifying, those after the *Sanctus* are to do with acclamation, confession and praise.[2] The significance of this is noteworthy from the theological perspective of this Prayer, which is closer to the doxological aspects of the ancient credal professions of faith than is the case in our other Eucharistic Prayers. In fact the main features of the style and theological approach of this Prayer resemble an *anaphora* of St. Basil and the Eastern tradition of liturgy from Antioch, on which it was modelled. These are characterized by: a Trinitarian profession of faith and confident celebration of human dignity in the work of salvation.[3] Both these features are developed around the *Sanctus*, which has an integral place — and is not an interruption — in the community's eucharistic song on behalf of creation. The *Sanctus* is the linchpin, as it were, holding the content and structure of this *anaphora* together. Hence, whenever this Eucharistic Prayer is used its own Preface must be employed.[4]

Praise in the name of every creation under heaven

All the ancient eucharistic liturgies begin with thanksgiving for creation before going on to praise and thank God for the work of redemption in and through Christ.[5] In this Prayer, which is truly a

---

[2] Mazza notes that the verbs used before the *Sanctus* are "thank" and "glory," whereas those following it are "acclaim" or "confess" (that is, "praise") and that the object of praise of God's greatness, i.e. transcendence, which is manifest in his creative actions of wisdom and love, which are perfect — cf. *The Eucharistic Prayers*, op. cit., p. 164.

[3] Cf. Mazza, *The Eucharistic Prayers*, op. cit., p. 170.

[4] Cf. GIRM, n. 322 d) & e); cf. Maloney, op. cit., p. 56; Mazza, op. cit., pp. 158 ff., 327, n. 46.

[5] Cf. McPartlan, op. cit., p. 296, quoting Zizioulas (fn. 47): "'In certain cases, like that of the eucharistic liturgy commented upon by St. Cyril of Jerusalem in his *Mystagogical Catecheses*, the thanksgiving for creation seems to be the only point of the eucharistic canon, with no mention at all of the sacrifice of Christ.' [. . .] Yarnold notes that there is sacrificial terminology and reference to 'offering the slain Christ' in the *Mystagogical*

credo of delight in God — a song of God's holiness — the Church on behalf of all creation participates in the Eucharist in reverent confidence. This eucharistic proclamation integrates the themes of creation and redemption in the revelation of God's loving care for humanity which leads to sharing in the eternal worship of his kingdom:

> . . . in your kingdom, freed from the corruption of sin and death, we shall sing your glory with every creature through Christ our Lord, through whom you give us everything that is good.[6]

But, already in the Church's eucharistic celebration we begin to realize and share in glorifying the work of God's love by uniting with the unceasing contemplation and praise of the *"countless hosts of angels"*:

> United with them and in the name of every creature under heaven, we too praise your glory . . .

The pre-Sanctus part or Preface of this Prayer presents briefly the overall motive for thanking and glorifying God the Creator, namely, his design to include humanity in the uninterrupted delight of beholding the splendor of his eternal beauty. While having a distinct place in the created order or hierarchy of being, humanity's voice of thanksgiving and praise harmonizes in the orchestration of the whole of creation's delight, complementing the song of the higher angelic intelligences and also the *"silent music"* of all that is lower than human

---

Catecheses (The Awe-inspiring Rites of Initiation, p. 91, n. 16). However, Zizioulas' point is simply to illustrate 'how central the reference to creation was in the ancient liturgies'."

[6] This ICEL translation has the verb in the indicative future tense ("we shall sing"), whereas the original Latin expresses a prayer to be united with the inheritance of the Blessed Virgin and saints in their worship: *"grant [. . .] that we may obtain an inheritance in heaven with the Blessed Virgin Mary [. . .] in your kingdom where, with all creatures, now freed from the corruption of sin and death, we may glorify you through Christ [. . .] ."* In other words, our version somewhat weakens the sense of the intrinsic link between prayer and the eschatological hope — a link that is evident in the Latin.

beings, *"all things bright and beautiful."*[7] This section of the *anaphora* may thus be regarded as providing a more rounded or complete and concise theological statement than what appears in other Prefaces. It expresses the essential quality and nature of creaturely worship and touches on the "pre-history" of salvation as a prelude to Christian worship. This proclamation is taken up after the *Sanctus* and becomes the motive for acclamation or praise. The beauty of worship pertains to the essence of God's creation: it springs from the heart of all creatures in which God has etched the instinct to praise him.[8] In praising God human beings realize their truest joy for they perform and fulfill their fundamental nature and work as the greatest labor of love. In this they reflect God's being as his image.[9] Ingeniously George Herbert relates the idea of image to the metaphor of window by alluding to the New Testament teaching on God's people becoming a living temple where his glory is worshiped not by mere words, but by *"Doctrine and life, colours and light, in one [/] When they combine and mingle"*:

> Lord, how can man preach thy eternal word?
> He is a brittle, crazy glass;
> Yet in thy temple thou dost him afford

---

[7] The phrase "silent music" comes from St. John of the Cross; the opening words of the lovely hymn by C.F. Alexander (1818-95) also seem apt here. Tertullian says that all things "pray," birds being raised to heaven on their two wings like the *orante's* extended arms in the classical Judeo-Christian posture of prayer — Cf. *De oratione*, 28; translation in the Ante-Nicene Christian Library, Vol. XI, T. & T. Clark, Edinburgh, 1869, p. 204 (near the end of the treatise — translation slightly amended): *". . . the birds too, rising out of the nest, upraise themselves heavenward, and, instead of hands, expand the cross of their wings, and say something sounding like prayer."* St. Francis of Assisi offers the best known teaching regarding the praise of the fraternity of all creatures in the *Canticle of the Sun.*

[8] Cf. St. Augustine's well-known theme at the opening of the *Confessions*, I.1.

[9] Strangely ICEL gives *"likeness"*! Much was made of the biblical and patristic doctrine of the "image and likeness of God" in the Second Vatican Council's positive and heartening teaching on Christians' relationship to, responsibility for, and role in this world, in which the Church itself must be involved. This is particularly elaborated in the great Constitution on the Church in the Modern World, *Gaudium et Spes* — cf. n. 12; and especially nn. 38-39 where human activity is related to its fulfillment in the celebration of paschal mystery in the Eucharist.

This glorious and transcendent place,
To be a window, through thy grace.[10]

"Eternity in an Hour"[11]

Eucharistic Prayer IV recalls the profound doctrine of St. Irenaeus on the recapitulation of all things in Christ.[12] This doctrine, which is based on Ephesians 1:10, has implications that have perhaps not been fully appreciated in a post-Augustinian perspective. This is because such a perspective for all its richness is somewhat limited by the concept of time which was imposed on Western thought by St. Augustine, whose fascination with human consciousness and the phenomenological account of psychological change tended to do little justice to the effects of sin or salvation on the material world.[13] In other words, by his, albeit brilliant, penetration into the workings of human awareness in which he sought the key to interpreting the meaning of time, Augustine nevertheless succeeded in severing

---

[10] *The Windows — The New Oxford Book of Christian Verse*, O.U.P., 1981, n. 60; cf. also *Church Monuments*; and also *Man*:

> *Since then, my God, thou hast*
> *So brave a Palace built; O dwell in it,*
> *That it may dwell with thee at last!*
> *Till then, afford us so much wit;*
> *That, as the world serves us, we may serve thee,*
> *And both thy servants be.*
>
> (*The Metaphysical Poets*, op. cit., p. 131.)

William Shakespeare's amazement at human grandeur is somewhat different in Hamlet's famous soliloquy: *"What a piece of work is man!"* — Cf. *Hamlet*, Ac. II, Sc. ii.

[11] Cf. William Blake, *Auguries of Innocence*:

> *To see a World in a Grain of Sand,*
> *And a Heaven in a Wild Flower,*
> *Hold Infinity in the palm of your hand,*
> *And Eternity in an hour.*

[12] Cf. my article, "The Glory of God, Man fully alive in the Eucharist" in *Adoremus*, vol. LXII, 1982, No. 2, pp. 14-21.

[13] McPartlan notes the amazing fact that in all his major writings St. Augustine makes no mention of Ep 1:10 regarding recapitulation —cf., op. cit., p. 292. He attributes de Lubac's inability to integrate all creation into a vision of the kingdom partly to Augustine's influence.

human beings from the rest of the material world. On the other hand, Irenaeus, who relied on St. Paul's insight regarding the recapitulation of all things in Christ, presented a broader, indeed universal approach to salvation and, hence, to worship.[14]

To take one example. In the following passage Irenaeus deals with the newness of worship, which consists not in our ritual (as differing from that of the Jews or pagans) but in the Christian use of God's gift of creation's first fruits:

> [Christ] counselled his disciples to offer to God the first fruits of his own creation; not that God needed this, but so that they might be neither unfruitful nor ungrateful. He took an element of creation, bread, and giving thanks said: "This is my body." In the same way he declared the cup, which is of the same creation as ourselves, to be his blood, and taught that it was the new offering of the new covenant. It is this offering which the Church has received from the apostles and which, throughout the whole world, it offers to the God who gives us food, as the first fruits of his own gifts under the new covenant.[15]

Just as in Irenaeus, for whom worship leads to and expresses the unity and peace or harmonization of mankind and the material world, so too in this Eucharistic Prayer there is no dichotomy between the community of human persons and nature.[16] This community realizes a new order coming about not merely through observation of the temporal order alone, but through celebrating the *mystery of faith* in time. The proclamation of this faith of the Church extends human awareness to realize the attitude of Christ's love.[17]

---

[14] McPartlan (ibid., fn. 20) instances five places in Irenaeus where the Pauline text is referred to: *Adversus Haereses*, I.3,3; 1.10,1; III.16,6; III.21,9; V.20,2.

[15] *Adversus Haereses*, IV.17.4; transl. in D.O. III, op. cit., p. 401.

[16] In a sense, perhaps more deeply than William Wordsworth meant, eucharistic worship enables us to recapture the youthful innocence of humanity's vocation to be "Nature's priest" — cf. *Ode, Intimations of Immortality*.

[17] As St. Paul constantly challenges Christian believers by calling for a "revolution" in their way of thinking/acting so that they "have in them the mind of Christ" and become "con-formed" to him — cf. especially Ph 2:1-11; also Rm 12:2; Ep 4:23; 5:10.

Such a proclamation in the Eucharistic Prayer itself expresses the coming about of this new awareness of Christ's consecration of all things in love. Love not only opens up, but is a new kind of awareness of the heart which exceeds rational knowing or understanding.[18] The *mystery of faith*, that is, the Church's proclamation of Christ's deed of passover love, gives us access to this awareness of the heart of God towards whom the human *heart in pilgrimage* tends. This pilgrimage is but a reflection of God's search for humanity, his heart's cherished creation:

> ... when through disobedience they [human beings] had lost your friendship, you did not abandon them to the power of death. In your mercy you came to the aid of all of them, so that they might seek and find you. You offered many covenants to human beings and taught them through the prophets to hope for salvation.[19]

The fact that the eucharistic proclamation leads to acknowledging what the change of the bread and wine signifies is more evident in comparing the Latin and ICEL texts of the eucharistic *epiclesis*, where the profound theological motivation is indicated by the phrase *"so that"* which governs the twofold request that follows — not only the transformation of the material elements, but also:

> so that [...] we may celebrate the great mystery which he left us as an everlasting covenant.[20]

Furthermore, as the original Latin of the words of the Institution Narrative in this Prayer clearly express better than the rather "choppy" ICEL translation, the Church's proclamation enters into the time-

---

[18] Pascal's famous dictum springs to mind: *"Le coeur a ses raisons que la raison ne connaît point"* ["The heart has its reasons which reason knows nothing of"] (*Pensées*, iv.277). Cf. also Newman's *Grammar of Assent*, Ch. IV on "Notional and Real Assent."

[19] This literal translation (as in Mazza, op. cit., p. 155) brings out aspects not in our ICEL version — e.g., God's tender mercy, human beings. This is well expressed in the words quoted from Pope John Paul II's first Encyclical Letter at the beginning of this chapter.

[20] Cf. Mazza's remarks on this in *The Eucharistic Prayers*, op. cit., p. 173.

transcending, history-transforming "Hour" of Christ's loving attitude:

LITERAL TRANSLATION:

ICEL TRANSLATION:

For when the hour had come for him to be glorified by you, holy Father, having loved his own who were in the world, he loved them to the end; and as they were eating ...

He always loved those who were his own in the world. When the time came for him to be glorified by you, his heavenly Father, he showed the depth of his love. While they were at supper ...

This Prayer explicitly refers to that "Hour" which St. John presents as the supreme realization of God's glorious and glorifying love.[21] The significance of the *anamnesis*, thereby, becomes all the richer for it "incarnates" Christ's awareness of love in which the Christian community is united by being faithful to his ordinance in carrying out his command: *"Do this in memory of me."*[22] In virtue of this proclamation of being united in a faith-awareness in Christ's love, moreover, the Church's intercessions reach out to all; they span all spatio-temporal gulfs of separation and sectarian or religious divisions by praying for:

all who seek you with a sincere heart. [...] all the dead, whose faith is known to you alone.

This does not imply that sincerity is all! Sincerity must not be identified with truth, whose *splendor* can never be compared to a subjective reaching for or even grasp of it. For as George Herbert says: *"Is there in truth no beauty?"*[23] But, in prayerfully acknowledging

---

[21] Cf. Maloney, op. cit., p. 78. The two Johannine texts combined here are: Jn 13:1 and 17:1.

[22] Mazza rightly insists on the theological importance of this as normative for the Church's liturgical action — cf. ibid., p. 173ff.

[23] Cf. Jordan (I) — somewhat different from the rather confused identification of John Keats: *"'Beauty is truth, truth beauty,' that is all [/] Ye know on earth, and all ye need to know."* (*Ode on a Grecian Urn*). He was perhaps nearer the mark at the opening of *Endymion*: *"A thing of beauty is a joy for ever: [/] Its loveliness increases; it will never [/] Pass into nothingness."* For do not aesthetics have deeper levels than those which are apparent in the dim light of the caverns of mere sensation?

others' sincerity in prayer the Church discovers the proper context for and opens the door to authentic dialogue.[24]

Spiritual revelation through the Incarnation

Our appreciation of the "incarnational" approach of this Prayer can be enhanced by comparing it to the teaching of St. John of the Cross about God gracing creation — a teaching which seems to be most relevant here. In his prose commentary on a stanza of his *Spiritual Canticle,*[25] the Spanish mystic theologian explains that the creatures of the world are "like a trace of God's passing"; God created them by "looking at" them:

> His look clothes the world and all the heavens with beauty and gladness, just as He also, upon opening His hand, fills every animal with blessing, as David says (Psalm 144:16).[26]

---

[24] *Vide infra* Chapter VII on reconciliation of different religious approaches. In his Encyclical Letter, *Redemptoris Missio* on the permanent validity of the Church's missionary mandate, Pope John Paul II clearly states: "I recently wrote to the Bishops of Asia: 'Although the Church gladly acknowledges whatever is true and holy in the religious traditions of Buddhism, Hinduism and Islam as a reflection of the truth which enlightens all, this does not lessen her duty and resolve to proclaim without fail Jesus Christ who is "the way, and the truth and the life" . . . The fact that the followers of other religions can receive God's grace and be saved by Christ apart from the ordinary means which he has established does not thereby cancel the call to faith and baptism which God wills for all people. Indeed Christ himself 'while expressly insisting on the need for faith and baptism, at the same time confirmed the need for the Church, into which people enter through Baptism as through a door.' Dialogue should be conducted and implemented with the conviction that the Church is the ordinary means of salvation and that she alone possesses the fulness of the means of salvation." (R.M., n. 55; translation (slightly amended) in CTS Do601, p. 39 —citing the Letter to the 5th Plenary Assembly of Asian Bishops' Conference, 23 June 1990, 4; also L.G., n. 14; A.G., n. 7; U.R., n. 3.)

[25] Cf. "Songs between the soul and the bridegroom" in *Poems of St. John of the Cross* (translated by Roy Campbell) Collins Fount, 1979, p. 15.

[26] *The Spiritual Canticle — Commentary in the Collected Works of St. John of the Cross* (translated by Kieran Kavanaugh and Otilio Rodriguez, Institute of Carmelite Studies Publ., Washington, D.C., 1979, p. 436.

He goes further in stating that God clothed creatures in beauty not only by creating them, but also by

> imparting to them supernatural being. This He did when He became man and elevated human nature in the beauty of God and consequently all creatures, since in human nature He was united with them all. Accordingly, the Son of God proclaimed: "If I be lifted up from the earth, I will elevate all things to Me' (Jn 12:32). And in this elevation of all things through the Incarnation of His Son and through the glory of His resurrection according to the flesh, the Father did not merely beautify things partially, but rather we can say, clothed them wholly in beauty and dignity.

In these days when attention is being directed to "ecological issues" — that is, human responsibility in caring for creation — it is well worth taking up the commentary of John of the Cross on the *"Spiritual Canticle."* For his capacity to see creation as sacramental, which made him a mystic and poet, also made him conscious of the delicate interdependence of the Creator's works. This interdependence or harmony of creation, as John of the Cross sees it, is only possible because all creatures are nurtured by God. Not even sin, which temporarily disrupts this harmony of creation, as Eucharistic Prayer IV brings out, can thwart God's ultimately positive purpose for his creation. For whereas we are capable of regarding creation and redemption as successive in time, God whose being is eternity, creates all things in full knowledge both of the Fall and the work of his Son's loving obedience to his will — the eternal will to save the beauty his heart creates. Creatures are rooted deeply in God who is in the deepest sense, then, their Culture of Life.[27]

---

[27] Despite its laudable concern about ecology and development of a sense of care for creation, the serious mistake of the California-based "New Age" movement consists in emphasizing grace without sufficient reference to what necessitates grace, namely, sin and our need for repentance from sin through traditional practices of confession, asceticism, etc. A much sounder approach is offered by the 18th century divine Humphry Primatt, whose neglected classic has recently been republished: *The Duty of Mercy and the Sin of Cruelty to Brute Animals*, Centaur Press. The teaching of this author, which inspired the foundation of the Royal Society for the Prevention of Cruelty to Animals (RSPCA), is solidly based on common sense and on Scripture, which he uses in a delightful way.

"Freed from the corruption of sin and death"

The theme of liberation, on which we focused above in dealing with Eucharistic Prayer II, is implicit throughout this Prayer. It is the other side of the coin of the cosmic canticle in praise of God for Christ the Word and for the power of his Spirit which comes to the aid of even the groanings of creation.[28] Eucharist is offered not only because the whole of the material world shares in the liberation realized by God's covenant with humanity in the mystery of Christ, but also because it is the first expression of *liberated being*. In other words, while *"it is right"* that God is praised by his creatures for this is his due, it is even more fitting that intelligent creatures offer this freely and joyously. Otherwise it would mean that they are unaware of being freed from sinful egoism and pride to acknowledge the Other as their loving Savior. Thus God's original design to establish human beings as rulers or caretakers of creation is proclaimed as restored in the new covenant of Christ. The celebration of this covenant in Christian worship communicates the true worth, dignity, joy and every spiritual gift and benefit which result from God's liberating love in Christ's unique sacrifice, by sharing in which humanity discovers the art of representing God in the world.

The whole Prayer is bathed in the light of God's patient revelation. This revelation gradually unfolds in the course of salvation history: it is adapted to our human condition of being slow learners because of sin and is shaped to accommodate the environment and circumstances of those with special needs — as, for example, the poor, prisoners, and those in sorrow. These are classical cases which the Good News of the Messiah addresses:[29]

> Again and again you offered a covenant to man, and through the prophets taught him to hope for salvation. Father, you so loved the world that in the fulness of time you sent your only Son to be our Savior. [. . .]
> To the poor he proclaimed the good news of salvation, to prisoners freedom, and to those in sorrow joy.

---

[28] Cf. Rm 8.
[29] Cf. Lk 4:1ff.

What all these diverse situations have in common is the darkness of sin which prevents enjoying the delight and freedom of worship; all share in common the essential need of Christ, *the Light of the Nations*.[30] His Good News of friendship, freedom and joy is for each and all who are drawn into God's offer of salvation so that in his kingdom *"freed from the corruption of sin and death"* we may freely join in the new and eternal canticle of creation.[31]

In a remarkable paragraph of his Encyclical Letter on divine mercy Pope John Paul II offers a fine meditative commentary on the theme of revelation which this *anaphora* presents as the dawning of the light of Christian awareness through worship. This paragraph is unmistakably inspired by the character of passover love celebrated in this Eucharistic Prayer:

> Although God "dwells in unapproachable light" (1 Tm 6:16), he speaks to man by means of the whole of the universe: "ever since the creation of the world his invisible nature, namely, his eternal power and deity, has been clearly perceived in the things that have been made" (Rm 1:20). This indirect and imperfect knowledge, achieved by the intellect seeking God by means of creatures through the visible world, falls short of "vision of the Father." "No one has ever seen God," writes Saint John, in order to stress the truth that "the only Son, who is in the bosom of the Father, he has made him known" (Jn 1:18). This "making known" reveals God in the most profound mystery of his being, one and three, surrounded by "unapproachable light." Nevertheless, through this "making known" by Christ we know God above all in his relationship of love for

---

[30] Cf. St. Vincent de Paul's *Letters and Spiritual Conferences*, Paris, 1922-1925 — e.g. n. 2546: *"We must not merely regulate our attitude to the poor by considering their external or interior needs. We should rather view them in the light of faith. [. . .] We must enter into the mind of Christ which we should make our own."* Cf. also the talk given by Sister Juana Elizondo Leiza, Superior General of the Daughters of Charity, at the 45th I.E.C., Seville: "The Social Challenge Flowing from Sharing in and Adoring the Eucharist" (to be published with other papers and Acts of this Congress by Éditions Paulines, Montreal).

[31] For an ecumenical parallel to this Prayer — *vide* the Church of England *Alternative Service Book* (1980) Holy Communion, Rite A: "Through him you have freed us from the slavery of sin . . ." — cf. *Baptism and Eucharist: Ecumenical Convergence in Celebration*, op. cit., p. 163.

man: in his "philanthropy" (Tt 3:4). It is precisely here that "his invisible nature" becomes in a special way "visible," incomparably more visible than through all the other "things that have been made": it becomes visible in Christ and through Christ, through his actions and his words, and finally through his death on the Cross and his Resurrection.[32]

The theme of liberation and human freedom is appropriately situated within the Christological section of this Prayer. It is related to the grace of discernment or wisdom which worship bestows. Wisdom is the essential condition for true liberation. But we must not forget that the beginning of wisdom is the *"fear of the Lord,"* which is the virtue of religion or true devotion—that is, the reverential awe of love which binds us to seek God in and through all things and to do his will.[33] We would be the poorer to forget that the fear of the Lord or a sense of awe is one of the seven-fold gifts of the Risen Lord's Holy Spirit,[34] for whom this Prayer gives the Father praise and thanksgiving. The folly of human disobedience of God and refusal to serve or worship — under the shoddy pretexts of exercising freedom, of achievement, of imagined fulfillment, of staking a claim for autonomy or whatever — is patiently corrected, or rather, transformed by Christ's gift of himself: *"In fulfillment of your will he gave himself up to death."* He wins us over by the logic of divine love through which he became *"a man like us in all things but sin."* This logic — or to call it by its proper biblical name: wisdom — would otherwise remain hidden from us *"in unapproachable light"* except that it is recognized through being manifested in the Eucharist by the Holy Spirit, Christ's *"first gift to those who believe."* By his Spirit Christ enables us to discern his Body in the Church's mystery of his sacrament and, thus, he draws us *"to live no longer for ourselves but for him."* Only by living for Christ do we

---

[32] Cf. D.M., n. 2; translation in CTS n. 526, p. 6f.

[33] Cf. Ps 111:10; Pr 1:7. The fear of the Lord is equivalent to the virtue of religion or devotion.

[34] Cf. Is 11:2. In three major works St. Augustine formally treats the links between the gifts of the Holy Spirit and the seven steps to the beauty of divine wisdom: cf. *De quantitate animae*, XXXIII, 70-76; *De Doctrina Christiana*, II. vii, 9-11; and *De Genesi contra Manichaeos*, I. xxv, 43; cf. also *Serm.* 216, 7.7, 8.8; *Serm.* 347; *De Trinitate*, XII. xv, 25.

live as adorers of the Father, who reveals the wisdom of his kingdom of love to those "little ones" receptive and faithful to his Word in their hearts like the Virgin Mary, the image and model of the worshiping Church.[35]

Exploration into God[36]

God's love reaching from eternity into time is beheld, contemplated, proclaimed, and celebrated with loving awe. In a splendid treatment of the Eucharist in the light of the paschal mystery, Martelet shows that the Church's liturgy presents "the unplumbed depths of the one unique hypostatic union,"[37] since here we are enabled to appreciate the dimensions of the cosmic reality of the whole eucharistic mystery (and not merely the "Real Presence" in a restricted sense) as the full extension of the incarnation. In other words, by God becoming incarnate, he has brought about a still more intimate relationship between the visible and the invisible — or in Balthasar's phrase: *"a unique hypostatic union between archetype and image."*[38] The paschal mystery of the incarnate Word of God enables a realization of the spiritual potential of matter and raises it to the level of sacrament. This is what is implied in this Prayer.

Thanks to the gift of the Holy Spirit, who continues to lead the Church to become aware of and explore the depths of God's truth and hidden wisdom, the Father's gift of Christ, "our passover," is never withdrawn from humanity.[39] But this awareness, this exploration is always in the spirit of praise and adoration — the spirit of divine worship — since the Holy Spirit enables and empowers us to acknowledge God as Father (*"abba"*) and Jesus Christ as "the Lord."[40] This

---

[35] Cf. Jn 4:23f.; Mt 11:25-27; 1 Cor 1:26-29, etc. Cf. also L.G., nn. 60-68.

[36] Cf. Christopher Fry, *A Sleep for Prisoners.* Cf. also T.S. Eliot, *Four Quartets — Little Gidding V: "We shall not cease from exploration . . ."*

[37] G. Martelet, *The Risen Christ and the Eucharistic World*, p. 143.

[38] *The Glory of the Lord*, I, op. cit., p. 432.

[39] Cf. Jn 14:16f.; 16:13ff.; 1 Cor 2:6ff.; 5:7. Cf. also 1 Cor 2:9-13.

[40] Cf. Rm 8:12-17; Gal 4:17 and Rm 10:9; 1 Cor 12:3; Col 2:6; also Jn 6:44; 1 Jn 5:1, etc.

Eucharistic Prayer is an exercise in this vital exploration which has its roots, as every eucharistic celebration does, in Christ's paschal mystery, that beginning which orientates humanity to its true end. The role of the Holy Spirit is thus described here as bringing about this end or ultimate purpose in God's saving design, namely, a community of worshipers:[41]

Before the first *epiclesis:* (Literal translation)	Ecclesial *epiclesis:* (ICEL)
[Christ] sent from you, Father, as the first fruits for believers, the Holy Spirit who would finish his work in the world and bring all holiness to completion.	Lord, look upon this sacrifice which you have given to your Church; and by your Holy Spirit, gather all who share this one bread and one cup into the one body of Christ, a living sacrifice of praise.

"Light invisible we praise you"[42]

Referring again to the words of Pope John Paul II's Encyclical Letter cited above, we are helped to appreciate better the unique role of Christ in revealing the mystery of the heart of God to humanity by becoming *"a man like us in all things but sin."* This is the great

---

[41] As appears more clearly in the Latin text.

[42] Cf. T.S. Eliot, *Choruses from 'The Rock'*, X, which presents a litany-like hymn in praise of the splendor of the Invisible God whose light mysteriously penetrates and plays through the variegated panes of human experience:

> *O Light Invisible, we praise Thee!*
> *Too bright for mortal vision.*
> *O Greater Light, we praise Thee for the less; [. . .]*
> *O Light Invisible, we worship Thee!*
> *We thank Thee for the lights that we have kindled,*
> *The light of altar and of sanctuary;*
> *Small lights of those who meditate at midnight*
> *And lights directed through the coloured panes of windows*
> *And light reflected from the polished stone,*
> *The gilded carven wood, the coloured fresco.*
> *Our gaze is submarine, our eyes look upward*
> *And see the light that fractures through unquiet water.*
> *We see the light but see not whence it comes.*
> *O Light Invisible, we glorify Thee!*

reversal: instead of human beings reaching up to resemble the likeness of God, Christ descends to take on human likeness; instead of remaining in the exclusive uniqueness of divine communion, the Eternal Word penetrates the sinful condition of human solitude and permeates it with the divine quality of communicability—love which enables human beings to dialogue at the highest level in the light of worship. God reveals himself as no solitary: Christian worship celebrates his being as communion. The Eucharistic Prayer — especially this proclamation — highlights sacramentality as the way leading to the mystery of God, as the truth of spirituality, as the life of authentic human being. It exemplifies well the necessity for sacramental spirituality being grounded in the proclamation of God's living Word. In St. Augustine's phrase, sacraments are the *"Word made visible"*[43] For, as this great-hearted Father teaches, on earth we cannot dispense with the condition of needing signs drawn from created realities.[44] This eucharistic proclamation especially expresses the fulness of Love's communication — that fulness which knows continuity in the Church's proclamation or *prayerful Word*.

This fulness and continuity is clearly evident at the end of the Christological section of Eucharistic Prayer IV which fittingly leads into the eucharistic *epiclesis*. The twofold action of the divine Word and Spirit is expressed by three Latin verbs concerned with fulfillment or completion (*impleret . . . perficiens . . . compleret*):[45]

---

[43] "Verbum visibile" — Cf. *Contra Faustum*, 19, 16; *In Joh. Ev.*, Tr. 80.3. This phrase must be the most concise and unsurpassedly rich description of what a sacrament is, especially when it is linked with the communication of the Word and Holy Spirit as Augustine's sermons amply illustrate: cf. *Serm.* 227, 1; *Serm. Denis*, VI, 1 & 3; *Serm. Guelf.*, VII, 1, etc.

[44] Cf. *De Doctrina Christiana*, II, 1-5 & III; cf. also *De Consensu Evang.*, IV, 10.20: *"Whoever thinks that in this mortal life a man may so disperse the mists of bodily and carnal imaginings as to possess the unclouded light of changeless truth [. . .] understands neither what he seeks, nor himself the seeker."*

[45] The ICEL version does well to translate *"dispensatione"* by will, for to say "dispensation," "economy," "arrangement," "design" or "plan" would probably mean little to people today, whereas "will" catches the sense of the concise biblical expression of the Latin.

ICEL:	LATIN:
In fulfillment of your will he gave himself up to death; [...] he sent the Holy Spirit [...] to complete his work on earth and bring us the fulness of grace.	Ut tuam vero dispensationem impleret, in mortem tradidit semetipsum [...] misit Spiritum Sanctum [...] qui, opus suum in mundo perficiens, omnem sanctificationem compleret.

The fulness revealed by the Word-made-flesh and communicated by the Spirit evokes and impels an appropriate response from us believers — a response that means a decrease of selfishness and increase of Christ's life of love: *"that we might live no longer* [non amplius] *for ourselves but for him."* This phrase, which refers to 2 Corinthians 5:15, is often quoted by the Fathers; St. Basil, for instance, cites it in a eucharistic context to define the nature of a Christian as one who increases in divine life by participating in the sacramental sacrifice of redemption.[46]

This notion of the continuity of Christ's communication of fullness, moreover, finds ample expression throughout this Prayer from beginning to end. The preface opens by glorifying *"the one God, living and true"*[47] — source of all abundant gifts, who *"fills* [adimpleres] *your creatures with every blessing."* The fulness of Christ's love *"unto the end"*[48] is manifest in taking the *"cup, filled with wine."* Before the doxology Christ is acknowledged as the channel *"through whom you give us everything that is good."*[49] To discern the truth, goodness, integrity and beauty in everything is ultimately to acknowledge the presence of God. The strain of reading, of trying to discern in the signs

---

[46] Cf. Mazza, *The Eucharistic Prayers*, op. cit., p. 168. Mazza refers to three places in St. Basil — *Moralia*, 80, 22 (PG 31:870); also, ibid., 21 (PG 31:739); and *Regulae brevius tractatae*, 172 (PG 31:1195).

[47] Strangely ICEL changes the sense somewhat by giving: *"You alone are God, living and true".*

[48] Again, ICEL lacks the rich biblical texture of the Latin, which states: *"so that he would love those who were his own in the world, he loved them unto the end."*

[49] Cf. Ep 1:10f. This sense of deep gratitude for the abundance of God's gracious gifts and blessings finds expression repeatedly in George Herbert's poems — cf. e.g., *The Pulley, Aaron, Easter Wings, Redemption.*

of the times God's presence is momentarily relieved, as it were, while the Church proclaims in praise and thanksgiving the mystery of its faith in what Christ accomplished and communicates sacramentally by his passover love.[50] Christ's glory is the depth of God's love in which Christians participate. He is loved as no one has been, is, or ever will be loved, as no one is worthy to be so loved — by his countless followers and, above all, by his Father. This atmosphere of love's light is what the proclamation of this Prayer magnificently creates.

The symbolism of light from time immemorial has fascinated the human heart in its religious imagination.[51] The Christian imagination no less has from the time of the Great Fathers of the Church called the two essential sacraments, Baptism and Eucharist, by the name of illumination (*"photismos"*). For in these sacraments especially Christ's faithful become "enlightened" by being mystically incorporated and brought into communion with the glorified body of the Risen Lord through the paschal mystery of his death and resurrection. The metaphors and imagery associated with illumination spread rapidly from the East to the West.[52] The significance of this language emphasizes the priority of God's grace or gift in communicating and clarifying the reality of his people's relationship with him through the sacraments.

Only in a secondary sense does this language refer to the enlightenment we attain by dint of our endeavors to learn the content of "the truths of faith" or to grasp the mystery of God to which they

---

[50] Hans Urs von Balthasar speaks of the "liquefying" of Jesus' earthly substance into that of the Eucharist — cf. *New Elucidations*, Ignatius Press, San Francisco, 1986, p. 111. He repeats the image when trying to describe the mysterious dynamic of total transformation which Jesus' passover introduces (p. 122): *"Above all, the boundary between oneself disposing (even in faith) and being at God's disposal must disappear. This is the essential eucharistic fluidity in which Jesus crosses the boundary into the actual Passion ('Not my will be done'), thus revealing the basic law of his existence that governed his entrance into this world ('I have come down from heaven, not to do my own will, but to do the will of the one who sent me': Jn 6:38). [. . .] This is both content and law of the 'hour' [. . .]."*

[51] Cf. Carl Jung, *Symbols of Transformation*, Routledge & Kegan Paul, London, 1907, pp. 85, 105, 220, 279, 315; cf. also Umberto Eco, *Art and Beauty in the Middle Ages*, Yale University Press, 1989 — Chapter IV on "The Aesthetics of Light," pp. 43-51.

[52] Cf. St. Cyril of Jerusalem, *Procat.*, 15; 16 (one of the names of Baptism); St. John Chrysostom, Baptismal Homilies in which the term *"neophotistoi"* ("newly-illumined") frequently appears; St. Augustine, *Enarr. in Ps 33, Serm.* II, 10 — re the Eucharist.

point when formulated and clarified by theologians — particularly when they are guided by the Church's Magisterium.[53] But the graced "language" of the sacraments holds a priority in that it illumines and transforms the heart of humanity by touching it in a way that no other method or language can. Indeed, the sacraments raise human language to an entirely new level — that of religious communion, which objectively speaking surpasses all other kinds of prayerful reflection and even the most rigorous method of meditation. To say this, however, does not at all mean that the authentic endeavors of human reason or the devotional practices of the great non-Christian religions cannot attain knowledge of God. Indeed every movement of the human heart is under the influence of the divine grace of providence. The distinctive quality of Christian prayer — particularly its proclamation in eucharistic worship, as this *anaphora* brings out — is that we are initiated and drawn into that circle or embrace of God's light, that is, personal relationship of dialogue with his eternal trinitarian communion of love.[54]

The focus of this Eucharistic Prayer on the *light of Christ*

---

[53] Cf. Congregation for the Doctrine of the Faith: "Instruction on the Ecclesial Vocation of the Theologian" (24 May 1990). Pope John Paul II has a special section on the role of theologians in the Encyclical Letter on morality: *Veritatis Splendor.*

[54] Cf. Letter to the Bishops of the Catholic Church on Some Aspects of Christian Meditation, (Sacred Congregation for the Doctrine of the Faith, 15 October 1989), n. 3 (translation published by Vatican City Press, p. 4f.): *"One must first of all consider, even if only in a general way, in what does the intimate nature of Christian prayer consist. Then one can see if and how it might be enriched by meditation methods which have been developed in other religions and cultures. However, in order to achieve this, one needs to start with a certain clear premise. Christian prayer is always determined by the structure of the Christian faith, in which the very truth of God and creature shine forth. For this reason, it is defined, properly speaking, as a personal, intimate and profound dialogue between man and God. It expresses therefore the communion of redeemed creatures with the intimate life of the Persons of the Trinity. This communion, based on Baptism and the Eucharist, source and summit of the life of the Church, implies an attitude of conversion, a flight from 'self' to the 'You' of God. Thus Christian prayer is at the same time always authentically personal and communitarian. It flees from impersonal techniques or from concentrating on oneself, which can create a kind of rut, imprisoning the person praying in a spiritual privatism which is incapable of a free openness to the transcendental God. Within the Church, in the legitimate search for new methods of meditation, it must always be borne in mind that the essential element of authentic Christian prayer is the meeting of two freedoms, the infinite freedom of God with the finite freedom of man."* Cf. also von Balthasar, ibid., p. 140ff. in regard to the theological (Trinitarian and personal) distinctiveness of Christian meditation.

enables us to contemplate what it is to be true to the name *Christian*. If we live what Christ is: our peace and our light, we reflect Christ the true light, who as the sun of justice delivers humanity from the darkness of error and vice and enlightens it to live the life of virtue "becomingly as in the light of day."[55] St. Augustine would say it is to participate in *"the Word's seeing of the Father."*[56] The Christian perspective of faith, hope, and charity — through the eucharistic proclamation (hearing the Word), contemplation (seeing the Word) and action (doing the Word) — are integrated into one. All creation is thus brought into the harmony of the light of Christ's presence.[57] George Herbert reinterprets St. Paul's imagery about *"putting off the old Adam and putting on the new, Christ"* and submission to the lordship of him who is head of the Mystical Body:

> Christ is my onely head
> My alone onely heart and breast
> My onely musick, striking me ev'n dead;
> That to the old man I may rest
> And be in him new drest.[58]

This Prayer finely expresses the delightful truth of the Eucharist: that being fully human means being a Christian, that being Christian means being a lover, such a lover whose whole life echoes and is creation's song. It gathers up the fragments of our lives and celebrates them in the Church's great mosaic of Eucharist, the living icon of Christ's community of love. As St. Augustine put it:

> Sing with your voices, sing with your hearts, sing with your lips, sing with your lives. [. . .] Do you ask what you should sing about to the one whom you love? Of course you want to sing about the one you love. Do you ask what you should sing in praise of him? Listen: "Sing to the Lord a new song." Are you

---

[55] Cf. Rm 13:13.
[56] Cf. *In Joh. Ev.*, Trs. 18 & 20; also *Serm. Den.*, 126.
[57] Cf. St. Gregory of Nyssa, *On Christian Perfection*; PG 46. 259-262.
[58] *Aaron.*

looking for praises to sing? "His praise is in the assembly of the saints." The singer himself is the praise contained in the song. Do you want to speak the praise of God? Be yourselves. Be what you speak. If you live good lives, you are his praise.[59]

---

[59] *Sermon* 34.6; *The Divine Office* II, op. cit., p. 538. This is what Julian of Norwich understood so well and summed up at the end of her *Revelations of Divine Love* (Chapter 86) where she discovered the secret of Christian joy: *"Love is my meaning."*

7

Prayers for Reconciliation

The Eucharist is revealed now to us as a sacrament which is marvelously adapted to the condition of the Church Pilgrim as the sacrament of the first step of the Salvation of the Church en marche. [...] In the dynamism of Christ's Pasch this Sacrament makes the Church pass little by little, adhere more to the goods of the resurrection, detaching itself more from the bonds of sin. This happens not in a single stroke, no longer in projecting it out of the world. But on the contrary, since it is the bread of love, in making it assume human values more and more in order to transform them (without destroying them) into Christ the Lord. By itself it can even purify these values, rid them of their worthless elements through contact with the glorious body. The Bread of the Koinonia is truly the bread which maintains the earthly Church in its Paschal state, in the awaiting of the great epiphany on the day of the Parousia.[1]

Sense of occasion

The two Eucharistic Prayers of Reconciliation provide the clearest example of our worship of God being focused by a basic theme in the word of God — both because of their title and also because of the occasion when they were first introduced (1974) for the Holy Year of 1975. In response to requests of Episcopal Confer-

---

[1] J.M.R. Tillard, *The Eucharist: Pasch of God's People*, op. cit., p. 209f. This translation unfortunately reads rather awkwardly in places — for instance, "Church Pilgrim" would be better rendered by "pilgrim Church," "goods of the resurrection"(!) by "the fruit/benefit of the resurrection."

ences these Prayers were prepared "to illustrate aspects of reconciliation which may be the *object of thanksgiving.*"[2] They are appropriate not only at special occasions of jubilee, penance, renewal — such as the Holy Year of 1975 or 1933 (the 19th centenary of the Redemption) — but also for privileged times of grace, prayer and renewal like Lent or retreats, etc. Though initially intended as an experiment in developing eucharistic liturgy, the "experiment" seems to have proved so worthwhile that the use of these *anaphoras*, which are patterned on Eucharistic Prayers II and IV, was approved for a second period of three years in 1977 and then definitively in 1980.[3]

Reconciliation is of the essence of evangelization and catechesis because it belongs to the center of Christ's mystery of salvation. The Church focuses on reconciliation and penance in inviting people today to rediscover the significance of the Lord Jesus' clear challenge early in his apostolic teaching: "Repent and believe in the Gospel" (Mk 1:15). This challenging invitation complements the announcement of what he came to realize in fulfillment of Isaiah's prophecy; in Luke's perspective Jesus proclaimed at the outset of his Galilean ministry:

> The Spirit of the Lord is upon me, because he has anointed me to preach the good news to the poor. He has sent me to proclaim release to the captives and recovery of sight to the blind, to set at liberty those who are oppressed, to proclaim the acceptable year of the Lord.[4]

Reconciliation in the light of the Gospel can be seen, thus, as integral to the agenda of the pastoral mission and ministry of the Church in proclaiming the passover mystery of Christ. St. Paul most clearly described the apostolic ministry in terms of communicating the reconciliation and peace of Christ:

> If anyone is in Christ, he is a new creation; the old has passed away, behold the new has come. All this is from God, who

---

[2] Cf. Sacred Congregation for Divine Worship, Decree 1 November 1974, Introduction, 1.

[3] Cf. Mazza, *The Eucharistic Prayers*, op. cit., p. 191ff.

[4] Lk 4:18-19; cf. Is 61:1-2.

through Christ reconciled us to himself and gave us the ministry of reconciliation; that is, God was in Christ reconciling the world to himself, not counting their trespasses against them, and entrusting to us the message of reconciliation. So we are ambassadors for Christ, God making his appeal through us. We beseech you on behalf of Christ, be reconciled to God.[5]

Reconciliation has perhaps never before been given such emphasis as in recent years in which it has become a most urgent need. Much deep healing of the human heart is required so that its distress caused by sinful divisions may be overcome — distress which is aggravated by industrial dispute, violence, war ... and which has been intensified by centuries-old political and, above all, religious polarization. For this healing to come about we are called to move — in prayer, dialogue and work — towards the reconciliation and unity of all humanity in the Christian Churches and also with all people of good will.

Genuine reconciliation in Christ in no way ignores or abolishes differences. Rather it enables us to respect one another more deeply; it fosters a deep appreciation of each one's characteristic qualities and respectively unique personalities. Through reconciliation in Christ we practically express the charity of Christ so that, in acknowledging that our diversity — of gifts, talents, functions, cultural and even religious traditions — is all God-given, we are enriched in discovering a sense of the Mystical Body both when we gratefully celebrate human existence brought under grace in the Eucharist and become thereby empowered to work together in the spirit of loving service. Indeed, God's gifts or *charisms* are bestowed in order that we may experience the joy of sharing and employing them in serving one another.[6] For Christ has penetrated the dividing wall of human selfishness and pride, which he has broken down once and for all particularly regarding a false sense of religious exclusivity and elit-

---

[5] 2 Cor 5:17-20. Cf. the notion of "newness" in the Scriptures e.g., creature/creation: 2 Cor 5:17; lump: 1 Cor 5:17; man: Gal 6:15; Ep 2:15; 4:24; Col 3:10; name: Rv 2:17; Ph 2:9; heart: Ezk 36:25; Jr 31:31; commandment: Jn 13:34 — although no new command because already given and exemplified by our Lord: 1 Jn 2:28.

[6] Cf. St. Paul's challenge to recognize and respect the contribution in constructing the body of Christ and in acting as its members for the good of the whole — 1 Cor 12:4-31.

ism, as the Apostle Paul says.[7] It is in this sense that we may understand the profound truth of Robert Frost's words about proper respect for individuality and the sacred zone of privacy:

> My apple trees will never get across
> And eat the cones under his pines, I tell him.
> He only says, "Good fences make good neighbors."[8]

But in revealing God's greatness to reconcile all differences, Christ's act does not sanction religious syncretism, which in reality shows little respect for the diversity of traditions, mentality, or conscience. Rather, Christ upholds the human heart's search for truth in all its splendor and challenges his followers to respect this in living his gift of reconciliation with others.[9] Especially in a pluralist society the recognition and cry of *human rights* as a common denominator has ironically become the license for indifferentism on the level of religious truth, and — on the level of moral action — introduced a lowering of standards and permissive individualism, which sanctions each one to "do his own thing." The result is that people become stereotyped in selfishness rather than to become creative and imaginative in seeking the common good with selfless dedication. In one way or another such an attitude breeds a casual disregard for the truth of revelation regarding the grandeur of human existence — a watering down of the very truth of the Good News of Christ's reconciling love.

---

[7] Cf. Ep 2:14ff. Though the Apostle's context refers to the universal extent of the Christian Gospel in contrast to the exclusive nature of Judaism, his words continue to be a proclamation of hope since the reconciling love of Christ conquers all human sectarian intolerance and the idolatry of institutions.

[8] *North of Boston. Mending Wall.*

[9] This is not the place to deal with the history of religious intolerance in the course of Christian history. But it is worth recalling that among the early Fathers of the Church, such as Justin and Clement, there has been a serious intellectual attempt to show that the essential truth of Christ is not absent from the human search for God, as the Second Vatican Council was to express clearly regarding our pluralist situation today — cf. A.G., n. 9; L.G. n. 17; cf. also Pope John Paul II, R.M., n. 55. For a study of the question of the early Church's attitude to its religious and philosophical milieu *vide* Professor C.N. Cochrane's unsurpassed work, *Christianity and Classical Culture*, Oxford University Press, London/Oxford/New York, 1968.

Praise and Thanksgiving for Reconciliation

Both of the Eucharistic Prayers of Reconciliation bring out the purpose of celebrating the sacrifice of Christ, which is to praise and thank God for his new and eternal covenant of reconciling love and, more deeply, his fidelity to his inner truth of love, his readiness to forgive, and his abundance of mercy. Insofar as these Prayers make this explicit they offer a fine example of the way the Eucharistic Prayer implies a catechesis of the mystery of salvation history, which does not alter, but rather enhances the primary quality of the Eucharist as the sacramental re-presentation of the redemptive mystery.[10] They richly employ the imagery and allusions of the progressive revelation of the mystery of God's love in the Scriptures. Throughout the Old Testament and especially in the New Testament God reveals himself to be "the God of tenderness and mercy/compassion [*'emeth hesed*]" (Ex 34:6);[11] he speaks only of peace to his people (Ps 85:9) and despite Israel's obstinate sinfulness and repeated infidelity he remains steadfast to his initiative in forging a covenant with humanity.[12] Thus, the Preface of the first Eucharistic Prayer for Reconciliation highlights the bond between the God's holiness and sinful humanity — a holiness, which is manifest through the continuity of God's gracious act of gratuitous reconciliation in Jesus:

> Time and again we broke your covenant, but you did not abandon us. Instead, through your Son, Jesus our Lord, you bound yourself even more closely to the human family by a bond that can never be broken.[13]

---

[10] Cf. Mazza, *The Eucharistic Prayers*, op. cit., p. 193.

[11] Cf. Pope John Paul II's excellent treatment of this biblical teaching in his Encyclical Letter *Dives in Misericordia*. In a lengthy footnote (32) he deals with the sense of the main twofold terminology for divine mercy in the Hebrew of the O.T.: *hesed*, which pertains to God's abundant and profound goodness; *rahamim*, whose nuance is different to the former word ("responsibility for one's own love," a masculine characteristic) insofar as it denotes the love of a mother and "constitutes an interior necessity: an exigency of the heart" (a feminine characteristic). The wealth of these Hebrew expressions is difficult to capture in translation, especially in the Greek Septuagint. However, the N.T. builds on the depth and richness of the O.T. inheritance.

[12] Cf. Jr 31:31ff.; Ezk 33:60-63, Cf. also Léon-Dufour, op. cit., p. 149 re *"new"* not "renewed."

[13] ICEL translation.

Whereas here the accent is placed mainly on the new and eternal covenant revealed in Christ to whose fulness the Holy Spirit invites us to open our hearts, the Preface of the second Prayer highlights God's "presence and action in the world" by the outpouring of Christ's Spirit, the description of whose work recalls the ordering of creation out of chaos in Genesis:[14]

> In the midst of conflict and division, we know it is you who turn our minds to thoughts of peace. Your Spirit changes our hearts: enemies begin to speak to one another, those who were estranged joined hands in friendship, and nations seek the way of peace together.
>
> Your Spirit is at work when understanding puts an end to strife, when hatred is quenched by mercy, and vengeance gives way to forgiveness.

These are the powerful motives for ceaseless thanksgiving and praise in which the Church joins with the heavenly choirs. The effects of the covenanted reconciliation revealed and manifested by Christ the Redeemer concerns the healing of relations both between humanity and God and between human beings themselves and even the rest of creation. This has been described in the image of the "vertical" and "horizontal" dimensions of the height and depth, breath and width of the mystery of love — the dimensions revealed by the mystery of the Cross (*mysterium Crucis*).[15]

---

[14] Cf. Gn 1:12: *"In the beginning God created the heavens and the earth. The earth was without form and void, and darkness was upon the face of the deep; and the Spirit of God was moving over the face of the waters."* Cf. Lk 1:35 — the overshadowing of the Virgin Mary by God's power is regarded as the presence of the Holy Spirit who overcomes her confusion and fear in bringing about the new creation of the One who is Holy.

[15] Cf. R.P., n. 7 (translation loc. cit., p. 27): *"It is precisely before the sad spectacle of the divisions and difficulties in the way of reconciliation between people that I invite all to look to the* mysterium Crucis *as the loftiest drama in which Christ perceives and suffers to the greatest possible extent the tragedy of the division of man from God, so that he cries out in the words of the Psalmist: 'My God, my God, why have you forsaken me?,' and at the same time accomplishes our reconciliation. With our eyes fixed on the mystery of Golgotha we should be reminded always of that 'vertical' dimension of division and reconciliation concerning the relationship between man and God, a dimension which in the eyes of faith always prevails over the 'horizontal' dimension, that is to say, over the reality of division between people and the need for reconciliation between them. For we know that reconciliation between people is and can only be the fruit of the redemptive act of Christ, who died and rose again to conquer the kingdom of sin, to reestablish the covenant with God and thus break down the dividing wall* (cf. Ep 2:14-16) *which sin had raised up between people."*

The imagery of a faithful spouse, which is poignantly expressed particularly by the prophet Hosea,[16] undergirds the theology of these Eucharistic Prayers as its principal *motif* in the Church's central act of thanksgiving, praise and perseverance in trusting God's loyalty to his sinful people. God is especially manifest, that is, he makes himself known precisely through his tender kindness — his "weakness," one might say, for sinners as an understanding and indulgent parent.

The visibility of God's mercy becomes incarnated *in and through Christ*.[17] This becomes characterized at the eucharistic banquet, which shares in his supreme event of reconciliation of the paschal mystery of his passion, death, and resurrection. Since reconciliation is an essential aspect of Christ's work of redemption as "the Mediator between God and mankind,"[18] we can rightly focus on the mystery of salvation from this viewpoint in the light of Pauline catechesis.[19] In the first of these Eucharistic Prayers Christ's mediatorial act is beautifully described in an image recalling the sign of the covenant given to Noah in the rainbow:

> . . . before he stretched out his arms between heaven and earth in the everlasting sign of your covenant . . .

Both Prayers bring out Christ's mission and ministry through which God manifests his will and design to reconcile the world of sinners to himself. In Eucharist Prayer I, "sinners" means all who are alienated and cannot be converted. The dire condition of our contemporary "godlessness" raises a serious challenge for evangelization and,

---

[16] Cf. Ho 2:16-22.

[17] In a passage from Pope John Paul II's Encyclical *Dives in Misericordia* referred to already in Chapter VI the full richness of divine mercy is linked with the doxology at the end of the Eucharistic Prayer: *"in Christ and through Christ, God also becomes especially visible in his mercy [. . .] He himself, in a certain sense, is mercy. To the person who sees it in him — and finds it in him — God becomes 'visible' in a particular way as the Father 'who is rich in mercy'* (Ep 2:4)." (D.M., n. 2). Cf. also, R.H., n. 9 (translation by Editrice Ancora, Milan, p. 20): *"This revelation of love is also described as mercy* (cf. St. Thomas, *Summa Theol.*, III, q. 46, a. 1 ad 3) *and in man's history this revelation of love and mercy has taken a form and a name: that of Jesus Christ."*

[18] Cf. 1 Tm 2:5.

[19] Cf. e.g. Rm 5:10ff.; 2 Cor 5:18ff,; Ep 2:15ff.; Col 1:20ff.

particularly, regarding the significance of the Eucharist itself as the proclamation of hope regarding the light of Christ's Good News penetrating the "dark night" of modern intelligence. As one author puts it starkly in regard to the note of hope and trust expressed in the first Prayer for reconciliation:

> We are at the central point in this opening paragraph: sinners are human beings who are disenchanted with God and no longer expect anything from him. What, then, can it mean to "trust in God" in a post-Christian situation in which the very idea of God is regarded as meaningless?[20]

The "answer" to this existential condition can lie not in recourse to any magical kind of *"ex opere operato"* approach, relying on the power of the Sacrament to work miracles! But, it must be in those who celebrate this powerful evidence of God's tender love towards us as sinners to attract those who do not believe in any hope for reconciliation or that hope itself exists: the lives of those who celebrate the Eucharist must be the clue and evidence of God's abundant reconciliation.

The Church's mission and ministry of reconciliation

The Church as a community of reconciliation must through the eucharistic celebration become ever more that environment of *"amazing grace"* of the *"heart in pilgrimage."* The fine theology of reconciliation means little until it is put to the test and meets the challenge of expressing the demands of eucharistic spirituality on every member of the Church — those demands which require every one (and the Church as a reconciling institution and instrument of God's grace) to offer others that very hope of reconciliation which has been received so abundantly and experienced. Indeed, this experiential dimension of knowing God who calls and prepares humanity for reconciliation is emphasized in the Second Prayer — an emphasis which regrettably does not appear so clearly in the ICEL translation:

---

[20] Mazza, *The Eucharistic Prayers*, op. cit., p. 197.

LITERAL TRANSLATION	ICEL TRANSLATION
For though the human race is fragmented by dissension and discord, we know by experience that you alter minds and prepare them for reconciliation ...	In the midst of conflict and division, we know it is you who turn our minds to thoughts of peace ...

While the stress on experience, *this experience*, is vitally crucial to human development, it is a far cry from that experimental or subjective kind of "experience" which is at the root of the sinful disruption of "common sense" or communion. A maverick desire for fulfillment only turns us inward to dwell on our own feelings irrespective of the common concerns and good of our brothers and sisters! But the genuine experience of being forgiven re-focuses on and shares in what Christ reveals of the purpose of the Father's unifying love. Even on a human level, anyone who has experienced the joyous relief of being reconciled with a friend — or, remembers as a child being embraced by its parent after many tears and fears! — will realize that restoration to a sense of wholeness renews also a sense of direction and purpose in living.

When reconciliation is experienced as an answer to prayer — *"forgive us our trespasses"* — the Church's thanksgiving and praise (or *Eucharist*) will then be valid because effective, that is, thoroughly transforming and transformative! Pope John Paul II dwells at length on this crucial aspect of experiencing both reconciliation and the need for forgiveness because herein lies our encounter with the tenderness of God's merciful love. He sums up the section of his Encyclical Letter on Divine Mercy regarding the Church's responsibility to put mercy into practice:

> Forgiveness demonstrates the presence in the world of the love which is more powerful than sin.[21]

Even more strongly in the post-Synodal Exhortation (*Reconciliatio et Paenitentia*) he stresses the Church's role as the dispenser of reconciliation and the environment where reconciliation should be

---

[21] D.M., n. 14; ibid., p. 73.

especially experienced by realizing (that is, "making real") Christ's paschal mystery in a sacramental way:

> [. . .] as Pope Leo said, speaking of Christ's Passion, "Everything that the Son of God did and taught for the reconciliation of the world we know not only from the history of his past actions but we experience it also in the effectiveness of what he accomplishes in the present." We experience the reconciliation which he accomplished in his humanity in the efficacy of the sacred mysteries which are celebrated by his Church, for which he gave his life and which he established as the sign and also the means of salvation.[22]

This experience is brought out well in the second Prayer for Reconciliation also in the language of friendship. Here the Church prays gratefully that Christ himself moreover calls and consecrates sinners to be his "friends." This special grace of intimacy and personal effect of meeting God through Christ is realized in his Holy Spirit. Here the notion of "friends/friendship" is featured in these Prayers.[23] It is particularly in the second of these Prayers that this beautiful aspect of the Eucharist as the Sacrament of Friendship is presented as transforming human relationships in such phrases as:

> enemies begin to speak to one another, those who were estranged join hands in friendship, and nations seek the way of peace together.

Thus, "we celebrate the reconciliation Christ gained for us" for he is the "Word," "hand," "way" leading to peace, as the second Prayer for Reconciliation expresses it in moving human imagery.[24] All these

---

[22] R.P., n. 8; English translation in CTS Do562, p. 28. The quotation from Pope St. Leo is: *Tractatus 63 (De passione Domini 12)*, 6; CCL 138/A, 386.

[23] Cf. *infra*, p. 173ff.

[24] The power of such figurative language cannot be underestimated in communicating the deepest mysteries of God. The image of "hand," for instance is frequently used in the Holy Scriptures: it richly expresses the generosity of God in nourishing his servants (cf. Pss 123 [122] & 145 [144]:15-16) or in extending his mercy as in the *Magnificat*. It was St. Irenaeus' cherished image for the working of God through the Son and the Spirit, the Father's "two hands" — cf. e.g. *Adversus Haereses*, IV, praef.3; IV.xx.1; V.i.23. The image of "way" is thoroughly biblical. While it applies first of all to

descriptive "titles" for Christ are rooted in divine revelation and signify communication, which is both the means to and achievement of the reconciliation that he alone uniquely realizes.

By sharing in the Eucharist, Christ's "sacrifice of reconciliation" which is the gift from the Father,[25] our hearts are opened "to the fullness of your Spirit" and, thus, enabled *"to serve the family of mankind."*[26] In other words, we are drawn by eucharistic sharing of reconciliation into the full scope and all dimensions of the mission and ministry of Christ. By being nourished and made the concrete sign of at-onement by both the sacrament of the Eucharist and the Word, the Church participates in Christ's mission and ministry of reconciliation, healing and freeing or liberation. Thus, the Church of the Spirit is incarnated in the *order* which manifests that God brings peace, not confusion.[27] Liberation by God's covenant is the necessary condition for authentic reconciliation and peace. In these Eucharistic Prayers thanksgiving and praise are offered for God's forgiveness of sin, healing of alienation, reconciliation of divisions, restoration of peace, friendship, and for empowering us to share in the joy of fellowship with the Blessed Virgin Mary and the saints. Immediately before the doxology in the first of these Prayers there is a significant statement of hope similar to that expressed at the end of Eucharistic Prayer IV:

EPR I	EP IV
Then freed from every shadow of death, we shall take our place in the new creation and give you thanks with Christ, our risen Lord.	Then, in your kingdom, freed from the corruption of sin and death, we shall sing your glory with every creature through Christ our Lord, through whom you give us everything that is good.

Christ, it also describes the Church, whose members, Christians, were originally designated as "followers of the way" — cf. Acts 19:9. It is the leitmotif of the *anaphora* composed and approved in 1974 for the Swiss Synod (and extended for use in Luxembourg, Austria, France and Italy). This beautiful Prayer has unfortunately not yet been adopted by the English-speaking world.

[25] EPR II.

[26] EPR I.

[27] Cf. 1 Cor 14:33 — Cardinal Basil Hume, *Towards a Civilization of Love: Being Church in Today's World*, St. Paul Publications, London, 1988, p. 46f.

Reconciliation and the Eucharist

We must now consider a particular way in which the Church experiences the mercy of God through the sacramental economy of reconciliation. The title of this chapter is no misnomer. Nor is it meant to mislead. The Eucharist is the "sacrament of reconciliation" *par excellence*, as Pope John Paul II makes clear in citing a phrase from Eucharistic Prayer III:

> With every good reason his Passion and Death, sacramentally renewed in the Eucharist, are called by the Liturgy the "Sacrifice of Reconciliation": reconciliation with God, and with the brethren, since Jesus teaches that fraternal reconciliation must take place before the sacrifice is offered.[28]

There is no dearth of patristic and theological witness regarding the power of the Eucharist to forgive sin.[29] Furthermore, repeatedly the post-communion prayers express the Church's belief regarding the effective power of the Eucharist to forgive sin and heal the effects of our sinful condition.[30]

The Eucharist must be distinguished, however, from that other specific means of sacramental grace, namely the Sacrament of Conversion, Penance, Confession or Forgiveness which since the revision envisaged by the Second Vatican Council is once again called by its proper name "the Sacrament of Reconciliation" as in ancient usage.[31] In summing up the work of the Sixth Synod of Bishops, which he had assembled, as he says, in sensitive response to shattered humanity's urgent yearnings as well as especially to the impulse of divine inspiration, Pope John Paul II relates the need for repentance and reconciliation to the theme of that penetrating "gaze" or contemplation of the mystery of existence which he had described in his first Encyclical Letter:

---

[28] R.P., n. 7; loc. cit., p. 26.
[29] Cf. Tillard, op. cit., p. 203ff.
[30] Especially during the Easter season.
[31] All these names are listed in the new *Catechism of the Catholic Church*, nn. 1423-1424.

The concern to know better and to understand modern man and the contemporary world, to solve their puzzle and reveal their mystery, to discern the ferment of good and evil within them, has long caused many people to direct at man and the world a questioning gaze. It is the gaze of the historian and sociologist, philosopher and theologian, psychologist and humanist, poet and mystic: above all, it is the gaze, anxious yet full of hope, of the pastor.[32]

Without this profound approach, the way to reconciliation and peace can hardly be discovered, appreciated, or followed. After describing catechesis — the first means for carrying out the Church's pastoral mission in communicating salvation — the Pope turns to outline the place of the sacraments and their relation to each other in bringing about reconciliation between God and ourselves and among one another:

In the mysterious dynamism of the Sacraments, so rich in symbolism and content, one can discern one aspect which is not always emphasized: each Sacrament, over and above its own proper grace, is also a sign of penance and reconciliation. Therefore in each of them it is possible to re-live these dimensions of the spirit.[33]

In particular he emphasizes the value and need for the use of the sacrament of reconciliation ("confession") as an integral and ordinary part of the sacramental life and piety of the Christ's faithful. The reason for attention being focused on this sacrament is evident from observing that during the last twenty years or so there has been a marked decrease in the use of this important means of grace while the numbers of people going to Holy Communion has grown considerably.[34] This latter fact should in itself be a matter of rejoicing and

---

[32] R.P., n. 1; loc. cit., p. 3f. Cf. R.H. n. 10.

[33] R.P., n. 27; loc. cit., p. 102.

[34] This concern was also expressed by Cardinal Paul Poupard in a talk to National Delegates preparing for the 45th International Eucharistic Congress of Seville — cf. "The Eucharist and the New Evangelization: A Challenge for Eucharistic Congresses," loc. cit., p. 73.

gratitude that a rigorist Jansenist mentality has been largely over-thrown and there is a return to the encouraging teaching of the Fathers about frequent and daily reception of communion.[35] However, in the pastoral context of a sharp decline in confessions, there are grounds for asking whether general reception of communion might possibly indicate the opposite tendency to rigorism, namely, the error of laxism and an overly casual approach to the sacred — an approach which stems from the loss of a sense both of the sacred (the process of "desacralization") and also of sin and objective morality. Furthermore, a widespread neglect of confession can only result in a distortion of Christian sacramental spirituality, whose integrity is preserved in faithfully observing the Church's teaching and discipline regarding the appropriate regular use of the sacraments as Christ's gifts to communicate the fulness of his life. The Church offers thanksgiving and praise for God's "unceasing call," or rather "challenge," in the Eucharist as the first Prayer for Reconciliation proclaims:

LITERAL TRANSLATION	ICEL TRANSLATION
Unceasingly you challenge us to a more abundant life and, since you are a good and merciful God, you continue to offer forgiveness and you urge sinners to commit themselves trustingly to your tender mercy alone.	You never cease to call us to a new and more abundant life. God of love and mercy, you are always ready to forgive; we are sinners, and you invite us to trust in your mercy.

Pastoral oversight and concern in reaffirming the Church's discipline regarding the use of the Sacrament of Reconciliation must be related to the doctrine regarding the relation of Eucharist to this

---

[35] An example of the Fathers' teaching is found in St. Isidore of Seville (c. 560-636): "Some say that unless sin stand in the way, the Eucharist should be received daily, as the Lord commands, when we say 'Give us this day our daily bread.' They are right about this, if they receive with religion and devotion and humility, and do not do it relying on their own righteousness with the presumption of pride" — *De Officiis ecclesiasticis*, Bk. 1, ch. 18 (PL 82, 754B), cited in *Corpus Christi*, op. cit., p. 102.

sacrament.[36] The development of this doctrine gradually came about as the Church became more finely sensitive to the purpose of God's mercy in entrusting it with the various sacraments as gifts appropriate to the different stages of its people's spiritual life and to the needs of their *heart in pilgrimage* towards the great banquet of charity, that communion in God's eternal life of love. This way of viewing the development of the relation of the sacraments of Reconciliation and Eucharist would seem to be far more preferable insofar as it expresses a sound Eucharist-centered Christian spirituality than that other approach which tends to focus primarily on considerations of individual self-perfection, worthiness or right dispositions. Thus, in reading Pope John Paul II's reaffirmation of the Church's discipline expressed in the Instruction on the eucharistic mystery regarding the need for the confession of mortal sin before receiving Holy Communion,[37] we must do so within the context of his pastoral solicitude in calling the whole Church to the conversion (*metanoia*) of love, repentance, and transformation through, with, and in the mystery of Christ's passover. Any other way of regarding the Pope's insistence on the Church's teaching would not only indicate an ignorance of his rich presentation of the context of the sacramental economy of redemption in his first Encyclical Letter, *Redemptor Hominis*, at the beginning of his Apostolic Ministry,[38] but it would also show a serious failure to grasp the significance of the pastoral charity authoritatively exercised by the legitimate successor of Peter, to whom Christ Jesus entrusted the *power of keys*.[39]

Honesty in admitting sin — not only personal sins, but the sinfulness inherent and sadly evident at times in the structures and institutions of the human dimension of the Church — received no little attention at the Second Vatican Council.[40] The constant need for

---

[36] The new *Catechism* very positively situates the discipline of the Church within the overall teaching regarding the constructive quality of penance in responding to the Christ's call and gift of his Spirit for conversion to the Father — cf. CCC, nn. 1422-1498.

[37] Cf. R.P, n. 27 — cites E.M., n. 35. Cf. also R.H., n. 20; *Dominicae Cenae*, n. 7.

[38] Cf. R.H., n. 20.

[39] Cf. Mt 16:18f. This passage is significantly referred to in the new *Catechism* in relation to the Sacrament of Reconciliation — cf. n. 1444f. Cf. also Jn 21:15.

[40] Regarding the Church *semper reformanda* . . . cf. Hans Urs von Balthasar, *Casta meretrix: Sponsa Verbi, Skizzen zur Theologie*, II, Einsiedeln, 1961, pp. 203-305, also K. Rahner, *Theological Investigations*, Vol. 6, DLT, London, 1969, p. 218ff.

reform and, more deeply, renewal not only of rites but of the whole of the Church's life was the positive challenge issuing from this Council. Martelet sees the Council's teaching on holiness shaped by St. Augustine's response to the Donatists' rejection of the Church of sinners. After quoting from one of the great African Doctor's sermons regarding the blessed but wounded Jacob, his favorite image of the true Church, Martelet says:

> This, again, is what the Council, under the direct guidance of Augustine, means when it says of such a Christ that "he remains indeed in the bosom of the Church," but, as it were, only in a "bodily" manner and not "in his heart." If we receive the Eucharist without being really "in our hearts" members of the Church, then we, too, are receiving a sacrament which has lost for us its reality and life. Our communion tends to become aimless, or rather, as happens when a love is betrayed, the presence of the other becomes for the betrayer the presence of denial. . . .[41]

Most significantly the introduction (*Praenotanda*) to new Rites of Reconciliation, which were drawn up after the Council, points to the need for constant conversion of heart. It situates reconciliation within the context of the Church's permanent responsibility to seek purification through acts of penance and an attitude of repentance and employs phrases with which Martin Luther perhaps would not have disagreed, as for instance in the following passage:

> The members of the Church [. . .] are exposed to temptation and unfortunately often fall into sin. As a result [. . .] the Church, which includes within itself sinners and is at the same time holy and always in need of purification, constantly pursues repentance and renewal.[42]

---

[41] Op. cit., p. 185 (cf. L.G., 14); Martelet quotes St. Augustine's *Sermo* 5, 6-8 (PL 36: 57-59).

[42] II.3; translation in *Instructions on the Revised Roman Rites*, Collins, London, 1979, p. 163. Cf. J.D. Crichton, *The Ministry of Reconciliation: A Commentary*. Geoffrey Chapman, 1974, p. 15 fn. 3: *"The Order is quoting Vatican II*, De Ecclesia, *8. The phrase is* 'semper purificanda' *which comes close to* 'semper reformanda' *and the two mean much the same thing. It reminds one of Luther's* 'simul iustus et peccator' *which if separated from Luther's theology is true: we are 'justified' but always (repentant) sinners."*

Towards a Civilization of Love

Reconciliation as these Prayers bring out in striking contemporary language is much more than a "process." It is God's gift of forgiveness which empowers us as Christians to be healers who witness to that wholeness coming from him. In the almost dramatic expressions of these Prayers this wholeness is multi-faceted and impels us to explore fearlessly and confidently ever greater depths of the mystery of God and mankind while our discovery of these depths leads us to adore, praise, and thank God for his Son so that "we might turn again to you and find our way to one another."[43] Reconciliation reveals the single movement of love — that love without which there is no quality of truly human life, without which human beings are lifeless. Or, in Pope John Paul II's words, because *"man cannot live without love, the Redeemer fully reveals man to himself"* in *"amazement."* In Christ we discover not only adoration of God, but a deep wonder of the meaning and mystery of self.[44] These Eucharistic Prayers proclaim clearly that the Church is at the service of "the family of mankind" — a service which expresses and brings us nearer to the reality of communion, of which Pope Paul VI said:

> We are called to be physicians of that civilization about which we dream, the civilization of love.[45]

On another occasion the same Pope brought out the crucial need for Christians to be witnesses in their lives to the reality which they celebrate and proclaim in the Eucharist:

> Modern man listens more willingly to witnesses than to teachers, and if he does listen to teachers, it is because they are witnesses.[46]

While celebrating the Eucharist and particularly in proclaiming the

---

[43] EPR II — somewhat different from the literal translation of the original Latin: *"we might turn back to you and might love one another"!*

[44] Cf. R.H., n. 10 — the most moving and profound paragraph in the whole Encyclical.

[45] Allocution on 31 December 1975.

[46] *Evangelii Nuntiandi*, n. 41.

Eucharistic Prayer, the Church reverses that terrible scenario of alienation which causes such fear despite all modern advances in means of communication facilitated by the technological revolution.[47] While there are many positive signs of hope regarding the movement towards unification of the world, there are *"other types of Christian behavior . . . which are an obstacle to evangelization, notably the continuing fact of Christian disunity as a major hindrance to the Church's work of spreading the Gospel."*[48] The Eucharistic Prayers of Reconciliation directly apply to such situations and celebrate the significant means pointing to fuller and deeper quality of life in God — communion, which is the *"new creation," "that new world where the fullness of your peace will be revealed"* since despite differences of *"race, language, and way of life"* people *"share in one eternal banquet with Jesus Christ the Lord."*

The Church appropriately expresses its yearning for this ultimate state of unity in the intercessions, whereas in the *epiclesis* it prays for the transformation of the community celebrating the Eucharist. In the intercessions of the first Prayer for Reconciliation, however, a significant point is made regarding the coming of God's kingdom which is implied as his eschatological gift rather than as something we are engaged in "building." This is a new idea not present in any other *anaphora*. The prayer asks God to *"help us to pave the way together for the coming of your kingdom . . ."* (rather than as in the ICEL translation: *"help us to work together for . . ."*) because the kingdom transcends everything else in which we are involved: participation in the work of creation, in the development of this world, or collaboration with and commitment to our brethren in the human family.[49] These intercessions show the integral place that the Church's

---

[47] Cf. R.H., n. 15. With stark realism, Cardinal Hume summed up the situation which the Gospel and Eucharist confront and challenge: *"Europe is divided; Europe is faithless; Europe is rich; Europe prides itself on its skill and technology; Europe is an armed camp..."* (Address to European Laity Forum, Dublin, 12 July 1984). When addressing the 6th Symposium of the European Bishops' Conferences he stated the vital importance of the "missionary charism of the laity" as the means of extending the grace of the Eucharistic life of reconciliation. He saw in the development of this charism, particularly in the work for justice and peace, signs which *"speak powerfully today in Europe"* since they express *"practical and effective relief of suffering of all kinds"* (*Briefing*, Vol. 15, No. 20, p. 306).

[48] Cardinal Hume's Final Address, *Briefing*, ibid.

[49] Cf. Mazza, *The Eucharistic Prayers*, op. cit., p. 204.

petitionary prayer holds in seeking the fulness of reconciliation, in looking forward to the kingdom of God while in the meantime through compassion realizing something of a *civilization of love.*

But the realization of this vision of a *civilization of love* involves the whole Christian people because of their baptismal consecration into the Body of Christ. The Eucharist presents the great challenge to all Christians to pray more fervently, hope more keenly and work together in love for the reality of eucharistic communion to be more clearly manifest and visible. Hence, the ecumenical implications cannot be missed in both Prayers significantly at the place where the Holy Spirit is requested to transform and unite Christians:

EPR I:

Father look with love on those you have called to share in the one sacrifice of Christ. By the power of your Holy Spirit make them one body, healed of all division.

EPR II:

Fill us with his Spirit through our sharing in this meal. May he take away all that divides us. May this Spirit keep us always in communion with N. our pope [. . .] and all your people. Father make your Church throughout the world a sign of unity and an instrument of your peace.

In a very poignant way Jesus' teaching about assuring brotherly reconciliation before offering one's gifts at altar can be seen as being more relevant to our situation of a divided Christianity.[50] The phrase "instrument of your peace" recalls the well-known prayer and teaching of the *Poverello* of Assisi, who has left a marked influence on the rebuilding of the Church and on the renewal of its inner life or spirituality.[51] These Prayers lay emphasis on the Church's commit-

---

[50] St. Irenaeus "applies the Lord Jesus' teaching" (Mt 5:23) to the Church's offering which he says implies the unity among Christians —Cf. *Adversus Haereses*, IV.18,12.

[51] The sentiments of the "peace prayer" (Lord, make me an instrument of your peace) express so well the conditions for reconciliation seeking to understand rather than be understood, etc., which St. Francis himself lived so perfectly. Although it is attributed to him, it could have been based on one of the *Sayings of St. Giles* or it may have been the other way round — cf. Fr. James Meyer, O.F.M., *The Words of St. Francis*, Franciscan Herald Press, Chicago, Illinois, 1952, p. 338. Cf. also Cecily Hallack & Peter F. Anson, *These Made Peace* (Studies on the Lives of the Beatified and Canonized Members of the Third Order of St. Francis of Assisi), St. Anthony Guild Press, Paterson, New Jersey, 1957.

ment to continual conversion through constant reformation. Indeed, particularly the words quoted above from the second of these *anaphoras* leave no room for complacency.[52] One of the first steps towards full reconciliation and unity among the Christian Churches consists in acknowledging that "we have all sinned." In this regard it is worth recalling the words of Cardinal Reginald Pole at the second session of the Council of Trent:

> Consider then the birth of these heresies which in these days are everywhere rife. We may indeed wish to deny that we have given them birth, because we ourselves have not uttered any heresy. Nevertheless, wrong opinions about faith, like brambles and thorns, have sprung up in the God's-garth entrusted to us. Hence even if, as is their wont, these poisonous weeds have spread of themselves, nevertheless if we have not tilled our field as we ought — if we have not sowed — if we took no pains at once to root up the springing weeds, we are no less to be reckoned their cause than if we ourselves had sowed them; and all the more since all these have their beginning and increase in the tiller's sloth. [. . .] If like our fathers we were suffering for justice' sake we should be blessed. But because the salt has lost its savour we are suffering justly yet not for the sake of justice. [. . .] "O Lord, to us is confusion of face, to our princes and to our fathers who have sinned. But to thee, O Lord our God, mercy and forgiveness, for we have departed from thee. [. . .] And on us is the malediction and the curse."[53]

Gerald Vann's comment on these words also give pause for prayerful reflection:

> Today we pay the penalty in the very immensity of the obstacles which prevent the reunion of divided Christendom. Behind us are all the years and centuries of divergent devel-

---

[52] Mazza states: it "disturbs our serenity, for it asserts that the Church is a sign of unity for all human beings" — *The Eucharistic Prayers*, op. cit., p. 211.

[53] *Causes of Christian Disunion*, Cardinal Pole's Legatine Address at the Opening of the Council of Trent, 7th January, 1546; with Introduction by Fr. Vincent McNabb, O.P. — cited by Gerald Vann, O.P., *The Heart of Man*, op. cit., p. 152f.

opment [. . .] But behind this intellectual problem there is the
deeper problem of the will: the legacy of the centuries of
enmity and hatred and distrust; and until these evils are
completely exorcized it is useless to hope for unity of mind.
And so we come — and it is one of the main themes of Cardinal
Pole's address — to the primary need of repentance and
humility, that the power of God may be able to work in us and
through us. Omnes nos peccavimus: we have all sinned; and
until we are all filled with that sense of sin, until we have gone
down into the depths of self knowledge and sorrow, we can't
serve the healing purposes of God, we can only resist them.[54]

Implied in these Prayers for Reconciliation — and indeed in every
celebration of the Eucharist — is the urgent responsibility both to
pray earnestly for the unity of the Christian Church and also to
acknowledge with utter honesty our part in the corporate nature of sin
which tends to tear the seamless garment of Christ's love into
fragments.

Passing from a sense of the corporate nature of sinfulness to
personal acknowledgement of it before God and our brothers and
sisters, we must avoid the tendency to regard admission of sin as a
symptom of some kind of morbid "guilt-complex," but, on the contrary, as a positive sign of seeking acceptance by love that heals and
makes us at-one or whole.[55] Ronald Rolheiser has expressed this
beautifully in challenging the widespread attitude which evades
responsibility by calling sin by some clever psychological term:

Today [. . .] there is a general hesitancy to use the word sin.
It is rare that we hear someone simply and humbly say,

---

[54] Vann, ibid., p. 153f.

[55] Cf. George Herbert's poems: especially *The Agonie* in which sin and love, "two vast,
spacious things," are mystically brought together in Christ's passion where sin is
overcome by love:
> *Love is that liquour sweet and most divine,*
> *Which my God feels as blood; but I, as wine.*

and also,
> *Love bade me welcome yet my soul drew back,*
> *Guilty of dust and sinne. . .*
> *You must sit downe, sayes Love, and taste my meat:*
> *So I did sit and eat.*

beyond any reference to circumstances or excuse: "I've sinned. There aren't any excuses . . . outside of being human." We are poorer for not being able to say that. First of all, we are poorer because our sense of sin is connected with our sense of love. To sin is to betray . . . in love. To have lost a sense of personal sin is to have lost a sense of being personally and deeply loved.

Lovers know that their immaturities, woundedness, and neuroses play a part in their struggles. They also know that, ultimately, there is something called betrayal, sin.

Secondly, more superficially, not to speak of ourselves as sinners is to lower the symbolic hedge under which we live. Bluntly put, psychological symbols — neuroses, immaturity, woundedness — do not link our actions to anything interesting, rich, or timeless. The symbol of sin does.[56]

A characteristic of sin — every personal sin of every individual —is that it impels the sinner to hide in the security of an anonymous group. And every group has its particular type of sin.[57] Sin — from the classic story of Adam and Eve — seeks accomplices. A subtle way of finding an accomplice is to cast the blame on others. This is commonly expressed in such familiar-sounding excuses: "But everyone does it," or, "I'm only human." Sin is the most social of human

---

[56] This is taken from one of Rolheiser's weekly pieces, "Be Brave, admit sin," which appeared in the Catholic Herald 1989 (?). Immanuel Jakobovits the Chief Rabbi in Britain (1967-91), attributes "the dramatic decline of moral standards" in our century particularly to a loss of a sense of shame: "The removal of shame has changed our moral vocabulary, encouraging the unacceptable to become accepted. [. . .] euphemisms are used, or intended, to overcome social disapproval. Can a sense of shame he restored?" He answers his question by suggesting that skilful propaganda can restore what is natural to humanity ("as the sense of shame is") — *The Times*, Wednesday, September 22, 1993, p. 16. Is this too naive a proposal? But, shame is out-shamed by divine Love, as George Herbert describes in that marvellous poem: *Love bade me welcome*.

[57] Hugh Lavery describes that of priests (*Sacraments*, DLT, 1982, p. 32f.): *"The priesthood is a group and the priesthood can have its own particular sin. A priest, in his preaching, can mislead, but he is called to lead. He is called to preach the good news; nothing else. He has no commission to air opinions, vent his prejudices, or preach a weird gospel of his own. 'Woe is me if I do not preach the gospel.' Anybody can preach. It is preaching the gospel that is hard. A priest must preach the good news and its light is the dawn of forgiveness. Christ is the luminous symbol and the sweet agent of absolution. This must be preached, day in and day out, week in and week out. To believe in God is to believe that I am loved. Few easily accept that they are lovable and are loved unconditionally. Yet they are around; they are the salt of the earth and the light of the world. They are the people of God."*

experiences while quite paradoxically it is the most anti-social of evils — implicating others, dragging them down, destroying them and oneself in the process not only in the "next world," but also in the *mean time* here on earth as well.

Sin is serious! It must be taken seriously. Sin dislocates us from reality — the reality of the transcendence of the sacredness of love, God's love. Sin is a gross misunderstanding of self, the world, neighbors and God because it refuses the beauty of relationship of fellowship and communion. Sin is not remembering or *being mindful* of God's wonderful deeds of loving kindness; it is thus *anti-memorial*. Sin is thus the ultimate ingratitude; it is thus a rejection of divine generosity and, hence, of the significance of all that we celebrate in *Eucharist*. Sin prefers self-sufficiency under one or other of its variegated camouflages which deceive into living a lie.[58] Reconciliation by God's mercy alone conquers sin — that mercy in which, as the Preface of the first *anaphora* states, God invites us to trust. But having no trust in God or acknowledging any dependence on him, sin looks forward to no future and has no sense of eternal life because it buries us in the attractiveness of our temporal condition and makes us settle complacently for the mediocrity of its narrow perspective. Sin is thus opposed to the paschal dynamism of the Eucharist. It slows down and, if unrepented, halts the movement of the *heart in pilgrimage*.[59]

Tragedy is made up of repeated acts of rejection of reconciliation, the refusal to recognize the need for forgiveness, and the obstinate turning away from the other — from the only Other ultimately who is *"rich in mercy."* All the great tragic figures of human drama, as depicted for example by Sophocles or Shakespeare, are flawed precisely because they refuse to admit their need to receive the mercy of others' generosity (forgiveness). They pride themselves

---

[58] Classically expressed as "the world, the flesh, the devil" — cf. 1 Jn 2:16: *"For all that is in the world, the lust of the flesh and the lust of the eyes and the pride of life, is not of the Father but is of the world."* Cf. also ibid. 1:8-10.

[59] In an early work the Canadian Dominican ecumenical theologian, Jean-Marie Tillard, says: *"The decisive battle is won in the paschal act of Christ, but [. . .] the fight is pursued in the daily acts of each faithful until the great victory of the Parousia. Such is the concrete situation of the Church Pilgrim. It is not a situation of peaceful repose, but of continual passage from the world of sin to the world of God, with the certitude, however, of the definitive victory already given in arrhes. In short, it is an essentially paschal situation."* op. cit., p. 199.

as being the givers, who hold others under the sway of their power to give or not give. But they themselves cannot admit being in the power of another's act of compassion or forgiveness. They die tragically alone, alienated from that personalizing experience of being reconciled. Jean-Paul Sartre expressed the tragedy of this rejection of reconciliation in his famous phrase which points to the ultimate alienation: *"Hell is others."* There is no alienation quite so terrible or comparable with that state of unfreedom and dis-grace of being compelled to live with others whom one rejects and by whom one is rejected.

Acknowledgement of our sinful condition is not merely a matter of knowing or being able to define the various categories or species of sin — original or actual, personal or social, mortal, grave, serious or venial. It demands a sense of genuine compunction. Compunction of heart needs to be experienced — as the great spiritual masters taught from Augustine to Thomas à Kempis, Ignatius of Loyola to Thérèse of Lisieux in order that true progress be made in piety and devotion, the soul of worship.[60] It is likewise an indispensable condition for expressing to others something of Christ's great compassion for humanity which needs to be healed and made whole. This compassion extends the mercy of God. Indeed, *"the quality of mercy"* is great — far greater than the meanness and self-centeredness of sin.[61]

Moreover, this compunction of heart is more than making excuses for ourselves or for others. This is not true contrition in seeking forgiveness but another form of escapism from moral responsibility.[62] Compunction of heart ultimately involves crying out: "Lord, have mercy," and not merely saying: "I am sorry."[63] This is quite different from what seemed to be the "message" of a film in the sixties, *Love Story*: "Love means not having to say I'm sorry." For this

---

[60] St. Augustine points out repeatedly that "confession" in the strong sense of the word means "praise of God," which itself is implied in confessing the sinner's need of him for forgiveness — cf. v. g., *Serm.* 29.2,2; Cf. also *The Imitation of Christ*, Bk. 1, ch. 21.

[61] William Shakespeare's famous eulogy in Portia's plea to Shylock highlights the gratuitous quality of mercy which redounds to the benefit of the giver of mercy — cf. *The Merchant of Venice*, Ac. IV, Sc. 1.

[62] C.S. Lewis' little essay "On forgiveness" merits re-reading —cf. *Fern-Seeds and Elephants*, Fontana/Collins, 1975, p. 39ff.

[63] Cf. Sheldon Vanauken, *A Severe Mercy*, Hodder & Stoughton, 1977, p. 20.

approach presents only half the truth (if that!); it brings out that love is understanding of weakness and patient with fickleness. But, rather than remain at the level of saying "I'm sorry," the cry for God's mercy recognizes that his love transcends not only our sentiments but also our sins. If we want to learn to love, we must not be afraid of approaching the dimension of sacred Love. This is the dimension of reality which our Lord opened to us on the cross. The dimension of *for-giveness*, which as the word itself indicates captures the most complete and intense *form of giving*.[64] The Eucharistic Prayers in general, and particularly those for Reconciliation, proclaim in different ways the central fact of the sheer largesse of God towards *giving* humanity what it most direly needs — the Savior's gift of himself "so that sins may be forgiven." In receiving and cherishing this "Gift of God," the Church rejoices in its Risen Lord's life, in which it ever seeks to share by rising above and giving up its condition of sinfulness. This very gift — not only the state of forgiveness but also the presence of the one who is its unique Giver —empowers the Church to become an instrument of God's will for peace,[65] a sign of hope and a channel of divine mercy for a world riddled with the misery and anguish of selfishness. The harvest of the human heart's hope grows from the Gospel-seed of the Eucharist, the Gift Christ gave us for the remission of sins and the life of a reconciled world. In Hugh Lavery's words:

> The wheat-germ of Christianity is forgiveness. That is what makes Christianity Christian. Forgiveness cannot be caught in words nor cased in a definition. The sublime truths find no words to contain them; each eludes analysis. Forgiveness can only be experienced. The sublime things cannot be spoken; they can only be acted. When we speak of forgiveness we speak of God, for forgiveness belongs to God. To err is human; to forgive divine. God is the totally personal because he is totally for. For what? For giving. Man is most personal when he is a being for; for giving [. . .].[66]

---

[64] This is likewise the root meaning of pardon, which derives from the French.

[65] Cf. Dante, *Il Paradiso*, Canto III: "In His will is our peace" (*"En'n in sua volontade è nostra pace"*).

[66] Fr. Hugh Lavery, *Sacraments*, DLT, London, 1982, p. 29.

"Do this in memory of me" — This is how Jesus wished to be remembered. He was a lover of friendship meals at which he created an atmosphere of acceptance and welcome of all and sundry. The eucharistic banquet is prefigured in the meals recorded in the Scriptures — especially those in the Gospel which Jesus frequently shared with others; among these meals a special place is occupied by those with sinners.[67] Sinners — especially the public outcast or "marginalized" as we say today — were made to feel at ease. The grace of his presence conferred dignity on those with a poor self-image. He treated everyone not merely as equals, for he identified with each one as his great parable of the last judgment poignantly brings out. To get across his message of the restoration of dignity through God's universal forgiveness he told his wonderful stories or parables.[68] These were not only for the guardians of public morality and order, the scribes and Pharisees, but also for those needing to learn confidence and a sense of their personal worth before others. His parables encouraged them to approach him with confidence, since a sense of reluctance to approach anyone with a reputation of holiness would have been part of their social and religious conditioning.

Today no less than in Jesus' time we need to realize, as the Second Vatican Council clearly emphasized,[69] that holiness is for all and that holiness is not a matter of strain or extraordinary feats of fasting, but of grace — the grace of knowing by experience of the eucharistic community's celebration of reconciliation that we are in the presence of the One who loves us more than we are capable of loving ourselves. In the end, there is only One who can say: where are

---

[67] Cf. e.g., Mt 9:9-13 (the call of Matthew); Lk 7:36-50; 19:1-10; etc. — Cf. Mazza, *The Eucharistic Prayers*, op. cit., p. 191ff.; Porro, op. cit., p. 188ff.; Della Torre, op. cit., p. 157f.

[68] Albert Nolan finely reinterprets the parables in terms of Jesus' lessons of forgiveness — cf. *Jesus Before Christianity: the Gospel of Liberation*, DLT, 1977, p. 37ff.

[69] This is one of the great insights of the Church which addresses and appeals to the whole of humanity in its situation of anguish through the Church as the sign of holiness, that is, of God's love — cf. L.G. nn. 39-42 (i.e., the whole of Chapter 5 of this Constitution on the universal call to holiness). Cf. also G.S., nn. 2, 12, 22, 24, etc. Pope John Paul II sees "the universal call to holiness [. . .] closely linked to the universal call to mission. Every member of the faithful is called to holiness and to mission. [. . .] The Church's missionary spirituality is a journey towards holiness." — cf. R.M., n. 90.

those who condemn you?[70] It is this uniquely patient One who, as George Herbert realized, stays the wrath of divine justice and calls us into the environment of love:

> Me thought I heard one calling, Child!
> And I reply'd, My Lord.[71]

For this One, who comes as Lord with all authority to judge the living and the dead, is our divine Redeemer, who knows the human heart and who is the Lamb of God *who takes away the sins of the world*. The Eucharistic Prayers in one way or another proclaim the unfolding of the mystery of forgiveness and reconciliation, the mystery of God who is *"rich in mercy"* and who in Christ reveals to the *heart in pilgrimage*: *"You would not be searching for me, if you had not found me!"*[72] The fount of this mercy is always the same: the immense charity of the heart of God which alone is capable of changing our hearts and transforming our lives —

> The love that moves the sun and the other stars.[73]

---

[70] Cf. Jn 8:10.

[71] *The Collar [Choler or Anger]*; cf. also his poem *Redemption*.

[72] Blaise Pascal, *Le Mystère de Jesus: Pensées*, 553 — this phrase inspired by St. Augustine is quoted by Pope John Paul II in his Apostolic Exhortation, *Catechesi Tradendae*, n. 60.

[73] Dante, *Divine Comedy — Paradiso*, XXXIII.145: *"L'amor che muove il sole e l'altre stelle."*

8

Formation of Children in Worship
(Three Eucharistic Prayers for Children)

The young especially need to be told that love is not a glamorous fairy tale but a lifework which involves all the patient toil that no great lifework, no great art, can avoid. But they need to be told too that it is a divine destiny, which the life of God within us can make both easier and more glorious.

They need to be told that in order to open their eyes and hearts God may lead them near to heartbreak; but they need to be told too of the deep abiding happiness and the moments of dazzling glory, of the joys that will come to them not in the next world only, when their troubles are over, but in this world too.

They need to be told of the greatness of the love of man and woman as ministers of God's omnipotence, as makers with God of what will not pass away. They need to be told to expect failures and misunderstandings, for the perfect work is not made in a day; but they need to be told too that the failures need never be final but on the contrary, like every evil, can be made the material of a deeper awareness and a more perfect love.

They need to be told that there may be times when they will cry their eyes out with fright or with sorrow; but they need to be told too that there will be times when they will cry their eyes out for joy. They need to be told not to be afraid of idolatry or of God's rivalry provided they love him faithfully; for their love is his will and their worship of him, and is only deepened and strengthened by their prayer if they pray, as they should, hand in hand.[1]

---

[1] Gerald Vann, O.P., *The Heart of Man*, Collins, Fontana, 1963, p. 69f.

Needs made difficult?

Long past are the days of the Victorian attitude: children should be seen not heard. Children are very much "on show" and being heard loud and clear — except the very little ones who are consigned behind the glass-panelled "crying room" at the back of some purpose-built modern churches. Never before this century have children been the focus of so much attention by such a welter of specialists in different fields: educationalists, psychologists, sociologists, and even criminologists. All this attention to the question of "child development" is itself an indicator of human development: it points to an overall awareness of the mystery of the human person and of the clue that children provide in confronting and unravelling the marvellous quality of growth which is a distinctive feature of being human. Attentiveness to the question of child development marks a stage of progress along the axis of human reflectiveness. Children are no longed considered and treated as miniature adults: their clothes are designed and fashioned to suite their various ages; they are even modelled and promoted by them — particularly in the hectic scenario of the teenage culture which has "pop stars" and idols drawn from its own peer group.

To find a balance in approach to the development of the human person from early childhood to adolescence and on to young adulthood, two extremes in attitude must be avoided. On the one hand, children must not be neglected as not having any rights to a fully human existence appropriate to their condition as human persons; their rights must be recognized and proclaimed in a culture of life. On the other, we should at all costs avoid idealizing the state of children especially by a sentimentality that both demeans their dignity and also shows up an immaturity on our part to accept them as persons rather than as favorite "pets" or possessions. If they are shown genuine Christian love their formation will be well grounded. Leo Tolstoy points to this fundamental principle of an education for life:

> People think there are circumstances when one may deal with human beings without love, but no such circumstances ever exist. Inanimate objects may be dealt with without love: we may fell trees, bake bricks, hammer iron without love. But

human beings cannot be handled without love, any more than bees can be handled without care. That is the nature of bees. If you handle bees carelessly you will harm the bees and yourself as well. And so it is with people. And it cannot be otherwise, because mutual love is the fundamental law of human life. It is true that a man cannot force himself to love in the way he can force himself to work, but it does not follow from this that men may be treated without love, especially if something is required from them. If you feel no love leave people alone. Occupy yourself with things, with yourself, with anything you like, only not with men. Just as one can eat without harm and profitably only when one is hungry, so can one usefully and without injury deal with men only when one loves them. But once a man allows himself to treat men unlovingly, there are no limits to the cruelty and brutality he may inflict on others.[2]

As experience shows this is especially true with regard to the treatment of children who, if abused, become abusers of others, but if properly loved develop into mature and responsible members of the community. What should also be avoided is an exaggeration of children's inability to understand.[3] For it must not be forgotten that human perception and understanding function at different levels, among which are the subliminal, emotional, affective or intuitional; through these the moral, spiritual or religious sense dawns. Children are a lot more religiously perceptive than we often give them credit

---

[2] *Resurrection* cited in *Words for Worship*, Edward Arnold Ltd., London, 1969, n. 674.

[3] Cf. e.g. in Edward Matthews' otherwise balanced and helpful introduction one comes across the following remarks regarding the notion of *anamnesis*: *"For the young child, however, it is a concept way above his understanding. The teacher need do no more than stress the fact that we celebrate the Mass because Jesus told us to and that Jesus is present together with the effects of his sacrifice"* (*Celebrating Mass with Children*, p. 17). First of all, this approach does not help the child to grow by attempting to answer its inevitable questions about how Jesus offers us the effects of his sacrifice. Moreover, it shows no appreciation for children's marvellous capacity to believe in and live out what they imagine and play. How easily adults forget what it is to think or be like a child! In their world of play children realize what they invent. Whereas children know how to be creative, often all that adults can do is create difficulties. Dare one disappoint or disillusion a child about his or her world of imagination not being real! Children need to be shown that the "playfulness" of liturgy is not mere make-believe, but faith's making-real of what Jesus invented or, rather, creatively gave us. —Cf. Romano Guardini's delightful and profound essay "The Playfulness of the Liturgy" in *The Spirit of the Liturgy*, Sheed & Ward, London, 1937, pp. 85-106.

for! The role of mothers in children's education is crucial for bringing about a sense of wholeness.[4]

The place of imagination cannot be gainsaid. Its rich religious dimensions were well realized by such writers as C.S. Lewis and J.R.R. Tolkien. It is impossible to estimate the moral and religious benefit many people have derived from reading their novels in childhood or early adolescence.[5] Children are naturally religious: they are full of a sense of awe and wonder; wide-eyed and curious, bristling with questions too! At the same time they are impressionable, vulnerable and inclined to imitate and come easily under the influence of what they see adults doing. Hence, it is vitally important for the adult community to show them an attitude of worship by its reverence for the sacred and the presence of God when celebrating the Eucharist. For much in our modern secularized urban society militates against the belief in the creative mystery of Christ's love and the values of the Gospel. A saturation with today's T.V. culture tends to wither up children's natural creativity, which is part of their innate religious sense. In such a superficial atmosphere they soon become blasé and easily sink into the common swamp of being merely spectators rather than participants in the creation of a new world. The religious poet and visionary William Blake insisted on the importance of perceiving through the eye rather than with it:

> This life's five windows of the soul
> Distorts the Heavens from pole to pole,

---

[4] Cf. *The Tablet*, 14 August 1993, p. 1047 — Margaret Hebblethwaite's review of Sally Cunneen's *Mother Church: What the Experience of Women is Teaching Her* (Paulist Press): *"Mothering . . . goes far beyond spoon-feeding. It is a matter of 'people-making' — and what could be more apt than that for 'the people of God'? Mother Church has made many mistakes beautifully summed up in the naive sermon of a keen young priest explaining the principles of Catholic education. 'We tell the children who they are, what they have to do, and where they're going,' he said. 'They never have to doubt or worry.' But then the splendid ideal of transition to independence is not an easy one to realize. Mothers 'would be the last to forget how thin a line it can be between over-control and an irresponsible absence of supervision.' At the end of years of slog and heartbreak, mothers are the first to recognize 'that they make lots of mistakes'."*

[5] For instance, Tolkien's penetration into the world of religious experience echoes through his description of the "long-expected party," which evokes the atmosphere of the Eucharist near the beginning of *The Lord of the Rings*. Tolkien baptizes human imagination in this great epic. — Cf. Stratford Caldecott, "Lord of the Imagination — Second Spring," the center section of *The Catholic World Report*, December 1992.

And leads you to believe a lie
When you see with, not thro' the eye.[6]

Is this sense of wonder too idealistic or stylized an approach to children today?

The process of human development is not usually realized in a series of leaps and bounds from one stage to the next, but rather through a gradual unfolding or evolving of awareness and attitude, which is an integral part of the stream of their inner experiences and also physical relationship with family, friends and environment at large. Gabriel Moran describes it as being

> not a straight line, but a constant circling back. [. . .] Being religious is a condition known to every child. Religious education of the young has little to do with instruction in belief; it has much to do with providing aesthetic form, stable environment and personal warmth that protects the religiousness of the child's experience.[7]

This statement does not imply that the religious formation of children — even the youngest — must be devoid of any content of belief. What is the point of getting them to genuflect when they enter a church if they are not focused on the presence of the Blessed Sacrament in the tabernacle? Or, what is the value of making them dip their hand into the holy water and bless themselves unless they are given some awareness of what Baptism means? Christian symbols and sacred signs communicate realities beyond the senses in a powerful way. But, they are not either magical gestures or expressions of irrational superstition. They are imbued with the faith of the

---

[6] *The Everlasting Gospel* — *y*. Perhaps Blake also had in mind Jesus' image of the "eye of a needle" through which all must pass into the kingdom of God, the new Jerusalem — cf. Mt 19:24. Elsewhere he states the same important truth in a similar vein: *"As a man is, so he sees. When the sun rises, do you not see a round disk of fire something like a gold piece? O no, no, I see an innumerable company of the Heavenly host crying, 'Holy, Holy, Holy, is the Lord God Almighty.' I do not question my bodily eye any more than I would question a window concerning sight. I look through it and not with it."* Cited in *Words for Worship*, op. cit., n. 672.

[7] Gabriel Moran, "Religious Educational Development," cited by Sister Maura McMenamin, art. cit., p. 17.

Church which itself derives from and responds to the living Word of Christ.

Formation for worship

Never before this century has the Church shown such pastoral care directed specifically towards children. At its beginning there was Pope St. Pius X's famous Decree in welcoming children to Holy Communion at an early age;[8] more recently, that is since the Second Vatican Council, the liturgical rites of Baptism were completely revised so as to provide a form for use with infants and little children which is entirely distinct from the adult liturgy of Christian Initiation,[9] and then the three Eucharistic Prayers for Masses with children were promulgated with a Directory on the use of these Prayers.[10]

The history of the compilation and promulgation of these Prayers is a rather complicated one. It dates back to the request made after the Second Vatican Council at the first Synod of Bishops in 1967 for an adaptation of the Mass to cater to the needs of children and teenagers.[11] Briefly, one of the main issues in the delay in producing suitable new Prayers was the principle pointed out by the Congregation for Divine Worship, namely, that the worshiping eucharistic community must not be divided. The Directory for Masses with Children pointed out that the focus must be on forming children for worship. This formation must hold a priority over the question of children's needs, as important and urgent as these may be. In forming

---

[8] Cf. Decree of the Sacred Congregation of the Sacraments, *"Quam singulari,"* 8 August 1910; DS 3530-3536.

[9] Cf. *Ordo baptismi parvulorum* (Decree 15 May 1969; 29 August 1973) and *Ordo Initiationis Christianae Adultorum* (Decree 6 January 1972).

[10] Cf. Decree of 1 November 1974. The importance of the Directory is all the more evident in the fact that it belonged to a new category of pastoral documents issued by the Holy See. It was preceded by only one other: The Directory on Masses with Special Groups (15 May 1969).

[11] This is not the place to describe the "history" of the wrangling between the Congregations for the Faith and for Divine Worship — cf. John Barry, "Eucharistic Prayers for Masses with Children" in Senn, *New Eucharistic Prayers*, op. cit., p. 53ff. For a detailed account of the development of these Prayers: cf. A. Bugnini, *La riforma liturgica* (1948-1973), Rome: CLV — Edizioni Liturgiche, 1983, pp. 470-475.

children for worship while attention must be paid to their backgrounds, needs, abilities, ages, etc.,[12] it is crucial to recognize that their deepest need is to be formed to participate in the worship of the whole Christian community. As one liturgical scholar comments:

> The first chapter of the Directory, following the priority set down in the Liturgy Constitution, is concerned to emphasize that our first priority in developing the participation of children in the Liturgy is not with adjusting and adapting the rite itself to suit their needs, but with their prior formation for worship. Only after eight solid and wise articles on the liturgical formation of children does the Directory move on in Chapters 2 and 3 to give particular guidance for celebrating Masses with children that is derived from the principles governing the reform of the Liturgy. The point is a simple one: that we must give more attention to Chapter 1 of the Directory than we give to Chapters 2 and 3. Tinkering around with the Order of Mass merely to hold the attention of children during what is seen fundamentally as an adult activity, will never be sufficient on its own. The Directory is indicting to us that that is doomed to failure unless we give great attention to the liturgical formation of children and regard it as an essential prerequisite of their participation in the liturgy, particularly the Liturgy of the Mass.[13]

Thanks to the interest and encouragement shown by Pope Paul VI in this question a commission was set up in October 1973 to prepare formularies to meet a genuine pastoral need. Eventually from the thirty-eight proposed texts, three were chosen — two from the French and one from the German groups — as the basis for discussion. Translations of these were made into English, Italian and Spanish and, after examination by national conferences of bishops and liturgical experts, they were reviewed, amended, edited and then approved on 1 November 1974 under the certain conditions, which

---

[12] Cf. Sister Maura McMenamin, "The Psychology of Sacramental Preparation" in *Liturgy*, Vol. 16, Number 3 (1992), p. 15ff.

[13] Cf. Anthony B. Boylan, "The Principles of the Directory on Children's Masses" in *Liturgy*, Vol. 16, Number 3 (1992), p. 4f.

incorporated those stated by the Holy See (through Cardinal Villot, the Secretary of State). Among these were the following:[14]

— that they may be used *ad experimentum* for a three-year period;
— that they may not be published officially nor printed in the Missal;
— that they may be sent to the bishops' conferences which requested them; that one text be chosen from among the three proposed drafts;
— that they may be freely translated into the vernacular where this was not already done (the ideas in the Latin being referred to as a guideline) and that the translation be approved by the Apostolic See . . .

In June 1975 the ICEL translation presented by the English-speaking national bishops' conferences was approved by Rome, which permitted all three Prayers to be published in a booklet together with the Eucharistic Prayers for Masses of Reconciliation for experimental use until 1977. This permission was extended for a further three years and in 1981 renewed without any time limit specified. All these Prayers are now included in the most recent editions of the Missal or Sacramentary in the vernacular.

Underlying the stages of the development of these Prayers are some important points which are significant in considering Christian spirituality in the light of the Eucharistic Prayer:

First of all, they highlight the pastoral concern or *"pastoral charity"* of the Church. Although the delay and difficulties presented by the Roman Congregations may be widely (and wildly!) criticized, we should acknowledge the need for the exercise of pastoral discernment on the part of those with the responsibility of pastoral oversight. This is no trivial matter especially since it concerns handing on the Faith of the Church-at-worship to children, who deserve to receive its richness and integrity rather than some "watered down" version. Hence the importance of authoritative teaching which involves taking into consideration the advice of experts in various fields — liturgical,

---

[14] Cf. Sacred Congregation for Divine Worship. Decree and Introduction to *Eucharistic Prayers for Masses with Children.*

theological, pastoral, catechetical, pedagogical, literary and also musical[15] — in order to provide vernacular texts which would faithfully represent the structure of the Eucharistic Prayer.[16] All this takes time despite no lack of good will, which must be accredited in charity and patience even to members of Church commissions and authorities! Anything less than this would only indicate a lack of competence and also a casual approach to the divinely entrusted responsibility to teach what is true and safeguard from error.

Next, there is the question of the use of the vernacular itself. Whether intended or not, whether envisaged or not, the fact that these Prayers were produced in modern languages and not in Latin heralds an important development in liturgical history. The Eucharistic Prayers for Masses with Children have no *editio typica* in Latin, which in all the other *anaphoras* is the reference point or normative basis for vernacular texts. In the case of the Prayers we are considering the Latin version was drawn up only after the original texts in French, German, etc., were settled. Furthermore, as is clearly stated, the Latin version may not be used; it is merely there as a universal reference-point.[17] These Prayers thus mark a unique step taken in the history of the Eucharist and of the liturgy: they set a precedent for our approach to worship today and for future generations.

What can we learn about eucharistic worship and, hence, Christian spirituality from the way it is presented in the Eucharistic Prayers for Masses with children? The introduction of these Prayers and especially their content, moreover, provide a definite enrichment in the understanding of Christian spirituality. We must turn now to consider some aspects of this enrichment.

---

[15] Cf. *Introduction*, n. 10.

[16] Cf. *supra*, Chapter II, p. 19ff.

[17] Cf. *Introduction*, n. 11: *"The committee of translators should always remember that the Latin text [. . .] is not intended for liturgical use. Therefore it is not simply to be translated. [. . .] Features proper to the Latin language (which never developed a special style of speaking with children) are never to be carried over into the vernacular texts intended for liturgical use [. . .] All aspects of the style of speech should be adapted to the spirit of the respective language as well as to the manner in which one speaks with children concerning matters of great importance. These principles are all the more pertinent in the case of languages which are far removed from Latin, especially non-Western languages. An example of translation for each eucharistic prayer is given in a Western language as a possible aid to the translator."*

Gospel values

These Eucharistic Prayers illustrate various aspects of the Gospel. Their tone reminds us of Jesus' attitude to children: his readiness to welcome them, his holding them up as a living "parable" of the kingdom of heaven, his identification with "these little ones" as his "least brethren," his severe reprimand of anyone who scandalizes, that is, places an obstacle to their growth in grace. Furthermore, there is Jesus' teaching on the necessity to be born again with the openness of the heart of a little child in order to possess eternal life which consists in knowing him and the Father. No one better than our Lord Jesus appreciated and shared in children's sense of wonderment, joy, spontaneity:[18] their *wonderment*, manifest in adoration and also the *simplicity* of freedom in asking questions; their capacity and *openness* to learn and develop; their sense of *dependence* on others/ God; their sheer *realism*; and their utter *vulnerability*. This is perhaps best summed up in Jesus' *hymn of jubilation*, his attitude at prayer which gives, as it were, a cross-section of his mind and heart:

> It was then that, filled with joy by the Holy Spirit, he said, "I bless you, Father, Lord of heaven and earth, for hiding these things from the learned and the clever and revealing them to mere children. Yes, Father, for that is what it pleased you to do." [Turning to his disciples he said:] "Everything has been entrusted to me by my Father; and no one knows who the Son is except the Father, and who the Father is except the Son and those to whom the Son chooses to reveal him."[19]

---

[18] Cf. R.H., n. 10; loc. cit., p. 21: *"In reality, the name for that deep amazement at man's worth and dignity is the Gospel, that is to say: the Good News. It is also called Christianity. This amazement determines the Church's mission in the world and, perhaps even more so, 'in the modern world.' This amazement, which is also a conviction and a certitude — at its deepest root it is the certainty of faith, but in a hidden and mysterious way it vivifies every aspect of authentic humanism — is closely connected with Christ. [. . .] The Church's fundamental function in every age and particularly in ours is to direct man's gaze, to point the awareness and experience of the whole of humanity towards the mystery of God, to help all to be familiar with the profundity of the Redemption taking place in Christ Jesus. At the same time man's deepest sphere is involved — we mean the sphere of human hearts, consciences and events."*

[19] Lk 10:21-22; cf. Mt 11:25-27; also Jn 10:15; 17:3ff. Significantly in Luke, Jesus' prayer to the Father is "inspired" and permeated by the joy of the Holy Spirit; it is placed a little before the pericope in which he teaches his disciples to pray the *Lord's Prayer*.

The Eucharistic Prayers for Children do not mention the theme of liberation as such, though there are frequent references to the beauty of relationship with God and among ourselves in family and friendship. So, the theme is certainly implicit throughout. In the second of these Prayers, sin is singled out as the root of evil and as preventing friendship, bringing hate and unhappiness in its wake: Jesus is praised for breaking this vicious circle. The third Prayer asks God's help "to work for peace."

True eucharistic worship[20]

The first point to note about the three Prayers is that each of them contains the eight elements required for the essential structure of a Eucharistic Prayer.[21] The way they are presented is not always the same as in the other Prayers as regards style or sequence. Furthermore, there are certain noteworthy differences which should be regarded as legitimate developments rather than unjustified innovations.

The third Prayer has no explicit intercessions for the dead, although this is implied in the commemoration of the saints and perhaps in the expression of eschatological hope at the coming of the Lord Jesus' kingdom when *"there will be no more suffering, no more tears, no more sadness."* This echoes the reference to the Book of Revelation which finds a place also in the special intercessions for the dead in Eucharistic Prayer III.[22] Death and suffering need not be kept from children while their Christian faith opens them to hope for a "happy ending" which is more enduring and real than that expressed by any fairy tale. The sense of trust in children would be deceived if they were deprived of being taught about so important an aspect of common human experience as death. This same trust, however, must be deepened by showing them how to integrate all experience to a personal and intimate relationship to Christ in prayer. Childhood is

---

[20] Cf. Mazza, *The Eucharistic Prayers*, op. cit., p. 240ff.
[21] Cf. *supra*, Chapter II.
[22] Cf. Rv 21:4.

the moment to begin learning that human life is a journey to God and prayer is the way of the *heart in pilgrimage*. When this approach is taken, then

> *All shall be well, and*
> *All manner of things shall be well.*[23]

The third Prayer does not mention the Holy Spirit as such in the first *epiclesis* before the consecration, but directly asks the Father *"to bless these gifts of bread and wine and make them holy."* It is interesting to note that the original version of the first Prayer has a similar omission whereas the English version includes a request for the sending of the Holy Spirit. The question of the *epiclesis* is a knotty one for theologians! But, what is important for children — and for all Christ's faithful — to appreciate is that all gifts come from God, the Father of love, and that Jesus' gift of himself in the Eucharist is a spiritual gift, that is, it is utterly unique and different from every other blessing bestowed on the human family. For this *"daily bread"* coming from the Lord nourishes our need and hunger for God; the gift of this food and drink is discerned in the prayer of faith which gives us access to the delight of holy communion in Christ's presence. The Holy Spirit, who is the personal love of the Father and the Son, enables the coming about of such a new creation of holiness, that is, the atmosphere of loving recognition in gratitude and praise of God who is the fulness of living love. This expression regarding the power of the Holy Spirit should remind us of his working in the sanctification of Christ's faithful through all the sacraments especially Baptism, Confirmation and Holy Orders.

The "offertorial" aspect of the *anamnesis* is replaced in the third Prayer by a request for the acceptance of the sacrifice or rather of the "beloved Son." It is helpful to see this section of each Prayer synoptically with the notion of acceptance in italics:

---

[23] Cf. T.S. Eliot, *Four Quartets — Little Gidding III*, citing Julian of Norwich's famous conclusion in the *Revelations of Divine Love*, Chapter 86. William Shakespeare perhaps alludes to this too when Puck repeats "the country proverb known" while squeezing juice on Lysander's eyes to induce sleep — cf. *A Midsummer Night's Dream*, Ac. III, Sc. ii; or perhaps he had in mind Ps 127 (126):2 — *"The Lord [. . .] gives to his beloved sleep."*

I	II	III
We remember his death and resurrection and we offer you, Father, the bread that gives us life, and the cup that saves us. Jesus brings us to you; *welcome us as you welcome him.*	And so, loving Father, we remember that Jesus died and rose again to save the world. He put himself into our hands to be the sacrifice we offer.	God our Father, we remember with joy all that Jesus did to save us. In this holy sacrifice, which he gave as a gift to his Church, we remember his death and resurrection. *Father in heaven, accept us together with your beloved Son.* He willingly died for us, but you raised him to life again . . .

Even in the first Prayer the offering is immediately followed by an implicit recommendation for the sacrifice to be accepted by God.[24] This is a most significant development for the theology of sacrifice because — instead of the accent being placed on ritual action and gestures — the focus is turned to God's loving acceptance of our personal union with Christ's sacrifice. It is highly significant as a consequence also for understanding Christian spirituality which realizes Jesus' fulfillment of the sacrifices of the Old Law in the spiritual sacrifice of the New Law of love. For in Mazza's words:

> Sacrifice is not an act but the entire person with his or her history of "life in Christ" and thus with his or her fundamental and most profound options. The person in all its complexity has become "cultic"; the person has even become the supreme cultic reality: a sacrifice acceptable to God. This is possible only in, with, and through Christ. That is why we ask to be accepted "together with your beloved Son."[25]

---

[24] Mazza refers to a passage in St. Irenaeus which is the basis of the formulation here (op. cit., p. 241f.: *"Thus the oblation* (oblatio) *which the Lord teaches is to be offered* (offerri) *throughout the world is said to be a pure sacrifice, acceptable to God. It is not that God needs our sacrifices; but those who offer are themselves glorified in what they offer, if their gift is accepted. The gift expresses honor and devotion to the King."* — cf. *Adversus Haereses*, IV,18.1 (SC 100/2:596).

[25] Op. cit., p. 241.

The phrase in the first Prayer *"Jesus brings us to you"* recalls the idea expressed in the Roman Canon regarding the Angel bringing the sacrifice to the altar of heaven.[26]

In the first Prayer a further development is evident in the way the *anamnesis* is presented in two phases: first, the Church is shown carrying out eucharistic worship in obedience to Christ's command and, second, the celebration itself is described as the proclamation of Christ's death until he comes in glory.[27] These two phases or aspects of the theology of celebration are not contrary to that of "Memorial," but rather enhance it and weave it into the rich fabric of Christian spirituality. For they underline the importance of the expectation of sure hope to which the certitude of the "obedience in faith" in Christ leads — hope for the fulness of eternal life, communion with God.

It is important that children be formed from their earliest years in the spirit of Christian sacrifice. This is particularly the case in materialistically minded society today when discipline — self-discipline — is unfashionable. But, such a formation would be incomplete and indeed wrongheaded if it were focused merely on "will-training," "self-mastery," or, worse, a return to a system of "repressiveness." On the one hand such a false "formation" at best would merely encourage an attitude of humanistic "voluntarism," the enemy of a genuine spiritual life of personal relationship with Christ the unique Savior; on the other hand, it would bring about a deformation of personal growth and crush and destroy a sense of individual worth. But by introducing the notion of personal sacrifice together with that of dialogue and intimate union with Jesus' sacrifice of love, these Eucharistic Prayers gradually lead children to the deepest and richest dimensions of a Christian spirituality. Little ones can be drawn to appreciate the beauty of giving themselves with amazing generosity to someone they love. Who cannot recall being deeply moved as a child when singing with great fervor George Herbert's beautiful lines?

> King of glory, king of peace,
> I will love thee [. . .]

---

[26] Cf. *supra*, p. 79f.

[27] Cf. 1 Cor 11:26. Cf. Mazza, op. cit., p. 250ff.

> Wherefore with my utmost art,
> I will sing thee.
> And the cream of all my heart
> I will bring thee . . .

Adolescents and youth are exemplary in their idealism. Albert Schweitzer was quite right to praise the youthful idealism of the human heart:

> Grownup people reconcile themselves too willingly to a supposed duty of preparing young ones for the time when they will regard as illusion what is now an inspiration to heart and mind. It is through the idealism of youth that man catches sight of truth, and in that idealism he possesses a wealth which he must never exchange for anything else. Grow into your ideals so that life can never rob you of them.
>
> At the present time when violence, clothed in life, dominates the world more cruelly than it ever has before, I still remain convinced that truth, love, peaceableness, meekness, and kindness are the violence that can master all other violence.[28]

But young people need to be attracted to recognize that the Christian community's focus of worship in reality concerns the very depths of human endeavors for betterment in this world — endeavors and betterment which are pointless and frustrated without the spirit of Christ's sacrifice. The dedication of their energies to just causes and human rights has much to contribute when channelled gently towards renewing the quality and vitality of the Church's worship. This is no plea to attempt to attract children and youth to take part in worship by using gimmicks, whose falsity they are the first to see through. Rather, it is a call for catechesis of the Church's understanding and representation of Christ's sacramental sacrifice whose mystery penetrates, involves, and transforms all human experience. For nothing could be more "relevant" to the anguish of our human condition than the eucharistic sacrifice through which we learn to appreciate the wide implications of the Gift of the "Bread of Life" —

---

[28] *Memoirs of Youth* cited in *Words for Worship*, op. cit., n. 675.

implications which point beyond a materialistic mentality to that of sacrifice and generosity, hope and collaboration, sharing, friendship and communion.

All children, but especially youth, respond to being presented a challenge. Their natural idealism and openness become fired by the opportunity to do great things when encouraged and sufficiently motivated by clearly defined objectives. Their reserves of energy and enthusiasm seem boundless. But even more than the challenge of giving of their time, energies, or refreshing enthusiasm, these Eucharistic Prayers focus young people on the exciting adventure of getting to know the Risen Lord Jesus Christ and our Father in the intimacy of personal relationship, which the Holy Spirit of love reveals. This above all is the heart of the eternal life he revealed in his great "high priestly prayer" to the Father during the Last Supper.[29]

Christ's Gift of himself as the "Bread of Life" fulfills the hunger of the human heart and even exceeds its hopes.[30] This Gift reveals the beauty and joy of friendship as each of these Prayers proclaims in a language easily grasped by children of all ages.[31] The second Prayer, for instance, links the words of the *Sanctus* very well with Christ's intention and deeds which express the most significant "preferential option" for the least of this world:

> Blessed be Jesus, whom you sent to be the friend of children and of the poor. He came to show us how we can love you, Father, by loving one another. He came to take away sin, which keeps us from being friends, and hate, which makes us all unhappy.

---

[29] Cf. Jn 17:3.

[30] Cf. Yevgeny Yevtushenko, *A Precocious Autobiography* cited in *Words for Worship*, ibid. n. 676: *"The old Biblical saying, 'Man does not live by bread alone,' has never had a more convincing ring than it has today. [. . .] If even the rich are sad if they have no ideals, to those everlastingly deprived, ideals are a prime necessity. Where bread is plentiful and ideals are short, bread is not a substitute for an ideal. But where bread is short, an ideal can be bread. Simply because such is human nature — because man is born idealist. And great ideals are born of great suffering."*

[31] It is suggested that the first Prayer be used with the very young; the second Prayer with children who are in the intermediate group; and the third Prayer with teenagers. The choice must obviously be a pastoral one which exercises sensitivity appropriate to the children's abilities and circumstances. Cf. Edward Matthews, op. cit., p. 11.

Most noteworthy is the inclusion of the notion of friendship in the context of the words of the Institution Narrative in all three Prayers. Thus in the first Prayer:

> Then he broke the bread, gave it to his friends . . .
> Jesus took the cup that was filled with wine.
> He thanked you, gave it to his friends.

This recalls Jesus' own explicit reference to friendship in the context of the Beloved Disciple's account of the Last Supper. More than a passing reference his words can be understood as his important teaching regarding the way in which divine revelation opens the human heart to the mysteries of God — a way of friendship; this teaching and his accompanying actions in the course of the Last Supper, especially that of washing the disciples' feet, are a revelation of the tenderness of divine love.[32] St. Thomas Aquinas points to the significance of friendship as integral to the way Christ reveals human salvation:

> Since friendship consists in a certain equality, things greatly unequal seem unable to be coupled in friendship. Therefore, to get greater familiarity in friendship between man and God it was helpful for man that God became man, since even by nature man is man's friend; and so in this way, "while we know God visibly, we may [through him] be borne to love of things invisible."[33]

The texts of these Prayers foster the involvement of the congregation by including various acclamations through which it can truly take an active and intelligent part in eucharistic worship. These acclamations do not merely serve to keep the interest of very young participants alive, but they also highlight certain key ideas and themes of the Prayers by repetition. This would be an obvious opportunity for youth

---

[32] Cf. Jn 15:12-17.

[33] *Summa Contra Gentiles*, IV.54.6; translation in *On the Truth of the Catholic Faith*, Image Books, Doubleday & Company, Inc., Garden City, New York, 1957, p. 231. St. Thomas refers to Aristotle's *Nicomachean Ethics*, VIII.1 & 5; the quotation is from the Preface of Christmas and of *Corpus Christi* of the liturgy in use in the 13th century.

to contribute to the worship by using their talents in music. In the second Prayer the *Sanctus* is broken up into three themes which may be related to corresponding parts of the eucharistic proclamation in the following way.[34]

Heaven and earth are full of your glory. Hosanna in the highest!	Thanksgiving for God the Father's work of creation.
Blessed is he who comes in the name of the Lord. Hosanna in the highest!	Praise for Christ's more wonderful work of redemption.
Holy, holy, holy Lord God of hosts. Hosanna in the highest!	Glorification in the Spirit of holiness for the Church and communion of saints.

Instruction on the structure of this Prayer would be an excellent way of leading little children into the mystery of the Blessed Trinity for it would help them to experience their relationship to God while celebrating the *"Mystery of Faith"* at every Mass.

"In my beginning is my end"

These words of T.S. Eliot might provide an appropriate heading to close this chapter. For they refer to our beginning in keeping with the goal or end ever before us.[35] While this chapter has been concerned with aspects of the Eucharistic Prayers for Masses with children, it has also brought out the importance of forming children to participate fully in eucharistic worship. The title of this chapter has

---

[34] Cf. Mazza, op. cit., p. 345 note 37. Cf. Edward Matthews, *Children Give Thanks*, op. cit., p. 14: *"The acclamation, 'We praise you, we bless you, we thank you,' underlines the very meaning of 'eucharist'."*

[35] Cf. *Four Quartets — East Coker I*. Near the end of this poem (*Little Gidding V*) Eliot reverses this: *"What we call the beginning is often the end [/] And to make an end is to make a beginning. [/] The end is where we start from."* But the reversal is only verbal. The reality of living is ever the same: the beginning must not lose sight of the purpose of life itself and the end of human existence issues into the fullness of eternal life — that fullness which is already begun in the Eucharist as Jesus promised in the discourse on the Bread of Life: *"He who eats my flesh and drinks my blood has eternal life, and I will raise him up at the last day"* (Jn 6:54).

a threefold sense: (1) that children be formed for worship (that is, to take their part in the worshiping community); (2) that their formation in Christ be realized as they become worshipers; and, (3) that worship forms the community of faith to become as little children, such as inherit the kingdom of God. One cannot and must not underestimate how young people contribute to the renewal of the Church by their inspiring example of the *heart in pilgrimage*.

There are important lessons to be learned by all Christ's faithful from children who paradoxically illustrate a "state" of continual development which pertains to the very essence or, rather, dynamism of being human.[36] Not insignificantly there is a lesson also for the celebrants of the Eucharist: they cannot merely gabble away these Eucharistic Prayers! For the tone and language of the Eucharistic Prayers for Masses with children require them to be prayed — particularly by the leaders (the official *pray-ers*) of the community. When this happens the Eucharistic Prayers reveal the truth of the *heart in pilgrimage*.

---

[36] The Anglican Bishop John Vincent Taylor drew on the religious experience of children in writing his splendid recent book, *The Christlike God* (SCM Press, 1993). To turn Newman's phrase, we would all do well to essay "consulting the Little Ones in matters of Doctrine and Worship."

9

The Worship of the Eucharist-Hearted Community

In the liturgy the Logos has been assigned its fitting prece-
dence over the will. Hence the wonderful power of relaxation
proper to the liturgy, and its deep reposefulness. Hence its
apparent consummation entirely in the contemplation, adoration and glorification of the fact that the liturgy is apparently
so little disturbed by the petty troubles and needs of everyday
life. It also accounts for the comparative rareness of its
attempts at direct teaching and direct inculcation of virtue.
The liturgy has something in itself reminiscent of the stars, of
their eternally fixed and even course, of their inflexible order,
of the profound silence, and of the infinite space in which they
are poised. It is only in appearance, however, that the liturgy
is so detached and untroubled by the actions and strivings
and moral position of men. For in reality it knows that those
who live by it will be true and spiritually sound, and at peace
to the depths of their being; and that when they leave its
sacred confines to enter life they will be men of courage.[1]

The Word — "A Living and Abiding Voice"

One of the most precious and exciting witnesses to the power
of the Risen Lord Jesus' presence as teacher in the Church is
contained in a fragment from Papias, who in the early second century
had the joy of visiting and consulting those who had known the

---

[1] Romano Guardini, *The Spirit of the Liturgy*, (trans. by Ada Lane), Sheed & Ward,
London, 1937, p. 148f.

apostles. Thanks to Eusebius of Caesarea this fragment has come down to us:

> For I did not think that I could get so much profit from the contents of books as from the utterances of a living and abiding voice.[2]

The phrase *"living and abiding voice"* might be seen as referring not only to those who gave first-hand reports or who narrated all they knew by experience of Jesus or of his teachings, but also to the "voice" of the Word of Life made flesh in the community of the faithful — especially at the eucharistic celebration. For here they give voice to the Word who abides in them, interpreting his gift of himself in the sacrament[3] and communicating through them — especially in the sacred liturgy — the life he shares with God the Father in the Holy Spirit. Jesus Christ's *"living and abiding"* voice calls and consecrates all who hear and keep his word in the Gospel of the Eucharist to become the embodiment of his love for the life of the world.[4]

The notion of being *"contemporary"* with Christ goes to the heart of Christian religious experience and spirituality.[5] It points the Christian community to the fact that God's love made Christ the contemporary of humanity. It was not merely that Christ entered a *"historically conditioned human existence,"* but in doing so he, the eternal Word of

---

[2] *Hist. Eccl.*, III.39 — *"living and abiding voice"* seems a better translation of the Greek (*"'para zóses phones kai menouses"*) than *"viva voce."*

[3] Cf. Karl Rahner, "The Word and the Eucharist," *Theological Investigations*, op. cit., Vol. IV, p. 284f.: *"A word of love, a promise, a threat still exist after their audible expression has passed away. And thus the words of consecration remain as an element of the sacramental sign even 'after' the actual moment of consecration, which was the reason for their being uttered, but not for their being permanently in existence. And so the Eucharist, even as a permanent sacrament which is 'reserved' in its special place, is constituted by the explanatory words of the Lord on the lips of the Church."*

[4] Cf. John Henry Newman, *An Essay on the Development of Christian Doctrine*, Chapter 1, at the end of Sect. II (Longmans, Green and Co., London, 1914, p. 54): "Taking the Incarnation as its central doctrine, the Episcopate, as taught by St. Ignatius, will be an instance of political development, the *Theotokos* of logical, the determination of the date of our Lord's birth of historical, the Holy Eucharist of moral, and the Athanasian Creed of metaphysical."

[5] Cf. *supra* Chapter 1, Fn. 15.

God (the *Logos*, as the Fourth Gospel proclaims), sanctified this temporal condition by his presence.[6] The mystery of Christ's passover refers not merely to his passing beyond the shadows of our experience of suffering and death, nor only to his transformation of a particular people's religious celebration of its historic moment of liberation from the oppression of slavery (namely, Israel's passover feast commemorating the Exodus and entry into the Promised Land), though this was undoubtedly the socio-religious and historical setting of his passover. But, there is much more to it than that! His passover, which the Eucharistic Prayer proclaims, points us further. It constantly points us towards Christ's passing beyond the frontiers of this world's limited attempts to discover meaning in human existence or to attribute to Christ's mystery a human meaning and motivation. By pointing us into the shadows of the night of the Last Supper in the Cenacle — not away from them — the Church's eucharistic celebration becomes the proclamation of supreme hope for humanity. For it invites us to recognize and rejoice that Christ's mystery reveals God's desire to be near his people in every facet of the material world — lilies of the field, birds of the air, the fruit of the earth. Moreover it shows us how God remains especially close to us in every dimension and pulse of human experience and activity — the trade and tackle of work, leisure, friendship, marriage, sickness and health, the daily round of eating and drinking, of sharing in giving and receiving, and in our very dying. But not only this. It consecrates us to become at-one both with him and "the least of our/his brethren."

---

[6] Cf. Crichton, *Christian Celebration: The Mass*, op. cit., p. 26 citing Mircea Eliade's description of the difference between primitive, non-Christian (and non-Jewish) worship and that of the Christian Church: *"When a Christian of our day participates in liturgical time, he recovers the* illud tempus *in which Christ lived, suffered, and rose again — but it is no longer a 'mythical time.' [. . .] When we make the memorial of what the Lord did at the Last Supper, when we recount the sacred history and perform the same gestures, when in short we do once again in symbol what he did long ago, we come into his presence or he makes himself present to us with all his power and love. There is 'epiphany,'* adest, *he is present."* — Cf. also Eliade, *Myths, Dreams and Mysteries*, Collins, Fontana, ed. 1968, pp. 301, to which Crichton refers (ibid., p. 28).

Conversion — not lacking in passover imagination

Being a *"contemporary of Christ,"* may take some imagination! To speak of our situation today in terms of a crisis of faith is really another way of referring to a lack of imagination. C.S. Lewis' various objections to Christianity vanished into thin air when he was brought to his senses quite starkly one day during a stroll when J.R.R. Tolkien gently made the observation: "Your inability to understand stems from a failure of imagination on your part."[7] Indeed, it is only the graced, spiritual power of the passover-imagination of Love alone which can bring about such a conversion of heart so that we become transformed and *"contemporaries of Christ."* We may see this conversion or "turning" as a response to the *"living and abiding voice"* of the Word-made-flesh. This response to the childlike simplicity of faith is realized through sharing and becoming immersed in the *"passover-imagination"* of the liturgy. From the moment of being plunged into the mystery of Christ at baptism until we have no more need of the sacraments of faith — that is, when we are immersed in the mystery of God's communion — *"the living and abiding voice"* of the "Word made visible"[8] in the eucharistic community challenges and empowers us to lift up our hearts (*"sursum corda"*) and turn towards the Father, the personal focal-point of Jesus' passover love. By proclaiming "the mind of Christ" in every Eucharistic Prayer, the Church sets before the faithful the pattern of Christian spirituality — that pattern of the deepest change, namely of the heart. This is the change which John Henry Newman advocates.[9] For, as Leo Tolstoy says, love

---

[7] The incident is related by Ronald Rolheiser — cf. *Catholic Herald*, April 12, 1991, p. 10.

[8] The expression derives from St. Augustine who often speaks of the sacraments as the *"verbum visibile"* (the "visible word") as indicated above: cf. p. 148, fn. 43.

[9] Cf. *An Essay on the Development of Christian Doctrine*, Chapter 1, Sect. 1 (at the end), op. cit., p. 40: *"Here below to live is to change, and to be perfect is to have changed often."* While this sentence is often cited, its context is scarcely known, namely, that principles remain the same though their expression takes different forms in the course of history. T.S. Eliot expresses a similar idea in *Four Quartets — Little Gidding V*:

> *With the drawing of this Love and the voice Calling*
> *We shall not cease from exploration*
> *And the end of all our exploring*
> *Will be to arrive where we started*
> *And know the place for the first time.*

brings about the greatest and only authentic revolution: the inner renewal of human existence.

Christ's passover-love is the supreme revelation of God making our path straight and enlightening our way.[10] Its proclamation in the Eucharistic Prayer is the celebration of our human path becoming pilgrimage. But, the proclamation of the paschal mystery is no easy shortcut to instant bliss or beatitude; it is not an escape from all that tests the human heart's capacity or quality to give of self in loving. Only by being tested can the deepest richness of our spiritual identity be uncovered. Furthermore, the way of Christ involves more than complete commitment, as vitally important as this is in genuine conversion of heart to follow him earnestly and truly. The paschal mystery portrays not merely the achievement of mankind; it is no symbol of a "muscular Christianity." If it were no more than this — a moral incentive — it would hardly qualify as being the perfect act of worship worthy of God, a *"pure sacrifice of praise"* and there would be no need for the grace of Christ's sacrifice! First and foremost, the celebration of the paschal mystery reveals the glory of God's love, the supreme gift of grace — the new and eternal sacrifice of the Lamb of God who takes away the sin of the world — in the banquet of love. The sacramental proclamation or celebration of this mystery encompasses also the way or manner in which Christ chose to communicate God's presence in our midst always. This mystery — no less than its sacramental manner of communication — manifests the magnificence of God's desire and imagination of love.

Though the Eucharistic Prayer is indispensable to fulfil Christ's command: *Do this in memory of me*, no mere words can adequately contain or express this mystery of God's Being-in-love with the world! Yet, the art of human imagination offers some vital clues — such as those depicted by a Russian monk, Andrei Rublev in the early fifteenth century in the *Icon of the Visitors to Abraham*, sometimes

---

[10] One recalls the poet Dante's words in *Divine Comedy* — *Paradiso*, XVII.58:

> You shall find out how salt is the taste of another's bread, and how
> hard a path the going down and going up another's stairs.
> Tu proverai si come sa di sale
> Lo pane altrui, e com'è duro calle
> Lo scendere e il salir per l'altrui scale.

called *The Trinity*. This is a splendid work of art, and, even more, it portrays the essence of what the Eucharistic Prayer proclaims. The most obvious feature, often pointed out about this lovely Icon, is certainly a sense of gracious hospitality in an atmosphere of pure communion, harmony of presence in an equal dignity of being. While this Icon is truly seen as a symbol of the eternal love-feast of the Holy Trinity, it also signifies the eternal moment of Love's desire to share intimately the cup of human suffering and sacrifice.[11]

This is the "dark side," as it were, of God, which is delicately insinuated into this Icon: the mystery of God's unbearable brightness, manifest in the light of Christ's sacrifice in love and for Love. It can, thus, be regarded as a celebration of the eternal Passover depicted in the cup before the Three Figures and in their gestures and inclination towards it. For in this cup, barely recognizable, is an image of the Paschal Lamb which signifies sacrifice at the heart of God's life. In other words, the Icon hints at God's desire to share his eternal love with us in the Eucharist, to which the whole "scene" opens, inviting us also to enter into the sacrifice of Christ which is never absent from the mind and heart of God.[12] How could God forget the gift of his love to his Beloved Son or to us, whom he created in love and re-created through sacrifice!

---

[11] Cf. Mgr. Pere Tena, loc. cit., p. 92; also ibid., article in *Notitiae*, 263, p. 405. Cf. Mary C. Grey, *In Search of the Sacred*, p. 72: *"The icon of the Holy Trinity of André Roublev, painted about 1450 in a Russian Monastery, depicts Father, Son and Spirit seated around the eucharistic table, based on the story of the angelic visit to Abraham. Here Roublev has presented us with an image of perfect communion and dialogue and it is focused on the eucharistic mystery. The table is that of the Lord's Supper, the cup is the sacrificial cup containing the blood of the Lamb. The table itself is placed on a rectangle symbolizing the cosmos, which draws its life-force directly from the eucharistic cup. At the heart of the mystery of the Trinity is suffering, eucharistic love. There is the suggestion in this icon that before the foundation of the world, God the Father looked to Christ, inviting him to take the Cup, the symbol of the way of sacrifice . . . 'Suffering is the bread which God shares with men,' said Paul Evdokimov, a sensitive Russian theologian — which adds another dimension to the symbolism of bread."*

[12] Henri J.M. Nouwen (*Behold the Beauty of the Lord*, pp. 21-23) speaks of how the silence of this Icon brought him inner healing at a difficult period of his life:

As I sat for long hours in front of Roublev's Trinity, I noticed how gradually my gaze became a prayer. This silent prayer slowly made my inner restlessness melt away and lifted me up into the circle of love, a circle that could not be broken by the powers of the world. Even as I moved away from the icon and became involved in the many tasks of everyday life, I felt as if I did not have to leave the holy place I had found and could dwell there whatever I did or wherever I went. I knew that the house of love I had entered has no

"Civilization of the Image"

This is truly the age of sacraments! People today are hungering for more than what materialism can provide; they are thirsting to learn once again the secret of the fulness of living — that secret which is communicated not by the plethora of words and sounds bombarding the senses through our highly developed technological means of the media, but by listening to God's "Good News" above all through the rich and deep resonance his sacred symbols or sacraments of the Church. In this regard it is well to recall Pope Paul VI's observation:

> We are well aware that modern man is sated by talk; he is obviously often tired of listening and, what is worse, impervious to words. We are also aware that many psychologists and sociologists express the view that modern man has passed beyond the civilization of the word, which is now ineffective and useless, and that today he lives in the civilization of the image.[13]

This Pope showed a remarkable sensitivity to the mood and condition of the malaise endemic in the present century. Its staleness and stagnation even in the arts has been referred to in literature as pertaining to an age of the *"deconstruction"* of language.[14] Pope Paul VI's intuition regarding constructing a *"civilization of love,"* about which he often spoke as the particular talent and task of the Christian community, is here linked with the means peculiar to this community, namely, the sacraments. For, the sacraments are guaranteed by Christ to communicate love — the Father's love which he bestows unto the end of time through the Holy Spirit; they manifest and bring

---

boundaries and embraces everyone who wants to dwell there. Within the circle of the Holy Trinity, all true knowledge descends into the heart. The Russian mystics describe prayer as descending with the mind into the heart and standing there in the presence of God. Prayer takes place where heart speaks to heart, that is where the heart of God is united with the heart that prays. Thus knowing God becomes loving God, just as being known by God is being loved by God." The new *Catechism of the Catholic Church* (n. 2691) recommends the practice of praying before an icon in a "prayer corner" set up in the home.

[13] E.N., n. 42 — cited by Cardinal Godfried Danneels in addressing the European bishops on the evangelization of "Secularized Europe" —cf. *Briefing*, Vol. 15, No. 20, p. 315.

[14] Cf. George Steiner, *Real Presences*, Faber & Faber, London, 1969, p. 94ff.

about[15] in a most special and profound way a *"civilization of the image."*

They not only image that abundance of life of sharing in the intimacy of eternal communion, but also enable us to respond fully to God's call to holiness since they provide the means to rediscover ourselves as created in the *"image and likeness of God."*[16] This rediscovery is experienced in the atmosphere of the Church's liturgy, the school of grace where all are moulded according to Christ's likeness until his image is formed in them.[17]

The eucharistic mystery *par excellence* images the *"civilization of Love"* since it contains and communicates the grace of Christ the Teacher, who is *"the image of the invisible God, the first born of all creation."*[18] The Church portrays the *"civilization of the Image"* insofar as at its eucharistic worship its mystery as the Body of Christ becomes realized and manifest. In virtue of this reality the Church is frequently referred to in the Second Vatican Council's Constitution on the Church as *"the sacrament or sign and instrument of intimate union with God and of unity for the whole human race."*[19] The Church is the extension in time of Christ, the primordial sacrament of the Father's communication of the eternal Word of Love. T.S. Eliot describes the paschal mystery as central to the revelation of the meaning of history and the development of religious awareness — an awareness through worship which, he laments, contemporary civilization rejects.[20]

---

[15] Or, *"signify and contain,"* in the classic scholastic language of St. Thomas Aquinas.

[16] Cf. Gn 1:26.

[17] Cf. L.G., n. 7 — cf. Gal 4:19.

[18] Col 1:15 cited in L.G., n. 2. Cf. also Rm 8:29.

[19] Cf. L.G., n. 1; cf. also, ibid., nn. 9, 59, 48; G.S., nn. 42, 45; and *Ad Gentes* (on missionary activity), n. 15. The expression occurs in the liturgy cf. v.g., the prayer of the second Tuesday after Easter referring to Christ in the Italian Missal not in our ICEL translation of the official Latin text.

[20] Cf. *Choruses from 'The Rock' VII*:
> *And the Spirit moved upon the face of the water.*
> *And men who turned towards the light and were known of the light*
> *Invented the Higher Religions; and the Higher Religions were good*
> *And led men from light to light, to knowledge of Good and Evil.*
> *But their light was ever surrounded and shot with darkness [. . .]*
> *Then came, at a predetermined moment, a moment in time and of time,*
> *A moment not out of time, but in time, in what we call history:*
> *transecting, bisecting the world of time, a moment in time but*
> *not like a moment of time,*

Proclamation of Being-in-Love

The words of Romano Guardini quoted at the beginning of this chapter deal with the primacy of *"the logos over ethos,"* that is, the priority of being over having, knowing and doing. The social teaching of the Church, particularly since the Second Vatican Council, has addressed itself to the age-old problem of human selfishness, which, because of its vast scale, has in recent times been appropriately called "consumerism." The roots of this problem, as Pope John Paul II states, can be traced to a failure to appreciate the important distinction between *"having"* and *"being"*:

> To "have" objects and goods does not in itself perfect the human subject, unless it contributes to the maturing and enrichment of that subject's "being," that is to say unless it contributes to the realization of the human vocation as such. [. . .] The evil does not consist in "having" as such, but in possessing without regard for the quality and the ordered hierarchy of the goods one has. Quality and hierarchy arise from the subordination of goods and their availability to man's "being" and his true vocation.[21]

A moment in time but time was made through that moment:
for without the meaning there is no time, and
that moment of time gave the meaning.
Then it seemed as if men must proceed from light to light,
in the light of the Word
Through the Passion and Sacrifice saved in spite of their
negative being; [. . .]
But it seems that something has happened that has never happened
before; though we know not just when, or why, or how, or where.
Men have left GOD not for other gods, they say, but for no god;
and this has never happened before
That men both deny gods and worship gods, professing first Reason,
And then Money, and Power, and what they call Life, or Race, or Dialectic.
The Church disowned, the tower overthrown, the bells upturned,
what have we to do
But stand with empty hands and palms turned upwards
In an age which advances progressively backwards?

[21] Cf. *Sollicitudo Rei Socialis*, n. 28; translation in *Briefing* 88, Vol. 18, No. 5, p. 98. The Pope refers to Pope Paul VI's Encyclical Letter, *Populorum Progressio*, n. 19 and G.S., n. 35. Cf. also P.D.V., n. 8. In Christopher Fry's words: *"What a man knows he has by experience, [/] But what a man is precedes experience." — Curtmantle —* Thomas à Becket's reply to the "action-man" Henry II.

So, what Guardini argued in the 'thirties holds good today:

> Here is the real source of the terrible misery of our day. It has perverted the sacred order of Nature. It was Goethe who really shook the latter when he made the doubting Faust write, not "In the beginning was the Word," but "In the beginning was the Deed."[22]

To rediscover this "sacred order" there is need to rediscover the spirit of the liturgy in which Christ the Inner Teacher re-creates the world — as in the beginning creation was realized by God communicating his Spirit-filled Word. Because he is the *Logos* he is the one who teaches with authority the real significance of creation.[23] Christ the Word of God teaches us, leading us by his Spirit, how to communicate by creating a new language — the sacraments. Since the mystery of Christ reveals the life of God who is love, what could be more appropriate than to employ the vast array of created things which all proceed from and are cherished by their loving Creator? It is he himself who pronounced them "good" in the beginning;[24] he reiterates this blessing, as it were, when the Word was made flesh. For Christ — *"the Light coming into the world . . . full of grace and truth"* — sheds new insight to discern in the divinely etched inner potential of all created realities God's presence and action to save all in love. In the light of his friendship, the Beloved Disciple with the hindsight of faith affirmed God's covenant in Christ's coming into the world:

> We have seen his glory, the glory of the only begotten son of God.[25]

The purpose of his coming and his historical existence was to proclaim a reinterpretation of human existence and of death itself. His

---

[22] *The Spirit of the Liturgy*, op. cit., p. 141. The passage in Goethe which Guardini refers to is in *Faust*, Erster Teil, 11.863-883, which C.H. Dodd cites in German as the front-piece of *The Interpretation of the Fourth Gospel*, CUP, 1953.

[23] Cf. St. Ignatius of Antioch, *Epist. ad Magnesios*, IX.2 cited by Pope John Paul II in C.T., n. 8. St. Augustine never tired of emphasizing —from his early treatises *De Magistro*, II.38ff. and *De Libero Arbitrio*, II.2 to his mature writings, e.g. *Confessions*, VII.19-25.

[24] Cf. Gn 1:3ff.

[25] Jn 1:14.

death represents the moment of Love's supreme triumph and glory over the terminal condition of sin, the enemy of abundant life.

We can thus speak of the Church discovering in the Eucharist its new language, the language of solidarity in sacrifice. *Communion in Christ's sacrifice* has myriad implications not only for a social welfare and liberation of the fundamental human right to free speech, but also, more radically, for humanity's vocation to live in his Spirit as his Mystical Body.

The moral and social implications of the Eucharist are unlimited! The baker's boy carrying the basket of five barley loaves could hardly have realized that his basket contained implications of immense love! These spiritual implications flow out from Jesus' words: *"Do this in memory of me."* This is the first Christian moral and spiritual imperative.[26] Eucharistic morality is thus an enabling or empowering morality because it contains and communicates the grace of holiness —the Author of holiness himself, truly *the grace of our Lord Jesus Christ, the love of God and the fellowship of the Holy Spirit.*[27]

Christ in his unique capacity as the Word-made-flesh imbues all symbols and art with the fresh vitality to communicate.[28] Thus the luminosity of divine substance is reflected through the Christian community's representation of his originality in the use of metaphor and every figure of speech in the gracious words of his parables and, especially, in his uniquely grace-filled deed of pronouncing bread and wine the symbols and reality containing and communicating the Gospel of his passover-love. Indeed, the "sign-language" of the Church's sacraments are countersigned by this love. In recent times discovery of the multilevel language of *sacrament* — and more

---

[26] Cf. Thomas Cullinan, O.S.B., "Eucharist and Politics" in *Justice Papers*, No. 2 — published by the Catholic Institute for International Relations (CAFOD). Cf. also David Morland, O.S.B., *The Eucharist and Justice — Do This in Memory of Me*, Inform, London, 1980.

[27] The conclusion of St. Paul's Second Letter to the Corinthians (2 Cor 13:14) is one of the greetings of the Eucharistic assembly.

[28] Cf. Kenelm Foster, O.P., *God's Tree*, Blackfriars Publ., London, 1957, p. 30ff. re Dante's traditional view of the Church's use of imagery and symbols: there is no new knowledge except through starting with the sensible. Thus, the poet receives Christ through Beatrice, who does not replace Christ, but only reflects and transmits him like a 'sacrament' of salvation.

importantly, its underlying power of symbolism to communicate reality — has highlighted that essential element of human existence: the spiritual quality of communication. This communication, which participates in the Word of Life (the *Logos*), has its source and fullness of expression, as the Council stated, in the eucharistic sacrifice.[29]

This *Logos* of communication — if we may speak this way — needs to be heard today during the *decade of evangelization*. Pope John Paul II's call for a "new evangelization" goes directly to the heart of the deepest sense of the Church's inner being itself, namely, the truth of the Gospel which is Jesus Christ, proclaimed and communicated in the mystery of the Holy Eucharist. The proclamation of the Eucharistic Prayer realizes or makes real to us that the Logos is the way, the truth, the life and beauty of the Church's *being in love*. To see the *"logos"* holding priority over *"ethos"* is to recognize the eucharistic mystery as *the parable* for our times. Through it we live the *passover-love* of Jesus: from aspiration to realization of hopes fulfilled, from ideals to deeds, from the imagery of the word of God to living, from the ritual of the liturgy to reality, from our stumbling endeavors to become holy to being-in-communion with Christ, from yearning and searching to "see God" and to experience the reality of Love to experiencing the delight of becoming transformed into the Mystical Body of Christ — that Body of Love-made-manifest in this world. And as a community proclaims and lives the Eucharist it becomes a *parable of solidarity* — openly "Good News" for fellow Christians, for the poor, oppressed and marginalized, for the aged and infirm, for the handicapped, for youth . . . and for all! Until this Good News becomes an experienced reality in the fullness of communion we must go on proclaiming the Grain of Wheat which in dying bears much fruit.[30]

The Eucharistic Prayer proclaims that evangelization or the proclaiming of "Good News" is essentially a bringing of light — God's light for all people in Christ Jesus, who in the perspective of the New Testament is seen as the "Light of the World."[31] It proclaims that Christ acting through the Eucharist is the *Sign of our times* who sheds light on the whole of our human condition: his Person is the "grace

---

[29] Cf. L.G., n. 11.
[30] Cf. Jn 12:24.
[31] This is most evident in Eucharistic Prayer IV.

and truth" for the meaning of becoming a fully integrated human being; he challenges every person and our communities about the necessity of sacrifice if values — and the supreme value of life — are to be upheld and achieved; he breaks through, purifies, illumines, transfigures and transforms the sin-darkened condition of our obstinate pride, materialism and selfishness. He alone is the Liberator of humanity — the Savior who uniquely can and does free us in our individual lives from the "sinful structures" in which we are implicated in our society.[32] The eucharistic proclamation of the Church's great Prayer realizes Christ's dynamic and transforming presence as continuing to be the world's First and Greatest Evangelizer! Participation in the Eucharist means responding to the Word of Christ, who is the Gospel; it means becoming at-one with God's splendid design of love. This design bears the name Jesus Christ.

In this perspective, our purpose in this book has been to discover the worth of being human by deepening our awareness and appreciation in experiencing *the inner reality of Christ's mystery*, which is communicated and realized at the center of the Christian worship, the Eucharistic Prayer. Here the Church announces and realizes the worth of human living as an expression of the relational life of communion in the Holy Trinity. In order that this may be most deeply lived, the Church upholds and fosters the dignity of every person, who by participating in the its Prayer truly becomes a *pray-er* — a *worshipper of the Father in spirit and truth*.

But, what do these mystical words of Jesus to the Samaritan woman by Jacob's well signify? Who is a "worshipper of the Father in spirit and truth"? What quality of living constitutes this worship that delights the Father's heart? The Spirit of the Risen Lord leads the Church to discern and proclaim that Baptism consecrates a person for worship of which the Eucharist is the source and summit.[33] In other words, the worthwhileness of all human life consists in being healed and made whole by the Father's love, gifted and empowered by the Spirit to be holy, that is, in communion with the Mystical Body of Christ. The worth of being human has its roots in worship. So, while

---

[32] As Pope John Paul II powerfully pointed out in his Encyclical Letter on Social Concern — cf. *Sollicitudo Rei Socialis* (30 December 1987), nn. 36-37.
[33] Cf. L.G., n. 11.

the common or usual meaning associates holiness with moral actions, this meaning is quite incomplete. For it falls short by a metaphysical mile of the mystery of God's gift of freedom. It does not do justice to God's grace! Nor does it duly realize the basis of any moral quality of attitudes or actions, intentions or motives. One is tempted to say that God is above such actions and intentions, being purely and simply all action and intention. He simply *is*. This is his freedom, his holiness, his uniqueness — freedom, holiness, uniqueness which he communicates to all who participate in *be-ing*. Before it is a moral quality, holiness is openness to "the ultimate Otherness." This is how the prophets and some saints perceived it in an instant of ecstatic vision or intuitive understanding.[34]

But being-in-the-world binds Christ's faithful also to be of service to the human family and to act for the betterment of the world. By being contemplatives of the Word-made-flesh — which pertains to *all* Christ's faithful, not only the "professionals" in cloisters — every Christian realizes that he or she is called to active service in some way or other: no one can be exempted as a "conscientious objector" from doing some charitable works of mercy, whether corporal or spiritual. While the path of tracking down or unravelling, tackling and finding solutions to the problems of our society is long and complex; while the solutions can never be adequately expressed in human words which are notoriously deceptive, slippery, open to misinterpretation, indicative only of an imperfect and partial grasp of others' cultural and historical background or of partisan interests and preoccupations; nevertheless, it is a path that cannot be evaded. If one wishes to remain true to one's calling to search for what it means to become truly human, to survive the critical test of putting the noblest language of ideals and values into practice, and, more than this, to become capable of perceiving and communicating the mystery of living as the communion of divine love which we attempt to proclaim at the Eucharist, the Sacrament of Love, how can one neglect the path of Christian service? For if human life is valued as a gift of God, can anyone honestly deny this to others and shirk the responsibility of enabling his sisters and brothers from enjoying this same gift? The path of life, the journey to enjoying it to the full involves responsibility

---

[34] See the classic work on this by Rudolf Otto, *The Idea of the Holy*, Penguin.

— such responsibility as no one can shed or shrug off except at the risk of opting out of being human, and of becoming irresponsible and utterly heartless.[35] Poverty, violence and child abuse, callousness regarding the gift of life: abortion, euthanasia, injustice, oppression, unemployment . . . The litany of woes is endless. The agenda of the Christian responsibility is vast. The path towards becoming human is one along which one can most surely travel only if enlightened by the light of Christian responsibility. For, of all the signs of this light — cultural conditioning and codes of decency, reason, ethical theories, intuitions arising from the natural religious instinct in peoples — there is nothing as clear and effective in pointing to and bringing about the needed change in the human heart as "the grace and truth" of Christ Jesus. Especially by abiding with and accompanying us in the Eucharist, Christ transforms the frustrations and uncertainties and failures of our journey for peace and justice in the world into the sure hope of realizing the fulness of his life. Of this fulness the Eucharist is the luminous pledge and the Eucharistic Prayer is the enlightening proclamation. Christian spirituality flowing from this proclamation of fulness in the Eucharist, the sign of unity and bond of charity, thus expresses the integrity or unification of all human experience and moral endeavor.[36]

The giving and manifesting of his glory — his Body and Blood for the life of the world — is essentially one and the same as his sacrifice on the cross because God is one, his inner being or essence being love — eternally unchangeable, one, and irrevocably faithful. The *Mystery of Faith* is the faithfulness of Love. At the Last Supper Jesus gently rebuked Philip for not knowing him as revealing God's nearness.[37] To "see" the Eucharist as the paschal mystery is to penetrate and behold the desire in the heart of God to restore us to his image and likeness as children born of his love.[38] The passover

---

[35] With fine sensitivity St. Augustine wrote: *"Let everyone, then, who thinks with pain on these great evils, so horrible, so ruthless, acknowledge that this is misery. And if anyone either endures or thinks of them without mental anguish, this is the more lamentable still, for he thinks himself happy because he has lost human feeling."* — *De Civitate Dei*, XIX.7.

[36] The Pauline doctrine of the Eucharist, the Sacrament of unifying Love, is poignantly commented on by many Fathers of the Church. Cf. e.g. St. John Chrysostom, *Hom. in Matt.*, 50:3-4 (PG 58, 508-509); St. Augustine, *In Joh. Ev.*, Tr. 31:13 (PL 35, 1613).

[37] Cf. Jn 14:9.

[38] Cf. Jn 1:13; 3:3ff.; 1 Jn 3:2; 1 Cor 2:9.

mystery and its proclamation in the Eucharistic Prayer involve the cost of searching for dialogue with God, whose love reveals the joy of finding that he is already and always present and ready to communicate all of himself. Every relationship is a costly matter — *costing not less than everything.*[39] Only the sacrifice of Christ's passover-love, which we proclaim particularly in the Eucharist, can sustain our endeavors to realize the depths of our Christian vocation to be worshippers, offering the spiritual sacrifice of ourselves which is required in any relationship that is enduring.

Communication proclaims Communion

There exists a great variety of liturgies in the East and the West.[40] This variety represents difference in mentalities, customs, temperaments and religious intuitions and traditions of people from the diverse cultures in which the seed of the Gospel, that is, the grain of the Eucharist, is sown. This variety manifests a wonderful sign of the catholicity of the spirituality of the Christian Church.

This spirituality expressed in the Eucharistic Prayer would be incomplete without commemoration of the Blessed Virgin Mary and the saints. The saints have an integral place in Christian spirituality which is always "eucharistic" — that is, full of a sense of praise, appreciation, gratitude and communion. The saints are integral also to the Church's doctrine of merit, which has been shaped by the New Testament proclamation of the grace and truth of Jesus Christ whose light brought the freedom and joy of God's Spirit exemplified in the lives of the saints. What we behold in them is more than some moral excellence. Why we honor them is not merely because of our tendency to hero-worship. We pray to them not because we do not have confidence in the unique Mediator and Lamb who readily gives us access to the Father by interceding on our behalf. But, inspired by their example, encouraged by their friendship, strengthened by their constant prayer and protection,[41] we above all find in them credible

---

[39] Cf. T.S. Eliot, "Little Gidding" — *Four Quartets.*
[40] Cf. Tillard, op. cit., pp. 306-311 for a useful reference table.
[41] Cf. Prefaces 69-71 — of Holy Men and Women and of All Saints (1 November).

witnesses to the form (*logos*) of Christ, whose light we behold reflected in world.[42] The saints are the Church's "experts in humanity"[43] because their gaze is fixed on contemplating the Word-made-flesh, because they know how to live the Good News of the Eucharist. How utterly different is the anguished picture of the dichotomy between ourselves and "the saints" that Graham Greene depicts:

> The saints, one would suppose, in a sense create themselves. They are capable of the surprising act or word. They stand outside the plot, unconditioned by it. But we have to be pushed around. We have the obstinacy of non-existence. We are inextricably bound to the plot, and wearily God forces us, here and there, according to his intention, characters without poetry, without free will, whose only importance is that somewhere, at some time, we help to furnish the scene in which a living character moves and speaks, providing perhaps the saints with the opportunity for their free will.[44]

Such a point of view is unacceptable to and unrepresentative of Christian faith. Its cardinal error is not so much that it misrepresents the saints as being outside and, indeed, above the common human scenario of change and conversion — temptations and doubts, hesitation and vacillation, compromises, mistakes and sin, struggles, frustrations and even failure —but that it attributes to them a superhuman capacity for creating themselves. Greene's outlook is that of an author who is struggling to cope with "runaway characters" — that is, characters who paradoxically while being entirely his own, while depending for their speech and actions on him, somehow escape, or rather, beckon to him to track down their own preexistent identity, which is buried deep in the unconscious zones of his inner emotional

---

[42] Cf. von Balthasar, *The Glory of the Lord*, I, op. cit., p. 28f.: *"The simple Christian knows this as he loves his saints among other reasons because the resplendent image of their life is so love-worthy and engaging. But the spiritual force necessary to have an eye for a saint's life is by no means to be taken for granted, and in our time our eyes (like those of Rilke's 'Panther' as he paces his cage) seem to be 'so tired from endlessly counting the bars' that even these most sublime figures of human existence can hardly snatch us from our lethargy."*

[43] Cf. *Sollicitudo Rei Socialis*, n. 41 — citing Paul VI's *Populorum Progressio*, n. 13.

[44] *The End of the Affair*, Penguin, p. 182.

and religious intuitions and in the hidden crevasses of his own imagination and creative genius.[45] A *fatal attraction*, as it were, for creativity allures Greene to indulge himself with the deception of putting the authorship of characters in a book on a par with God's mysterious dialogue with his human creatures in whom the divine Author creates an incredibly wonderful capacity to become free. Greene's "saints" can have no place of honor or admiration on the calendar of time or on history's honors list: they are so utterly inhuman! More terrible than this, however, is their heinous crime of apparently having opted out of and of being beyond the pale of the struggle of the history of salvation. Greene exalts this as their heroic virtue, though it is hardly "virtue" if they could not help being so creatively free! For, because of their sheer creative freedom, as Greene claims, they have no need for fellowship with other people or even for communion with God, as our Savior and Redeemer.

Quite different, indeed, is the picture left us by another author, Georges Bernanos. On the very last line of his celebrated novel about the anguished struggle of a priest to respond to God's call to holiness despite his experience of the weight of human weakness and despite a feeling of disgust for the heaps of "dust" surrounding him (and in him!), Bernanos tersely states the Catholic creed of freedom, that is, gratitude for the ultimately transforming power of God's at-oneing love: *"Does it matter? Grace is . . . everywhere?"*[46]

If George Herbert is correct in praising Prayer in many beautiful names, there is one title which belongs both to the Church's Eucharistic Prayer and to us, its pray-ers: *"heart in pilgrimage."* Emptied of all pretensions, trusting entirely in the love of God, forgetting themselves in the vision of God, it is the saints who are the truest artists, the truest scientists, the "seers" or prophets of beauty and truth. They are the real founders of the culture of life! Among the many saints of the Eucharist, St. Peter Julian Eymard, a priest in nineteenth century

---

[45] Dostoevsky, for instance, states the he discovered aspects of himself in his characters, whose innermost motives and mental anguish he penetrated in his psychological method of writing. Thus, he confesses in his *Notebooks* how he himself was startled at the unexpected murder in *Crime and Punishment*, a novel which turned the scene "into one of the most terrible of literary truths" — cf. Malcolm Bradbury, *The Modern World's Ten Great Writers*, Secker & Warburg, London, 1988, p. 47.

[46] *The Diary of a Country Priest*, Collins, Fontana, 1963, p. 253.

France, has a special place. His heart was drawn by Jesus' passover-love, which he contemplated as an adorer and whose "fire" he zealously sought to spread abroad; he was truly an evangelist of the Eucharist *"always on the move."*[47] Addressing the Bishops of Europe, Pope John Paul II said:

> We need heralds of the gospel who are experts in humanity, who know the depths of the human heart, who can share the joys and hopes, the agonies and distress of people today but who are at the same time contemplatives who have fallen in love with God. For this we need the saints of today.[48]

Christian contemplation is not merely an exercise of the heart which focuses on human fulfillment. It pertains to the whole Church — to all Christians who are called, like the Virgin Mary, to ponder the Word in their hearts. The Word received and contemplated in the Church's liturgy leads to forming in the community the "new heart" of which the prophets spoke — that heart of interior life in which the Holy Spirit inscribes the pattern of covenanted Love. Baldwin of Ford, Archbishop of Canterbury, in the twelfth century appreciated this and offers a rich spiritual doctrine especially regarding the Sacrament of the altar.[49] Citing a famous passage from St. Gregory the Great which was a fundamental text in forming the approach of medieval monastic theologians, he teaches that full maturity of knowing consists in love:

> For you, O God, are charity, and how far he is from salvation who hates charity, and who is rejected by charity! O what folly is this, to hate love! Folly, for this is to hate wisdom! You, Lord, are highest Wisdom. To get to know you is perfect under-standing (cf. Ws 6:16); coming to know you is love, a love

---

[47] Cf. Retreat Notes, Rome, 5 February 1865: *"I have been somewhat like Jacob always on the move."* — Cited in the lively and realistic biography of the saint by Norman Pelletier, Superior General of the Blessed Sacrament Congregation, *Tomorrow Will Be Too Late: A Life of Saint Peter Julian Eymard (1811-1868)*, Emmanuel Publishing, Cleveland (Ohio), 1992, p. 12.

[48] Cited in *Briefing* 85, Vol. 15, No. 20 (25 October 1985), p. 317. Cf. Paul VI, E.N., n. 41; CTS S 312, p. 52: *"Modern man listens more willingly to witnesses than to teachers and if he does listen to teachers, it is because they are witnesses."*

[49] Cf. my article in *Adoremus*, Vol. LXX, No. 2 (1990), pp. 14-27.

which is itself knowledge (qui amor ipse notitia est).[50] He who does not love you, cannot know you as he ought, or who you are even though he glorifies in his flowery eloquence, or prides himself on his knowledge of wonderful things, or shows off a wealth of rich desirable objects. He is foolish and stupid (cf. Ps 48:11), if he does not love you, wretched and poor (cf. Ps 69:6), if he fails to love you. For the "abundance of salvation, wisdom and knowledge" (Is 33:6), is that wisdom which savors and cherishes you, and is "more precious than jewels; and nothing desirable can compare with her" (Pr 3:15).[51]

Freedom is where the horizons of history merge

Authentic spirituality must lead to freedom which is exercised in our temporal condition. It must therefore address itself to the constant problem experienced as the fragmentation of existence by change. Time is problematic! Who has not felt in some way or other the fever of being goaded on to engage at breakneck speed in an impossible venture to become a success — an "achiever"! And who has not been caught out in a "race against time" whether in turning in an assignment by some impersonal "deadline" or in finishing the scones before the arrival of some important guests for tea! *"Hurry up, please; it's time"* is the weary cry not only of the barman or barmaid at the end of day.[52] The pressure of modern conditions leave little room for that leisure which the ancients appreciated as the basis of creating an environment of culture favorable to fostering genuine human relationship.[53] Existence is punctuated and crammed into digital

---

[50] Cf. William of St. Thierry (an earlier contemporary of Baldwin), *Expos. in Cant.* I.7,76: *"Amor ipse intellectus est"* ["Love itself is understanding"] — cited in the Instruction on contemplative life, *Venite Seorsum*, 15 August 1969.

[51] *Cenobitic Community Life* (*De Vita Coen.*), 6 — Interim translation based on PL 204:516-562, Nunraw, October 1985, which the Rt. Rev. Abbot Donald Glynn, O.C.S.O., kindly sent me.

[52] As in T.S. Eliot's *The Waste Land*, III.

[53] Cf. Josef Pieper, *Leisure, the Basis of Culture* (translated by Alexander Dru), The New American Library (Mentor-Omega Book), 1963.

flashing atoms of experience which are not apparently related to the context of the whole of an hour or even to other parts of it. Time and the passing of things, loved and lovely, is indeed poignantly problematic as the poet Virgil lamented long ago.[54] Something is needed not to "put the clock back" or to "make time stand still," as we might sometimes wish, but to transform our *approach* to the experience of the transience of all things. While our observation of change yields an important clue, the very idea of change must be deepened or transformed. That is, our notion of change must become transformed as we are, as our hearts are changed or converted.

But how? *Conversion* through Christ's passover-love is the key to the discovery of the real significance of being human. As we saw above,[55] the biblical significance of the appropriate hour (*kairos*) is uncovered through revelation — that is, Christ's call to respond to the "sacrament of the present moment" in which he is present to all and all is present in him. The proclamation of the Eucharist, the Sacrament of unity, reveals presence. The remembering or *anamnesis* of the Church's Eucharistic Prayer challenges us to break through our habitual way of viewing experience, which is constricted into the categories of past-present-future so that we may discover and live *being-in-Love*. This is the stance of the Christian *"heart in pilgrimage"*!

The mystery of the Passover concerns the eternal moment of Love's thoughtfulness — love's capacity never to forget, love living ever in the presence of the other. Love keeping the beloved ever present in one's eye, after all, is frequently a poignant theme in great love-poetry.[56] Our Judeo-Christian tradition expresses its response to God's love for his creation in the religious act of recalling with thanksgiving and praise or rather, re-presenting *"the wonderful deeds of God."* This manner of responding to the presence of divine love reaches its perfection especially in our Eucharistic celebration as the *"anamnesis"* or memorial of Christ's eternal passover, which he

---

[54] Cf. *Aeneid*, i, 461: *"Sunt lacrimae rerum et mentem mortalia tangunt"* (Mortality has her tears and touch the heart of man).

[55] Cf. Chapter VI, p. 140f.

[56] This can be illustrated from both the Western and Eastern traditions — cf. Shakespeare, *Sonnets* 27, 30, etc., or the Sufi mystic Fakhruddin Iraqi, *Divine Flashes*, V.1.

himself revealed and enjoined his disciples to carry out. *Anamnesis* is not merely retrospective remembering; it has nothing in common with nostalgia, which — although at times delightful — may also be an evasion or escape from responding to reality. In the biblical and liturgical sense the significance of *anamnesis* is essentially that of *remaining* in God's love through Christ's becoming our contemporary —that abiding which the Beloved Disciple reminds us was Jesus' behest at the Last Supper. This love is the basis of understanding anything![57]

In the *anamnesis* of the Eucharistic Prayer we give thanks for the living presence of Christ. His *action* in the passover mystery expresses the whole liberating vitality of his *Being-in-love*. For it is this that frees us from our tendency to become complacent with our "dead-end" condition of selfishness and pride — that condition which even infects our "good works." We are enabled to passover to eternal life, that is, to become committed to one another and concerned for the values of the Gospel: truth, trust, dialogue, justice, love, freedom, friendship and peace in human relationships. The worth of giving thanks in the *anamnesis* is not merely a matter of recalling as history God's saving deeds in the Exodus or in Jesus' life, death and resurrection. But, insofar as it reveals that the present comes to us "from" the future (as in the uncanny way our past not only influences who we are, but also shapes the way we shall be) the *anamnesis* proclaims the goal of hope for our future that is eternal. The worthwhileness of our struggle for the great evangelical values of the Beatitudes is thus already signified by the Lord Jesus Christ's unique and eternal sacrifice which is represented or made present sacramentally in the eucharistic worship of the Church, ever the community of faith, hope and love.

---

[57] Cf. von Balthasar, *The Glory of the Lord*, Vol. I, op. cit., p. 30: *"The spiritual eyes of the disciples were indeed held in check as long as he had not died and risen from the dead, and they required a certain distance not only somehow to 'believe' the divine content of Christ's reality, but to 'see' it in its self-evidence. And yet, this content was already to be found expressed in the man Jesus, and, for all its abstraction and contemplation, the retrospective remembering and* anamnesis *of what had been seen — the* conversio ad phantasma *(verissimum!) constitutes the basis of understanding anything."*

Understanding liberation in the light of the Eucharistic Prayer, we can make our own the words of Pope John Paul II, who writes as a poet, priest, pastor, and man of exquisite sensitivity:

> Freedom has continually to be won, it cannot merely be possessed. It comes as a gift but can only be kept with a struggle. Gift and struggle are written into pages, hidden yet open. You may struggle for freedom with all your being; then call this your freedom, that paying for it continually you possess yourself anew. Through this payment we enter history and touch her epochs. Which way runs the divisions of generations, the divisions between those who did not pay enough and those who had to pay too much? On which side are we? And exceeding in so many self-determinations, did we not outgrow our strength in the past? Are we upholding the burden of history like a pillar with a crack still gaping?[58]

Today, more than ever we have a great need to re-discover that condition of utter simplicity which integrates mind, heart and feelings. Rather than turn our religious approach and thinking of everyday realities into abstractions or generalizations, God's revelation in the Holy Scriptures shows how he enabled his people to discover his nearness to them through the various circumstances and experiences of human existence. Yet, for whatever reason — anti-semitism, infatuation with the patters of Hellenistic neoplatonic intellectualism, a fatal obsession with Manichaean dualism, or perhaps a mixture of all of these and other reasons as well — we seem for too long to have forgotten or neglected "a poetical view of things," which Newman regarded as "a duty" pertaining to Christians.[59] The Holy Scriptures, bathed in the light of the divine Word's taking flesh, call us afresh to experience what Dylan Thomas (not without a wisp of nostalgia) remembered of his childhood religious experience:

---

[58] From Karol Wojtyla's poem "I reach the heart of drama," in *Collected Poems* (translated by Jerzy Peterkiewicz), Random House, 1982.

[59] Cf. J.H. Newman, "Poetry with reference to Aristotle's Poetics" in *Essays, critical and historical*, I, 1857, p. 23.

And I saw in the turning so clearly a child's
Forgotten mornings when he walked with his mother
Through the parables
Of sunlight
And the legends of the green chapels . . .[60]

Sursum corda — Lift up your hearts!

This summons implies an image signifying not an escape, but the sense of dynamism and urgency about entering the movement of Christ's passover. Christ's Spirit uplifts and inspires our hearts which respond to this stirring invitation before every Eucharist Prayer. All depends on the response we make both during this great Prayer and in our lives. All depends on our response today to the Word who desired to raise all creation to the Father as it did on the response of the Blessed Virgin Mary.[61] Only the passover-imagination of faith can liberate our hearts from the heavy downbeat of this world's materialism and hedonism. In the joy of praising God for his gift of Christ's mystery of passover in the Eucharistic Prayer we rediscover with the freshness and innocence of childlike simplicity the world's true value — its reality as the sign of God's nearness in creative love. The attractiveness of his living and abiding voice in this Prayer exercises its power over our hearts which continue to be drawn — at whatever age we may be — through the capacity and love he imbues in them to listen to and celebrate the greatest parable of all that Love told: *the parable of the Eucharist*. In a splendid passage in Pope St. Leo the Great's second sermon for the Ascension, the rich significance of the mystery of Christ's passover is lucidly expressed:

> This is the strength which is given to great minds, this is the light of those who are truly the faithful, that unhesitatingly they can believe what they cannot see with the bodily sight,

---

[60] *Poem in October.*

[61] Cf. St. Bernard's Sermon on the inner drama of acceptance of the angelic message at the Annunciation — *Hom.* 4, 8-9 in *Laudibus Virginis Matris; Edit. Cisterc.* 4 (1968), 53-54; D.O., Vol. I, p. 141f. (20 December).

and focus their longings beyond the array of visible things. How could our hearts sustain such devotion, how could anyone be justified by faith, if our salvation were based solely on those things which meet our gaze? The visible presence of the Redeemer has passed over into the sacraments [transivit in sacramentis]; and to confirm and ennoble faith, it is now grounded not on sight but on doctrine. The hearts of the faithful follow this doctrine by a light which comes from above.[62]

In addressing the National Delegates for the International Eucharistic Congress on 11 March 1989 Pope John Paul II stressed the central place that prayer ought to have in preparing for the world event of the Forty-fourth International Eucharistic Congress, which was to be held in Seoul, South Korea:[63]

It is altogether appropriate that there be intense spiritual preparation through reflection and prayer for the forthcoming Congress, with a sincere opening of hearts and minds to welcome the gift of Christ's peace.

Prayer especially ensures spiritual participation in any such event and, indeed, in living itself — since it takes us into the heart of all human experience and endeavor. The *Catechism of the Catholic Church* links all aspects of Christian living to the Eucharistic Prayer, for here the essential relationship with God becomes the proclamation of the Christian spirit. The *Catechism* develops its description of the prayer-life of the Church in terms of a response to the gift of God, to his covenant, to communion.[64] The Eucharistic Prayer most richly

---

[62] Cf. *Sermon 74*, 23.

[63] St. Peter Julian Eymard (1811-68) may rightly be honored as the inspiring figure behind these events, as was acknowledged in the processes of his canonization by Pope John XXIII (on 9 December 1962, at the end of the first session of the Second Vatican Council). For he had been the Spiritual Director of Emilie Tamisier (1834-1910), whose undaunted zeal and energy brought about Congresses 1881-1991: "Origin and Development" in *The International Eucharistic Congresses for a New Evangelization*, Vatican Bookshop, Vatican City, 1991, pp. 7-61.

[64] Cf. CCC, n. 2558.

expresses and realizes the depth and extent of the Christian response or spirituality of relationship.

As was brought out in different ways at the 45th International Eucharistic Congress of Seville in June 1993, the eucharistic celebration is the Church's primary and essential source and summit of evangelization.[65] In his eloquent and deeply stirring talk, for instance, Cardinal Sin of Manila said that the Eucharist is "the greatest intensification of the Word" for the "Word and Sacrament are constitutive dimensions of evangelization."[66] In the words of the Basic Text proposed for reflection on the Congress theme, *"Christ, the Light of the Nations"*:

> The themes of "light" and "life" are intimately bound together because life which was in Christ the Word of God is revealed as light for humankind.[67]

The Eucharist-hearted Community

The Eucharistic Prayer at the heart of the Church realizes the proclamation not only of the purpose and content of all evangelization, but also of *the beauty of worship which saves.*[68] Evangelization,

---

[65] The theme of this Congress: *Christus, Lumen Gentium*, was developed in the various talks and round table discussions, apart from the pastoral preparations, devotional activities, and homilies during the eucharistic celebrations. Thus, for instance, in the following discourses: Cardinal Joachim Meisner, *Eucharist and Evangelization*; Cardinal Carlo Maria Martini, *The Eucharistic Celebration: Summit of Evangelization*; Cardinal Jaime Sin, *The Eucharist: A Call to the Missions*; Fr. Anthony McSweeney, s.s.s., *The Evangelizing Richness of the Eucharist*; Prof. Guzmán Carriquiry, *The Eucharistic Source of the True Christian Spirit*; Sr. Juana Elizondo Leiza, *Social Implications of Participation in and Worship of the Eucharist*; etc. The main talks and conferences of this Congress are published and made available in English and French by Éditions Paulines, Sherbrooke, Quebec, Canada.

[66] Cf. Sin, loc. cit., p. 10.

[67] *Basic Text*, op. cit., n. 5; op. cit., p. 20.

[68] Dostoevsky held that "Beauty will save the world" — Cf. Pavel Evdokimov, *Gogol et Dostoevskij*, Éd. Paulines, p. 173ff. Cf. also, Stratford Caldecott & Michael L. Gaudoin-Parker, "The Eucharist: Source for a Culture of Life" in *Adoremus*, Vol. LXXIII, No. 1, pp. 21-19.

whose theme is Christ, "culminates in the Eucharist."[69] There is no question here of mere aestheticism — that is, it is not a matter of the "holiness of beauty," but rather of *"the beauty of holiness."*[70] George Herbert pointed to the harmony that worship ensures — between being and saying, knowing and doing the truth:

Beauty and beauteous words should go together.[71]

The eucharistic community offers a culture of life because through faith it discerns in worship the invisible mystery of God's presence penetrating, permeating and transforming the visible created realities which we handle. This community, however, is constantly threatened by the seductions of a world or culture of death, which is aptly called a *"consumer society"* because, instead of nourishing and fostering genuine human growth, it devours the human quality of life. This culture of death, pretending to live by appearances, the only "reality" it acknowledges, manipulates and glorifies appearances in order to imitate life. It constructs an increasingly artificial world: surrounding us with a false sense of security, comfort and uninterrupted entertainment. In fact the verb "construct" is hardly appropriate in an environment pretentiously boasting of having "deconstructed" everything — all inner meaning in speech, art, and living itself.

The eucharistic community draws its strength from Christ, the *Alpha* and *Omega* who holds all creation in being. His words are "spirit

---

[69] Cf. E.N., nn. 27-28.

[70] Drawn by aesthetic sense, William Pater admired the Mass as *"the greatest act of worship the world has seen"* and *"the liturgy of the church came to be — full of consolations for the human soul. [. . .] worship — 'the beauty of holiness,' nay, the elegance of sanctity —was developed, with a bold and confident gladness, the like of which has hardly been the ideal of worship in any later age. The tables in fact were turned: the prize of a cheerful temper on a candid survey of life was no longer with the pagan world. The aesthetic charm of the Catholic Church, her evocative power over all that is eloquent and expressive in the better mind of man, her outward comeliness, her dignifying convictions about human nature: — all this, as abundantly realized centuries later by Dante and Giotto, by the great medieval church-builders, by the great ritualists like Saint Gregory, and the masters of sacred music in the middle age — we may see already, in dim anticipation, in those charmed moments towards the end of the second century."* — Cf. *Marius the Epicurean,* Oxford University Press (The World's Classics), 1986, p. 210ff.

[71] George Herbert, *The Forerunner.*

and life" for all. While such a community needs people of vision artists, poets, musicians, and organizers, too — it is essentially an environment of grace where the least of Christ's brethren can feel at home and wanted — the house-bound, the old-age pensioner, the disabled, those "marginalized" by a society which only recognizes those who are useful or successful. Such a community is truly *eucharist-hearted* insofar as the hidden but real form of all its members' vitality is the same Christ in his Sacred Sign, the Bread of Life, which unites them in worship and love. Receiving into their bodies this Sacrament, which they all adore, this community in holy communion nourishes in itself a life that cannot be overcome by death — a life that heals the sinful "body of death" and preserves it from falling a prey to the surrounding environment of a culture of death.

"Eucharist-hearted" would seem an appropriate way of describing the quality of community life envisaged in the new culture of life. For this expression points to nothing short of the radical shift of values implied and required by sharing Christ's *"gift of self"* in the eucharistic sacrifice. It complements (and corrects) the impression given by the expression frequently employed today, *"community-building,"* an expression which, albeit Pauline in origin, is too often interpreted as laying emphasis almost exclusively on the external dimensions of human sociability. Without gainsaying the need and importance of expressing greater friendliness and fraternity both in participating in the liturgy and also in our relationships in ordinary living, the question is: what is the solid basis and deep *raison d'être* of this accent on human relatedness?

From the Eucharistic Prayer, on which we have been meditating throughout this book, it is clear that the radical *source, center and summit* of the whole life of a eucharist-hearted people is the mystery of Christ's presence, which is most fully manifest in his *"gift of self"* in the eucharistic sacrifice. At the Last Supper, Jesus did not merely say: "Love one another"; he added those significant and vital words: "as I have loved you." Thus, the task in bringing about the "wholeness" of this new culture of life does not consist merely in our human striving to do away with poverty and disease or to overcome divisions and class distinctions, but rather, in realizing our unity in woundedness — a unity with Christ the Savior who heals our deepest wound of self-centered pride by becoming one with us in his own *"gift of self."*

Evangelization, which is intrinsic to the reality of our life together in Christ as brothers and sisters, therefore, takes on a profound *"eucharist-hearted"* significance in this environment of the grace of Christ's presence to humanity in the eucharistic sacrifice: it becomes a matter of "one beggar telling another beggar where to get bread."[72] A truly eucharist-hearted community discerns and values the indispensable hidden contribution of so many of its members who do not seem to be involved in "building up community" — or are incapable of any obvious involvement in it.[73] The deeper colors of suffering, stained by the Blood of the Lamb, are crucial to balance the brighter tones of the Church's celebration of the culture of life so that its worship may be realized in spirit and truth.

Christians who are truly catholic are utterly realistic. They cherish the vital significance of the present moment; they call its great sacrament the Mass the sacrament or most sacred sign of Memorial, in which all past experience and all yearning for future expectation and hope regarding justice, peace, and joy are gathered into an instant of religious celebration in the present moment. The present moment, especially at this celebration, is richly precious for it draws on the consciousness of God who communicates through Christ how he is present to all, in all and through all creation — particularly in all creatures who are open to the reality of presence. The sacramental celebration of the present moment in the Mass touches, transforms, consecrates the best of our deepest longings. It is the transfiguration of what lies at the heart of human living where there is but one vital impulse — the instinct that is characteristic of human life, namely, the godlike dynamism for eternity. This is far more than a nostalgia for a golden age of immortality! It bespeaks a dynamism for mystery — the mystery of presence, that is, the revelation which communicates being enfolded in love, the fulness of intimacy. In a word, it points us

---

[72] This is the way evangelization is defined by Dr. Heather Ward in a challenging study of "self" in Christian spirituality — cf. *The Gift of Self*, DLT, London, 1990, p. 50. This book provokes a reappraisal of many commonly-held assumptions in modern approaches to spirituality (e.g. notions of human development/growth/wholeness as in the Myers-Briggs or Enneagram systems).

[73] Cf. ibid., p. 89: "Those whose lives are a struggle with difficult temperaments, with emotional and psychological distress, are equally enabling the Body to function, their acceptance of their poverty providing its continuing openness to life." It is timely to hear this kind of affirmation!

to communion. In this mystery of remembrance or Memorial we are pledged to eternal life, the glory of being-present in full communion with God and one another as is proclaimed in the Christian Creed: *the communion of saints [. . .] the resurrection of the body,* of which the Eucharist, the Mystery of Faith is proclaimed as a foretaste since it is the sacrament *par excellence* of the Mystical Body of Christ.

At the end of his quest for true beauty St. Augustine realized that the human heart was made for God and remains restless until it discovers true peace in being set on fire in confessing or proclaiming the glory of God:

> the price of my redemption is before me. I eat it and drink it and proclaim it to others.[74]

This is precisely what is at the heart of the Church's eucharistic proclamation! This is what the Church's Eucharistic Prayer realizes: the *heart in pilgrimage.*

The Eucharistic Prayer proclaims that the Word who creates all things — the Word of Life — through becoming our sacrifice and praise and prayer has become our language of communication perfectly acceptable to God and the Good News comprehensible to anyone open to his Spirit to be moved by the love shown us by the Father. In the eucharistic celebration we hear Christ the Evangelist *par excellence* and have access to God since we are united and in communion with him, the eternal Liturgist and perfect Mediator, in the work of integrating worship into the fabric of human living and vice versa. George Herbert exquisitely penetrated this mystery of communication which we are hard-pressed to express. Only by surrendering ourselves in the Church's great Eucharistic Prayer to the deed of the Word's sacrifice do we discover the truth of the *"heart in pilgrimage"* and the beauty of the Word:

> We say amisse,
> This or that is:
> Thy word is all, if we could spell.[75]

---

[74] *Confessions,* X.47; cf. I.1; X.27. Cf. ibid., IX.12,32. The expression "price of our redemption" occurs also in Augustine's other writings — e.g. *Quaest. Evan.,* 11.23 (PL 35, 1346); *Contra Faust.,* 20.17 (PL 42, 380).

[75] *The Flower.*

Further Reading

Aldazábal, J., "La Eucaristia" in *La Celebracion en la Iglesia*: II Sacramentos (Lux Mundi 58), Ed. Sigueme, Salamanca, 1990, esp. pp. 303-335.

Anamnesis — Eucaristia teologia e storia della celebrazione, Marietti, 1983.

Basic Text of the 45th International Eucharistic Congress in *Eucharist: The Heart of Evangelization*, Éd. Paulines, 1992, pp. 10-60.

Bouyer, L., *Eucharist*, Notre Dame, 1968.

———, *Introduction to Spirituality*, Liturgical Press, Collegeville, MN, 1961.

Brilioth, Y., *Eucharistic Faith and Practice: Evangelical and Catholic* (tr. A.G. Hebert), S.P.C.K., London, 1965.

Bro, B., *The Spirituality of the Sacraments: Doctrine and Practice for Today* (tr. by Theodore DuBois), Sheed and Ward, New York, 1968.

Burnaby, John, *Amor Dei: A Study of the Religion of St. Augustine*, The Canterbury Press, Norwich, 1991.

Burton, J.R., (ed.), *The Richest Legacy: The Eucharistic Hymns of John and Charles Wesley*, P. Cross & Sons Ltd., Norwich.

Buxton, R.F., *Eucharist and Institution Narratives — Study of Roman and Anglican Traditions* (Alcun Club Coll. No. 58) Mahew-McCrimmon Ltd., Great Wakering, 1976.

Casel, O., *The Mystery of Christian Worship*, DLT, 1962.

Catella, A. & Cavagnoli, G., *Le Preghiere Eucaristiche*, Ed. Paoline, 1989.

Clark, F., *Eucharistic Sacrifice and the Reformation* (2nd ed.), Blackwell, Oxford, 1967.

Coughlan, P., *The New Mass: A Pastoral Guide*, Geoffrey Chapman, 1970.

Crichton, J.D., *Christian Celebration: The Mass*, Geoffrey Chapman, 1971.

Daly, Robert J., *The Origins of the Christian Doctrine of Sacrifice*, DLT, London, 1978.

_____, *Christian Sacrifice: The Judaeo-Christian Background before Origen*, Studies in Christian Antiquity 18; Washington — The Catholic University of America Press, 1978.

Danielou, J., *The Bible and the Liturgy*, DLT, 1964.

Deiss, L., *It's the Lord's Supper*, Collins, 1980.

Della Torre, L., *Pregare l'eucaristia*, Queriniana, Brescia, 1983.

De Lubac, H., *Corpus Mysticum*, 2nd ed., Aubier, Montaigne, Paris, 1949.

_____, *Meditation sur l'Église*, 2nd ed., Aubier, Montaigne, Paris, 1954.

Dix, G., *The Shape of the Liturgy*, Adam & Charles Black, London, 1970.

Flannery, A. (ed.), *Vatican Council II. The Conciliar and Postconciliar Documents*, Dominican Publications, Dublin, 1975.

_____, *Vatican Council II. More Post Conciliar Documents*, Fowler Wright Books Ltd., Leominster, Herefords, 1982.

Forte, B. *La Chiesa nell'Eucaristia*, M. D'Auria ed., Napoli, 1988.

Gaudoin-Parker, M., *Adore What You Receive*, Falcon Press, Stockton-on-Tees, Cleveland, 1989.

_____, *The Real Presence Through the Ages: Jesus Adored in the Sacrament of the Altar*, Alba House, Staten Island, N.Y., 1993.

_____, The Beauty of the Eucharist — St. Augustine's experience of the Mystery of Faith" in *The Clergy Review*, Vol. LXXI, No. 12 (December 1986), pp. 438-444.

_____, "Augustine's 'Conversion' considered in the light of the Eucharistic imagery in his hymn of Beauty" in *Adoremus*, Vol. LXVI, No. 2, 1986, pp. 19-29.

_____, "St. Ignatius' Sacrifice for Unity" in *Adoremus*, Vol. LXI, No. 1, 1981, pp. 60-73.

_____, "The Mystery of the Passover: The Catechesis of Melito of Sardis" in *Adoremus*, Vol. LXII, No. 1, 1982, pp. 33-42.

_____, "The Glory of God, Man fully alive in the Eucharist. The Eucharistic teaching of St. Irenaeus" in *Adoremus*, Vol. LXII, No. 2, 1982, pp. 14-21.

_____, "The Flesh: The Pivot of Salvation. Tertullian's insight into the Eucharist" in *Adoremus*, Vol. LXIII, No. 1, 1983, pp. 20-34.

_____, "Hymn of the Word's Creation. The Alexandrians' Spiritual Understanding of the Eucharist" in *Adoremus*, Vol. LXIII, No. 2, 1983, pp. 28-37.

_____, "Cyprian's Cup of delight" in *Adoremus*, Vol. LXIV, No. 1, 1984, pp. 33-38.

Giraudo, C., *La Struttura Letteraria della Preghiera Eucharistica. Saggio sulla genesi letteraria di una forma. Todah veterotestamentaria — Berakah giudaica — Anafora cristiana* (Analecta Biblica, 92) Rome, 1981.

Griffiths, A., *Focus on the Eucharistic Prayer*, Kevin Mayhew, Bury St Edmunds, 1988.

Guzie, T., *Jesus and the Eucharist*, Paulist Press, New York, 1974.

Hänggi, A. & I. Pahl, (eds.), *Prex eucharistica. Textus e variis liturgiis antiquioribus selecti*, Spicilegium Friburgense 12, Fribourg, 1978.

Jeremias, J., *The Eucharistic Words of Jesus*, ET, London, 1966.

Johnson, C. & Ward, A., "The Sources of the Roman Missal . . ." in

Notitiae, Vol. 22 (1986), pp. 445-747; andJ ibid., Vol. 24 (1987), pp.413-1009.

Jungmann, J., *The Early Liturgy*, DLT, 1963.

_____, *The Eucharistic Prayer* (Revised), Anthony Clark, 1978.

_____, *The Mass of the Roman Rite* (2 vols.), Benzinger Bros., New York, 1955.

Kilmartin, E.J., *The Eucharist in the Primitive Church*, Prentice-Hall Inc., Englewood Cliffs, N.Y., 1965.

Lash, N., *His Presence in the World*, Sheed and Ward, London, 1968.

_____, *Theology on the Way to Emmaus*, SCM, London, 1986.

Léon-Dufour, X., *Sharing the Eucharistic Bread: The Witness of the New Testament* (tr. Matthew J. O'Connell), Paulist Press, Mahwah, New Jersey, 1987.

Ligier, Louis, *Magnae Orationis Eucharisticae*, P.U.G., Romae, 1964.

_____, *Textus Selecti de magna oratione eucharistica*, P.U.G., Romae, 1965.

_____, "The Origins of the Eucharistic Prayer," *Studia Liturgica* 9 (1973), pp. 161-185.

McKenna, J.H., *Eucharist and Holy Spirit*, Mayhew-McCrimmon, Great Wakering, 1975.

McPartlan, P., *The Eucharist Makes the Church: Henri de Lubac and John Zizioulas in Dialogue*, T. & T. Clark, Edinburgh, 1993.

Maloney, R., *The Eucharistic Prayers in Worship, Preaching and Study*, Domincan Publ., Dublin, 1985.

Martelet, G., *The Risen Christ and the Eucharistic World*, Collins, 1976.

Martimort, A.G. (ed.), *The Church at Prayer: Eucharist*, Geoffrey Chapman, 1986.

Masure, E., *The Christian Sacrifice: The Sacrifice of Christ our*

Head (tr. Illtyd Trethowan), Burns Oates and Washbourne, London, 1944.

Matthews, E., *Celebrating Mass with Children*, Collins, 1978.

Mazza, E., *The Eucharistic Prayers of the Roman Rite*, Pueblo Publ. Co., N.Y., 1986.

_____, *Mystagogy: A Theology of Liturgy in the Patristic Age* (tr. Matthew J. O'Connell), Pueblo Publ. Co., N.Y., 1989.

Mysterion — Nella celebrazione del Mistero di Cristo la vita della Chiesa, Elle di Ci ed., Leumann, Torino, 1981.

Nichols, A., *The Holy Eucharist from the New Testament to Pope John Paul II*, Oscott 6, Veritas, Dublin, 1991.

Nouwen, Henri, *Behold the Beauty of the Lord: Praying with Icons*, Ave Maria Press, Notre Dame, IN, 1987.

O'Carroll, Michael (ed.), *Corpus Christi: An Encyclopedia of the Eucharist*, Michael Glazier, Inc., Wilmington, DE, 1988.

O'Connor, J.T., *The Hidden Manna: A Theology of the Eucharist*, Ignatius Press, San Francisco, 1988.

O'Neill, C.E., *Sacramental Realism: A General Theory of the Sacraments*, Dominican Publications, Dublin, 1983.

Pennington, M.B., *The Eucharist Yesterday and Today*, St. Paul Publ., 1985.

Rattenbury, J.E., *The Eucharistic Hymns of John and Charles Wesley*, Epworth, London, 1948.

Schillebeeckx, E., *Christ the Sacrament*, Sheed & Ward, London, 1963.

_____, *The Eucharist*, Sheed & Ward, London, 1968.

Schmemann, A., *The Eucharist: Sacrament of the Kingdom*, St. Vladimir's Seminary Press, Crestwood, New York, 1988.

_____, *For the Life of the World*, St Vladimir's Seminary Press, Crestwood, New York, 1988. [Originally: *The World as Sacrament*, DLT, London, 1966.]

Schökel, L. Alonso, *Celebrating the Eucharist: Biblical Meditations*, St. Paul Publications, Slough (U.K.), 1988.

Senn, Frank C. (ed.), *New Eucharistic Prayers: An Ecumenical Study of Their Development and Structure*, Paulist Press, Mahwah, N.Y., 1987.

Stevenson, K., *Eucharist and Offering*, Pueblo Publ. Co. Inc., New York, 1986.

Tatre, R. (ed.), *The Eucharist Today*, P.J. Kenedy and Sons, New York, 1967.

Thurian, M., *L'Eucharistie Mémorial du Seigneur: Sacrifice d'action de grâce et d'intercession*, Delachaux et Niestlé S.A., Neuchatel, 1963.

_____ & G. Wainwright (eds.), *Baptism and Eucharist: Ecumencial Convergence in Celebration*, World Council of Churches, Geneva, Wm B. Eerdmans, Grand Rapids, 1983.

Tillard, J.M.R., *The Eucharist: Pasch of God's People*, Alba House, Staten Island, N.Y., 1967.

Vagaggini, C., *The Canon of the Mass and Liturgical Reform*, Alba House, Staten Island, N.Y., 1967.

_____, *Theological Dimensions of the Liturgy*, 2 vols., Collegeville, 1959.

Vonier, A., *Key to the Doctrine of the Eucharist*, Burns Oates & Washbourne, London, 1925.

Wainwright, G., "Recent Eucharistic Revision" in *The Study of the Liturgy*, (ed. Cheslyn Jones et alii), SPCK, 1978, pp. 280ff.

Yarnold, E., *The Awe-inspiring Rites of Christian Initiation*, St. Paul Pub., Slough (U.K.), 1973.

Young, F., *Sacrifice and the Death of Christ*, SCM, London, 1983.